PEARSON

ALWAYS LEARNING

Compiled by John S. Szczechowski Ed. D.

The Wilmington University Guide to Writing
English Composition 102

Third Edition

Taken from:

Expressways for Writing Scenarios: From Paragraph to Essay, First Edition
by Kathleen T. McWhorter

The Longman Reader, Seventh Edition
by Judith Nadell, John Langan, and Eliza A. Comodromos

A Brief Handbook: Conventions and Expectations for Writing, Second Edition
by Barbara Fine Case

The Longwood Reader, Sixth Edition
By Edward A. Dornan and J. Michael Finnegan

Cover photo courtesy of Wilmington University.

Taken from:

Expressways for Writing Scenarios: From Paragraph to Essay, First Edition
by Kathleen T. McWhorter
Copyright © 2007 by Pearson Education, Inc.
Published by Longman
New York, New York 10036

The Longman Reader, Seventh Edition
by Judith Nadell, John Langan, and Eliza A. Comodromos
Copyright © 2005 by Pearson Education, Inc.
Published by Longman

A Brief Handbook: Conventions and Expectations for Writing, Second Edition
by Barbara Fine Case
Copyright © 2005 by Pearson Education, Inc.
Published by Longman

The Longwood Reader, Sixth Edition
by Edward A. Dornan and J. Michael Finnegan
Copyright © 2006 by Pearson Education, Inc.
Published by Longman

Pearson Learning Solutions, 501 Boylston Street, Suite 900, Boston, MA 02116
A Pearson Education Company
www.pearsoned.com

Printed in the United States of America

4 5 6 7 8 9 10 V202 16 15 14 13 12 11

000200010270779198

RG

ISBN 10: 1-256-27715-0
ISBN 13: 978-1-256-27715-6

Copyright Acknowledgments

Contents

Chapter 5   Revising and Editing   41

A Brief Handbook

Chapter 6   The Active Reading Process   53

Taken from Expressways for Writing Scenarios

Chapter 7   The Term Paper   73

John S. Szczechowski, Ed. D.

Chapter 8   Cause and Effect   75

Expressways

Readings

Chapter 9　Process　123

Expressways

Readings

Chapter 10　Argument　177

Expressways

Readings

PART ONE

A Practical Guide to Writing Essays

CHAPTER 1
Structuring the College Essay

Custom, then, is the great guide of human life.
—David Hume (1711–1776), Scottish philosopher and historian

1a CONVENTION AND THE COLLEGE ESSAY

Writing is an important part of college studies. Instructors in almost every discipline ask students to use writing to explore their own ideas, evaluate the ideas of others, explain what they have read, and report research findings. More often than not, when instructors assign writing, they expect it to be in the form of a conventional college essay. This chapter and the ones that follow focus on the college essay and its components, including what makes an effective paragraph.

THE EXPECTATION
Like most important writing, most college writing requires a certain seriousness and formality. Whether you are writing a position paper in a law enforcement class, a brief essay in a food services class, a book review in a political science class, or an essay in a composition class, your instructor will expect your writing to follow the format typical of college writing. The format is important because it allows you to present information in a clear, efficient way. If you depart from that format—for example, if you write your essays like e-mail to friends or like a résumé—your instructor may question how serious and competent you are.

MEETING THE EXPECTATION
Formal situations are more structured than casual ones. Thus, for a formal wedding, dress is highly structured and guests have only a few options: Men wear tuxedos, but may pick the style; women wear fancy dresses, but may choose long or short. For a casual gathering of friends, more freedom is possible: Guests may wear shorts, jeans, dress slacks, T-shirts, sweaters, or other items. College writing and serious writing outside the classroom are more like the formal wedding than the casual gathering, so for these writing tasks you should conform to the essay structure explained in this chapter.

1b ESSAY STRUCTURE

Imagine life without structure. What if there were no structure at an airport, and planes landed and took off whenever they wanted? What if products were not grouped by category in a supermarket and the pickles were next to the deodorant, the cake mix next to the roach killer? Structure helps us cope with a complex world: Workplaces are more efficient with the structure of assigned tasks; students get a well-rounded education with the structure of graduation requirements; and busy metropolitan areas are safer with the structure of road signs and traffic laws. Without structure, we would have confusion—even chaos.

THE EXPECTATION
Just as we need structure in the world at large, we need structure in writing. We need structure in writing so readers understand the progression of ideas. If they do not, they will become confused, find the material too difficult to follow, and stop reading.

MEETING THE EXPECTATION

Although essays can be structured in more than one way, most have three parts. Each part plays an important role.

- **The introduction,** which is the opening paragraph or paragraphs, states the central point of the essay—which is called the **thesis**—and gives information to spark interest in that thesis. A strong introduction makes readers want to read on and find out more.
- **Body paragraphs,** which come after the introduction, support the thesis by giving all the ideas that explain, illustrate, or prove it. Effective body paragraphs leave no doubt about the truth of the thesis.
- **The conclusion,** which comes at the end of the essay, wraps things up for a strong finish. A satisfying conclusion provides a sense of closure.

NOTE: For an extended explanation of the thesis, see page 17. For an extended explanation of the introduction, body paragraphs, and conclusion, see Chapter 4.

To better understand the parts of an essay and how each helps writers achieve their purpose, read the following essay and study the comments in the margin.

Banning Alcohol on College Campuses

Paragraph 1
This is the introduction. It sparks reader interest by asking intriguing questions and with dramatic examples.

The last sentence is the thesis. Notice that the thesis give the topic (drinking on college property, at off- campus housing, and at fraternity and sorority houses) and the writer's viewpoint (drinking should be banned). Can you tell that the writer's purpose is to persuade?

1   When you think of the Massachusetts Institute of Technology (MIT to most of us), does your mind call up images of computer nerds and engineering geeks who spend every waking hour of every day bent over their textbooks or glued to their computer monitors? Do you think of super-intellectuals on their way to the library in pants a few inches too short, revealing white socks and an inch or so of skin at the ankle? Even if these are not the images the school conjures up for you, I doubt you think of wild fraternity parties and nonstop drinking. After all, those are the images of a party school, and MIT is certainly not that—or is it? Just last year Scott Krueger, a fraternity pledge at MIT, did what far too many college students do. He drank himself to death. In Baton Rouge, Louisiana, in 1997, Louisiana State University student Benjamin Wynne died from an overdose of alcohol, and in 1995 Matthew Farofalo, a sophomore at the University of Iowa, died because he drank too much. These are not isolated cases. Drinking on college campuses is legendary, but it is time it stopped because students are dying. Colleges must ban all alcohol consumption on college property, at off-campus housing, and in fraternity and sorority houses.

Paragraph 2
This is a body paragraph. It presents the first idea to prove the thesis: Colleges know they have a responsibility to protect their students. Since other efforts to protect students from death by alcohol have failed, a ban is necessary.

2   Colleges know that they have a responsibility to protect students. That is why they have police and security forces, locks on residence halls, evening safe-escort services, and emergency call boxes. Now that they know students are dying from drinking, colleges must do what they can to prevent the deaths. In the past, schools have sponsored alcohol awareness programs and responsible drinking seminars, but these measures have not worked, since students are still dying. During my freshman orientation, the dean of students lectured us about drinking, but most of us just laughed the lecture off. No one takes the talk seriously,

so tougher measures are called for. Perhaps more to the point, since colleges know their students have a drinking problem, they contribute to that problem if they do not take adequate measures to solve it.

3   If alcohol were banned on campus, I know students would still find a way to drink. However, they would drink less because it would be harder to find a way to "party hearty," and the penalties would deter many people. Of course, these penalties would have to be stiff to serve as a real deterrent. I recommend a single warning followed by suspension. Students threatened with suspension are not likely to risk drinking.

4   Students think that drinking is part of the privilege of going to college, and that they cannot enjoy themselves unless they drink. What is called for here is some old-fashioned attitude adjustment. Students need to learn that the so-called privilege is a killer, and that they can have a great deal of fun without drinking, maybe even more because they won't be throwing up, passing out, and nursing hangovers. I am confident that after some time without alcohol, students will easily become accustomed to enjoying themselves sober.

5   Alcoholism is a serious problem in this country. When colleges allow drinking, particularly heavy drinking, they are contributing to that problem. Frankly, that is immoral. Of course, when schools ban alcohol, it cannot be just for students. There can be no drinking in the president's box of the football stadium, no drinking at faculty mixers on college property, and so on. The statement must be made from the top down: Drinking is dangerous and cannot be allowed.

6   Many students say the dangers of drinking are overrated, that they are adults who can drink in moderation. They rebel at the idea of being policed. However, most freshmen and sophomores (the students who I believe are doing the majority of the heavy drinking) are not adults. They are not 21, which is the legal drinking age. They are 18, 19, and 20. Furthermore, they do not drink in moderation, and they do not act like adults. They drink to excess, act like drunken fools, and risk their lives.

7   College students are still young people, for the most part, and that means they do not always make wise choices. In the case of alcohol, too many are choosing to drink too much. They risk a lifetime of alcoholism and even death. Colleges cannot stand by and be content that "safe drinking" lectures fulfill their obligation. They need to protect students with a bold measure. They need to ban drinking altogether.

Paragraph 3
This is a body paragraph. It presents the next idea to prove the thesis: Threatening students with suspension if they violate the drinking ban will prevent many students from drinking.

Paragraph 4
This is a body paragraph. It presents the next idea to prove the thesis: Students need to learn that they can enjoy themselves without drinking. The paragraph discusses a point that people who disagree with the author are likely to make. Think about how that discussion advances the writer's persuasive purpose.

Paragraph 5
This is a body paragraph. It presents the next idea to prove the thesis: By allowing alcohol consumption, colleges contribute to the problem of alcoholism. Therefore, they should ban drinking by the entire campus population, not just by students.

Paragraph 6
This is the last body paragraph. It presents the next ideas to prove the thesis: Many students who drink are breaking the law because they are not 21. Also, students do not drink in moderation. The paragraph discusses a point that students might make to contradict the thesis. How does that point advance the persuasive purpose?

Paragraph 7
This paragraph is the conclusion. It provides closure by restating points made in the body paragraphs and by restating the thesis.

1c TRY IT OUT 1

Analyze an Essay

At your campus library or online, locate any copy of *Newsweek* magazine from the last two years. Find the essay in the section called "My Turn" (listed in the table of contents) and copy or print that essay. Then, read the essay and answer these questions:

   a. Does the introduction spark your interest in reading further? Why or why not?
   b. Is there a sentence or sentences that state the thesis? If so, which one(s)? If not, write out the thesis in your own words.
   c. Do the body paragraphs do a good job of explaining, illustrating, or proving the thesis? Explain.
   d. What do you think of the conclusion? Why?

1d TRY IT OUT 2

Discover Teacher Expectations

Speak to two instructors who teach classes you expect to take before you graduate. Ask the following questions and report your findings to the class.

   a. How often do your students write essays?
   b. How much do those essays affect students' grades?
   c. What qualities do you expect student writing to exhibit?

1e CONVENTIONS AND EXPECTATIONS AT LARGE

The Importance of Format

The structure of college and other formal essays makes sense because it allows writers to present a considerable amount of information in an accessible and efficient format. Format is important in many other situations as well.

- Your degree requirements are arranged so that you take introductory courses first and in-depth courses afterward. This structure allows you to learn the basics so you can understand the more sophisticated material.
- A good workout is structured so that you first do a warm-up, then the strenuous activity, then a cooldown. This format makes for a safe workout.
- In a movie theater, the screenings are sequenced so you view the coming attractions before the feature film. This structure ensures that you do not walk out on the previews.
- The requirements for earning a driver's license in many states are formatted so that you must first pass a written exam to earn a learner's permit, then take driving lessons, then pass a road test. This progression helps ensure that motorists can operate their vehicles safely.

Activity

Select something you wrote in the past—either in or out of the classroom. Explain the extent to which it does or does not conform to the structure explained in this chapter. If it does not conform very much, explain whether the piece would be better if it conformed more, and why or why not. If it does conform, explain whether the structure is important, and why or why not.

Writing Topic

Pick a situation and explain the role of structure in it. For example, you can consider a date, a job interview, driving, a funeral, or a meeting with your advisor.

CHAPTER 2

Generating Ideas

The secret of getting ahead is getting started.
The secret of getting started is breaking your complex, overwhelming tasks into
small manageable tasks, and then starting on the first one.

—Mark Twain (1835–1910),
American writer, journalist, and lecturer

2a   CONVENTIONAL WISDOM ABOUT GETTING STARTED

Beginnings can be difficult. Painters know the frustration of the empty canvas, potters stare down at the shapeless lump of clay, interior designers puzzle over the empty room, people on a first date struggle to make conversation—and writers face the blank page or computer screen. If the blank page or screen causes writer's block, take heart, for this chapter will show you how to break through the block.

THE EXPECTATION

Why are writers so tortured by the blank page? Usually, the answer is that we expect too much of ourselves too soon. We look for polished work far too early, and the pressure causes writer's block.

To avoid writer's block and make beginning easier, have a single modest expectation at the outset: to produce enough rough preliminary material to get you started. This means that when you write a first draft—and engage in all the activities leading up to that draft—you must not judge your early efforts too harshly. Instead, accept what you produce for its promise—no matter how rough it is—knowing that you can improve the material later.

MEETING THE EXPECTATION

To minimize anxiety and produce enough raw material to get you started, follow Mark Twain's advice at the opening of this chapter and work in a series of stages. Think of writing as a process, as something that develops gradually—not as an entity that springs forth fully formed and reader-ready. The following chart presents stages of writing. These stages are explained in this chapter and ones that follow.

THE STAGES OF WRITING

STAGE 1	Determine your reason for writing. Assess the characteristics of your reader.
STAGE 2	Use idea-generation strategies to come up with a writing topic and ideas to develop that topic.
STAGE 3	Decide on a suitable order for your ideas and outline them if doing so is helpful.
STAGE 4	Write a first (rough) draft that is subject to change.
STAGE 5	Revise your draft to improve it.

Note: Although the stages are numbered, writers often work out of order, and they often return to an earlier stage one or more times.

2b ESTABLISHING YOUR PURPOSE AND ASSESSING YOUR AUDIENCE

My college-student son wanted to travel to Spain for a week to see his friend, who was studying there for several months. However, he would have to travel in the middle of the semester. To go, he had to (1) convince his parents to pay for the trip, (2) convince his instructors to allow him to make up the work he would miss, and (3) convince his employer to give him the time off. He said one thing to his dad and me, another to his instructors, and a third to his employer. In each case, he said something different because in each case his audience and purpose were different. (By the way, my son must understand purpose and audience very well, because all parties agreed to the trip!)

THE EXPECTATION

Your **purpose** is your reason for writing; your **audience** is your readers. Both purpose and audience affect what you say and how you say it—just as they did for my son. Will an e-mail to a friend to convince that person to see a movie with you be the same as a letter to the editor of your campus newspaper urging students to contribute to the United Way campaign? Will an essay you write in your history class for a good grade be the same as a thank-you note you write to your aunt to express appreciation for a birthday present? Will a letter you write applying for a job be the same as one you write complaining to a store manager about poor service? Each of these writings must be different because each is written to achieve a different purpose, and each is written for a different reader.

You may be thinking that establishing purpose and assessing audience are easy tasks because your reader is your teacher and your purpose is to earn a good grade. However, knowing that outside the classroom you will write to many people for many reasons, your instructor will evaluate your success in writing for a variety of audiences and for a range of purposes.

To appreciate that purpose and audience affect what you say and how you say it, let's contrast an e-mail to a friend about the poor food in a residence hall with a letter to the Director of Housing on the same topic.

E-MAIL ABOUT POOR FOOD IN RESIDENCE HALL

purpose: to complain about how unhappy the writer is with the food in order to express and vent feelings

audience: a friend at another college

sample sentence from the e-mail: It's so bogus that we are forced to eat this slop. We cough up big bucks for room and board, and all we get is garbage.

LETTER ABOUT POOR FOOD IN RESIDENCE HALL

purpose: to convince reader to take steps to improve the food

audience: Director of Housing

sample sentence from the letter: The morale of residents is suffering because we are forced to eat unappealing items such as chipped beef on toast, even though we pay the second-highest room-and-board fee in the state.

The sample sentences illustrate how purpose and audience affect what writers say and how they say it. Consider the sentence from the e-mail to a friend written to express feelings:

It's so bogus that we are forced to eat this slop. We cough up big bucks for room and board, and all we get is garbage.

- The sentence does not give an example of the kind of food because the reader will likely accept a friend's word that the food is bad, even without specific evidence.
- The language is casual and includes slang, which is appropriate between friends.
- The writer sounds angry because friends can share emotions.

Now consider the sentence from the letter written to persuade the Director of Housing:

> The morale of residents is suffering because we are forced to eat unappealing items such as chipped beef on toast, even though we pay the second-highest room-and-board fee in the state.

- The sentence includes specific details (chipped beef on toast; second-highest room-and-board fee in the state) to back up claims, because this reader requires proof.
- The sentence cites the effect of the food (poor morale) to give the reader a good reason to act.
- The language is formal and respectful because the reader is in a position of authority.
- Emotions are kept in check; no anger is shown.

Certain expectations surround different audiences and purposes. Thus, you would not use slang in a letter to the Director of Housing if you want to convince that person to take steps to improve the food, and you would not hesitate to show your anger and frustration in an e-mail to a friend if you want to vent those feelings.

MEETING THE EXPECTATION

- **To establish purpose.** Sometimes you will write for just one purpose, and sometimes you will write for a combination of purposes. To establish your purpose for writing, you can answer these questions:
  1. Do you want to give your reader some information (such as information about how to choose a suitable advisor)? If so, what do you want to inform your reader about? Your purpose here is *to inform.*
  2. Do you want to tell your reader about your experience (such as the time you were arrested by mistake)? If so, what experience do you want to relate to your reader? Your purpose here is *to relate experience.*
  3. Do you want your reader to understand how you feel about something (such as your parents' divorce)? If so, what feelings do you want to express? Your purpose here is *to express your feelings.*
  4. Do you want to make your reader laugh by writing something funny (such as the time you tried to cook a gourmet meal)? Your purpose here is *to entertain.*
  5. Do you want to convince your reader to agree with you about something (such as what should be done about global warming)? If so, what opinion do you want your reader to adopt? Do you want to convince your reader to do something (such as vote for a particular candidate)? If so, what do you want your reader to do? In both cases, your purpose is *to persuade.*
- **To assess audience.** Some readers will be more interested in what you have to say than others. Some readers will be easier to convince, easier to inform, and easier to entertain. For example, convincing parents of school-age children to support a school levy that increases taxes will be easier than convincing retirees on a fixed income to do so. Writers must suit what they say and how they say it to their audience if they are to achieve their writing purpose. Thus, to persuade parents, you might emphasize that the levy will improve their children's education. However, to persuade retirees, you might emphasize that passing the levy will improve property values.

  To understand your readers so you can tailor your writing to their needs and expectations, you can answer these questions:
  1. What is your audience like? (Consider age, gender, ethnicity, political persuasion, geographical location, biases, economic level, education, and anything else that characterizes the reader.)
  2. How interested will this audience be in your topic?
  3. How hard will it be to achieve your purpose with this audience?
  4. Do any of the answers to numbers 1–3 suggest that you have to shape your material a particular way?

2c TRY IT OUT   1

Identify Audience and Purpose

For each writing topic given, indicate a possible audience and purpose. Then identify a publication that might include the essay with that audience and purpose.

> EXAMPLE: *topic:* an explanation of how to prevent gum disease
>
> *possible audience: patients in a dental office*
>
> *possible purpose: to inform the reader*
>
> *possible publication: a brochure in a dental office*

1. a comparison and contrast of the job descriptions of a physical therapist and an occupational therapist
2. an explanation of how to give a successful speech
3. the reasons to vote for changes in the zoning laws of your city
4. the problems associated with body piercing
5. a humorous story about your first day as a college student

2d GENERATING IDEAS

Inspiration is an appealing notion, much like "love at first sight" and "one size fits all." It happens occasionally, but you cannot rely on it, so do not wait for ideas to leap into your head. Instead, try one or more of the strategies described in this chapter.

THE EXPECTATION

In the absence of inspiration, use the strategies described next to discover topics and ideas. Just remember, you are looking for raw material with potential. If you keep rejecting ideas because they are not perfect, you will never get anything written. Take the very best you can come up with at the time; later you can polish the material until it gleams.

MEETING THE EXPECTATION

Maybe you think that you cannot write until you have something to write about. However, writing is an act of discovery, so you can use it to discover ideas to write about in greater length. The strategies that follow, called **idea-generation techniques,** are ways to *use* writing to discover topics and ideas *for* writing.

Keep your expectations for idea generation reasonable. Strive to discover a suitable writing topic and a few ideas to develop that topic. As you work, remember these points:

1. **Limit your topic.** Your topic should not take in more territory than you can write about comfortably, or you will never be able to cover it adequately.

UNSUITABLE (NOT LIMITED):	the differences between men and women
SUITABLE (LIMITED):	the differences between the way men and women view friendship
UNSUITABLE (NOT LIMITED):	general education requirements
SUITABLE (LIMITED):	the problems with the college's general education requirements
UNSUITABLE (NOT LIMITED):	pets
SUITABLE (LIMITED):	the benefits of pets in nursing homes

2. **Present a debatable issue or new information.** If you write about something everyone already knows or agrees with, your readers will be bored. Try to come up with an interesting, fresh viewpoint or angle.

UNSUITABLE (NOT DEBATABLE):	children need a good education
SUITABLE (DEBATABLE):	why charter schools provide a good alternative to traditional public schools
UNSUITABLE (EVERYONE KNOWS):	the need to provide children with an education
SUITABLE (PROVIDES NEW INFORMATION):	how home schooling works

Freewrite

A good way to discover topics and ideas is **freewriting.** For about fifteen minutes, write about whatever occurs to you, either at the computer or with paper and pen. Do not worry about how good your ideas are, whether your grammar is correct, or whether your spelling is right. As one thought leads to another, write those ideas down the best way you can as quickly as you can. If you dry up and run out of ideas, write anything you want—the alphabet, how you feel at this very minute, a list of your favorite foods—and soon new ideas will surface for you to write.

When time is up, read your freewriting. The material will be rough but you will find one or more ideas with potential. These gems indicate that a topic is taking shape and ideas are coming to the surface. This material can be shaped to include in your writing.

In the following example of freewriting, notice that the writer recorded a free flow of thought without worrying about grammar, spelling, abbreviations, or any other matter of refinement. Also notice that the writer discovered a topic (banning alcohol on campus) and ideas for developing that topic (students pass out, drive drunk, attend class hung over, can't study, and even die; colleges are responsible for the deaths).

> I'm suppose to write about a campus issue which shouldn't be to hard b/c there's enough of them. Parking, the cost of books, drinking, tuition ect. Which one? Parking isn't such a serious issue. It doesn't seem worth writing about. Who cares? Drinking is serious. Parents would never believe how much their kids are drinking. Its pretty dangerous actually. Kids passing out, driving, hung over in class, generally trashed. I don't drink so I'm left out a lot. I think banning alcohol on campus is a good idea but most kids would freak out. They'd even transfer. I could also write about the insane cost of books but that's soooooooo boring. I could interview the book store manager and get good ideas though. I don't really care that much b/c I have a scholarship. I really want to write about alcohol I think. It's a big problem, a big issue, even a matter of life and death. There's lots of reasons to ban it. It kills students who binge drink and kids are so trashed half the time they can't really study. Let's see what else? I gotta think of more stuff. She said I could research so I could look up newspaper articles about students who died from drinking. Oh, I know, I could write about how colleges that don't ban drinking are responsible for the deaths.

You may need only one freewriting to get you going. If not, freewrite again, but this time write about the good ideas in your first freewriting. Between the two freewritings, you are likely to discover enough ideas to move you forward.

COMPUTER TIP

Turn the brightness dial on your monitor until the screen is dark, and then freewrite. With the screen dark, you are less likely to censor yourself, so ideas will flow better.

Make a List

Listing is an excellent way to generate writing topics and ideas for developing topics. With paper and pen or at the computer, list words, phrases, or sentences that occur to you. Do not worry about how "good" or "correct" the items are; just allow a free flow of thought. If necessary, write multiple lists. For example, here is a first list to find a topic about computers:

expensive

laptops vs desktops

PDAs

Internet

Internet dangers

porn sites and sexual predators

e-mail

spam—I'm sick of it

chat rooms

computer dating

copying music—Napster should be legal

research for classes

crashes

The above list offers many possible topics. You can pick one of them and write a second list for ideas to develop the topic. Here's a list of ideas to develop an essay about one of the list topics, computer dating.

People think it's tacky but it's not.

scary

dangers—people lying about themselves, creepy people

take precautions—meet in public place, talk on phone first

dangers exist in traditional dating too

It's hard to meet people if you work fulltime.

Daryl met a great woman with a computer service.

When you exhaust your ideas, review your list. Cross out ideas you do not want to include and add new ones that occur to you—but remember, you are looking for raw material with potential, not brilliance.

COMPUTER TIP

E-mail your idea-generation list to another student or reliable reader and ask that person to add ideas that he or she thinks of.

Cluster

Clustering, sometimes called **mapping** or **webbing,** can help you find a topic and ideas to develop that topic. To find a topic, write an idea in the middle of a page and draw a circle around it.

As related ideas occur to you, connect them to the circle, like this:

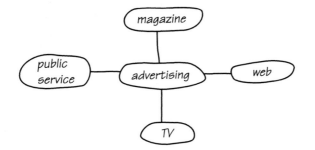

Next, connect additional ideas to the appropriate circles. Some circles will have more ideas connected to them than others, and some ideas may be connected to more than one circle. As always during idea generation, accept anything with potential; do not censor yourself.

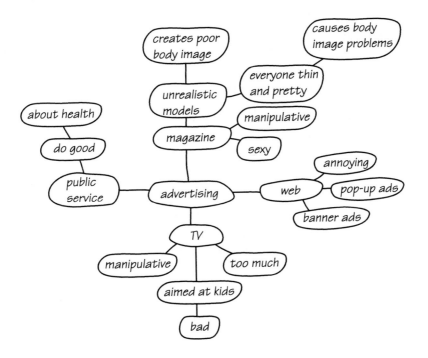

You can write about the cluster that has the most circles or the one that is the most interesting. For example, after studying the previous cluster, you might decide to write about how magazine advertisements contribute to body image problems. If you need more ideas, you can cluster again, with "magazine ads and poor body image" in the center.

Answer Key Questions

Once you have your writing topic, answering key questions about that topic can help you discover ideas for developing it. The following questions are good ones, but feel free to develop your own.

What story can I tell?	What can I describe?
Why is it important?	What is its cause?
Who cares about it?	What is its effect?
What does it mean?	What is it similar to and different from?
Who would disagree?	What examples are there?
Why would people disagree?	In what groups or categories can it be placed?
How does it work?	Will it matter in ten years?

COMPUTER TIP

Save a list of key questions—like the one above—as a file to use whenever you generate ideas.

Discuss Your Ideas with Others

Mention your ideas to a trusted friend or classmate, and ask that person to comment, suggest other ideas, and ask questions. Respond to that person's remarks and questions to continue the dialog. The exchange can help you discover additional ideas and refine the ones you already have.

Combine Techniques

Sometimes one idea-generation technique is all you need. Other times, combining techniques works better. For example, you may begin with a list and then freewrite about one of the ideas on the list. Or you may freewrite and then cluster to develop one of the ideas from the freewriting.

2e   TRY IT OUT   2

Discover a Topic and Ideas

1. Freewrite on one of the following subjects for about fifteen minutes to discover a suitable topic and some ideas to develop that topic.
   college life   friendship   politics   sports   raising children
2. Assume you must write about holiday celebrations. Make one or more lists to discover a topic and some ideas for developing that topic.
3. Cluster one or more times on one of the following subjects to discover a topic and some ideas to develop that topic.
   money   shopping   television   stress   technology
4. Select one of the topics you discovered from your freewriting, your listing, or your clustering, and answer some key questions to discover more ideas to develop that topic.
5. Of the idea-generation techniques you have tried, which ones do you like the best? Why?

2f   CONVENTIONS AND EXPECTATIONS AT LARGE

Preliminary Activities and Rituals

For writers, idea generation is important preliminary work. However, writing is not the only activity that involves planning and preliminary actions. Consider sports, for example. Basketball players perform shooting drills prior to the start of a game, runners stretch and stride out before the race, and sailors test the wind before they sail. Golfers find preliminary activities particularly important. They arrive at the course early enough to practice chipping and putting. Before stroking the ball during match play, they crouch down to study the green and determine how it breaks between the ball and the hole. Then they take a practice stroke to try out their shot. Only after that do they attempt the putt.

Some preliminary rituals have more of a psychological benefit than anything else. Consider a bowler who will only wear a favorite shirt, a baseball player who will not change socks during a winning streak, a student who will not take an exam without a good-luck charm, or a writer who can produce only after taking a long walk. Russian novelist Leo Tolstoy was an extreme case. He sat naked in a locked room with no food until he generated a certain number of pages. His wife was under orders not to bring him food or clothes until he reached his goal.

Activity

Ask ten people what preliminary activities they engage in when they write, play sports, or take an exam. Record their responses.

Writing Topic

Based on what you learned from your interviews and any other information you have, explain the role and importance of preliminary activities.

CHAPTER 3
Outlining and Drafting

I hate to write; I like to revise. . . . I like to get the draft out of my system.
—Malcolm Cowley (1898–1989), writer and editor

3a CONVENTIONAL WISDOM ABOUT FIRST ATTEMPTS

Imagine you are a parent watching your child try roller skating for the first time. You make sure your child is prepared, with skates laced and knee pads on, and then you stand back. You know those first glides will be shaky, that there will probably be a fall or two, and that is fine. You do not expect perfection the first time out, so you encourage your child to keep trying. Writing a first draft is not much different. It will be shaky and imperfect, like most first attempts.

THE EXPECTATION

A **first draft,** also called a **rough draft,** is nothing more than a first attempt to write ideas. It is supposed to be full of trouble spots, so do not despair if your first drafts are nowhere near ready for a reader's eyes. Everything at this point is subject to every kind of change, large and small. Remember when you draft, your work can be polished during revision.

MEETING THE EXPECTATION

When you understand that your first draft is supposed to be rough, writing it will go more smoothly. In addition, the drafting process will be more productive—you will produce more material suitable for later revising—if you

- understand how to write a thesis
- write an outline before you draft

The next sections take up these concerns.

3b DRAFTING A THESIS

Rose, a character on the old TV situation comedy *Golden Girls,* was fond of telling long, elaborate stories that had no readily apparent point, invariably leading one of the other characters to ask in frustration, "What's your point, Rose?" If you have had the misfortune of listening to someone like Rose, you know that confusion or frustration result when discourse has no central point.

THE EXPECTATION

Readers expect what they read to have an easily identifiable central point. In an essay, that central point is called the **thesis**. A thesis is a convention, a courtesy a writer extends to readers to let them know what is in store. As you shape the early version of your thesis, you should consider your topic, purpose, and audience.

MEETING THE EXPECTATION

To meet your readers' expectations, draft your thesis with the following in mind.

1. **State your topic and a viewpoint about that topic.** You can decide on your topic and viewpoint by considering your idea-generation material, your audience, and your purpose.

YES:	Extending the school year to eleven months will improve the quality of education.
TOPIC:	extending the school year to eleven months
VIEWPOINT:	it will improve the quality of education
NO (LACKS VIEWPOINT):	The board of education is thinking about extending the school year to eleven months.

2. **Limit your thesis, so you can develop it in an essay (not a book!).**

YES:	College students experience more stress than many people realize.
NO (TOO BROAD):	People have too much stress in their lives.

3. **Write a thesis that is debatable or in need of explanation.**

YES:	For the best possible workout, hire a personal trainer.
NO (NO ONE WOULD DISAGREE):	Exercise is important to good health.

4. **If it helps you achieve your purpose, preview the points you will develop in your essay, in the order you will present them.**

SAMPLE THESIS:	More students should consider a liberal arts degree.
SAMPLE THESIS WITH POINTS OF DEVELOPMENT:	More students should consider a liberal arts degree because it provides a solid general education, skills desirable in the job market, and preparation for graduate and professional schools.

STRATEGIES FOR DRAFTING

Your Thesis

1. Review your idea-generation material to determine whether many or most of your ideas center on a particular viewpoint.
2. If your idea-generation material does not suggest a thesis, list your best ideas from that material. The act of listing may lead you to a thesis idea.
3. If you still lack a thesis idea, do additional idea generation, perhaps focusing on one or two of the ideas you have already generated.
4. Think about your audience. Do your readers' expectations suggest a particular thesis?
5. Remember that your thesis can change, so do the best you can with what you have at the moment. You will have ample opportunity to rethink and revise.

SOME IMPORTANT CONVENTIONS

Drafting Your Thesis

1. In essays for your writing class and most humanities courses, avoid announcing your thesis with words like "this essay will explain," "the following paragraphs will show," "in the rest of this paper, I will prove," and so forth.

NO:	My essay will demonstrate that student athletes do not get the respect they deserve.
YES:	Student athletes do not get the respect they deserve.

In many science and social science disciplines, however, these wordings are accepted conventions.

EXAMPLE: The purpose of this experiment was to determine the relationship between learning styles and test scores.

2. State your viewpoint in specific language, avoiding general terms such as *great, nice, interesting, awesome, bad,* and *terrible.*

   NO: Cross country running is a great sport.

   YES: Cross country running teaches perseverance and self-reliance.

3. In most cases, avoid expressions like *in my opinion, it seems to me,* and *I think.* Since you are the writer, your reader will assume, unless told otherwise, that the ideas are your thoughts and opinions.

3c TRY IT OUT 1

Identify the Topic and Viewpoint in a Thesis

For each thesis, identify the topic and the viewpoint.

EXAMPLE: Although a certain amount of animal experimentation is necessary in medical research, animals should not be used to test cosmetics.

topic: using animals to test cosmetics

viewpoint: It should not be done.

1. The summers I spent at Lake Erie as a child were always a time of discovery.
2. Despite what our state senator claims, tax cuts are not the best way to stimulate the economy.
3. Although they are twins, Matthew and Michael have very different personalities.
4. Unless it is an economic necessity, high school students should not work during the school year.
5. Advertisements can cause both males and females to have negative self-images.
6. Because of recent violence at high school football games, the board of education should cancel the remainder of the season.
7. Because an emergency can occur anywhere at any time, everyone over fifteen should take a CPR and first-aid class.
8. Before hiring a babysitter for your children, investigate the individual thoroughly.
9. Most magazine advertisements sell an image more than a product.
10. Rather than award football and basketball scholarships, colleges should pay their players outright.

3d TRY IT OUT 2

Evaluate Thesis Sentences

Evaluate each thesis. If it is acceptable, write *okay* next to it. If it is not, note what the problem is and rewrite the thesis to eliminate the problem.

EXAMPLE: *thesis:* The United States should revise its foreign policy.

evaluation: The thesis is not limited.

revision: The United States should not trade with any country guilty of human rights violations.

1. *Good Morning America* is an early morning news program.
2. The quality of public education would improve if all students were required to wear uniforms.
3. No one should drink alcohol and drive a car.
4. Litchfield Beach is a great place to vacation.

5. Men and women approach dating with very different attitudes.
6. I will demonstrate that legalizing drugs is the best way to reduce the crime rate.
7. Modern technology has improved our lives in countless ways.
8. Shopping for a computer does not have to be a difficult process.
9. At your medical checkup, you should ask questions if you have them.
10. A new high school is being built on the west side of town.
11. Trying juveniles younger than fifteen as adults—even for violent crimes—is bad.
12. If more young couples received premarital counseling, the divorce rate would drop.
13. As the next paragraphs will illustrate, HBO's original programming includes an excessive amount of violence.
14. Until we can eliminate unjust convictions, we should abolish the death penalty.
15. Many people oppose stem cell research on moral grounds.

3e TRY IT OUT   3

Write Thesis Sentences

Select five of the following topics and write one thesis sentence for each. Remember the criteria for an acceptable thesis. If you need ideas, try freewriting or listing.

1. family life
2. violence in the media
3. college athletics
4. American politics
5. attitudes toward the elderly
6. the Internet
7. college life

3f OUTLINING YOUR IDEAS

Outlining is not required, but it is a useful tool. Some writers mistakenly think that outlining takes too much time and is too much trouble. In fact, the opposite is usually true. The time and energy you put into outlining are worthwhile because the outline makes writing the first draft go much more smoothly.

THE EXPECTATION

People expect the material they read to be in an easy-to-understand, logical order. If they cannot tell why one idea comes after the one before, or how ideas relate to each other, they become confused and frustrated. They may even stop reading. Outlining can help you arrange your ideas to ensure an easy-to-understand order.

MEETING THE EXPECTATION

The outline techniques explained next can help you meet your readers' expectation for logical order. They can also make writing your first draft go more smoothly by giving you the order of ideas for that draft. The techniques are not necessarily interchangeable. Some will work better than others for you; some will work better for certain kinds of essays. If one technique does not work, try another.

1. **Write a scratch outline.** Look over your idea-generation material; list the ideas you will use in the order you will write them up in your first draft.
2. **Use index cards.** Write one main idea to explain, illustrate, or prove your thesis on the top of an index card. Under that idea write the points you can make to develop or support that idea. Write your second main idea to explain, illustrate, or prove your thesis on another index card, with the supporting points below it. Continue until you have a card for each main idea to explain, illustrate, or prove your thesis. (Each of these cards gives you the content for a body paragraph.) Arrange the cards in the order you want to write the main ideas in your draft.
3. **Use an outline form.** You can photocopy the following form or keep a copy of it on your computer to use as needed.

```
                          Outline Form

Thesis _____
_____

Main Idea 1 to Explain, Illustrate, or Pr    ove Thesis _____
_____

Points to Develop or Support Main Idea 1    _____
_____

Main Idea 2 to Explain, Illustrate, or Pr    ove Thesis _____
_____

Points to Develop or Support Main Idea 2    _____
_____


Main Idea 3 to Explain, Illustrate, or Pr    ove Thesis _____
_____

Points to Develop or Support Main Idea 3    _____
_____

_____

(Continue in this fasion until you exhausted all your        idea s
to explain, illustrate, or pr    ove your thesis.)

Idea for Conclusion    _____
_____
```

4. **Generate additional ideas if necessary.** If you have trouble completing an outline, you may not yet have enough ideas. Try one or more of the idea-generation techniques explained in Chapter 2.

COMPUTER TIP

- To develop a scratch outline, list your idea-generation ideas. Then use your Copy and Move functions to place those ideas in the order you want for your first draft.
- Use your word-processing program's outline feature by filling in the various levels with your idea-generation material. If necessary, generate additional ideas to complete the outline.
- Create a blank outline form and save it as a file. You can easily complete the form each time you write an essay.

3g TRY IT OUT   4

Develop an Outline

1. Using the topic and ideas you generated in Chapter 2 for number 1 of Try It Out 2, write a scratch outline. If you need more ideas or if you did not complete that exercise, use one or more of the idea-generation techniques.

2. Using the topic and ideas you generated in Chapter 2 for number 2 of Try It Out 2, complete an outline form. If you need more ideas or if you did not complete that exercise, use one or more of the idea-generation techniques.

3. Using the topic and ideas you generated in Chapter 2 for number 3 of Try It Out 2, write an outline using index cards. If you need more ideas or if you did not complete that exercise, use one or more of the idea-generation techniques.

4. Of the outlining techniques you tried, which did you prefer? Why?

STRATEGIES FOR DRAFTING

1. **Use an outline.** Regardless of the kind of outline you wrote, it can serve as a roadmap by indicating what ideas you will write in your draft and the order you will write them in. However, the outline is not an ironclad contract. You can depart from it any time you have a better idea.

2. **Write your draft in one sitting.** Do not linger too long over anything—if you get stuck, leave some blank space and push on, concentrating on what you *can* write rather than what you cannot write. Do not polish as you go or check spellings or try to think of just the right word. Express yourself the best way you can and keep writing. You will able to revise later.

3. **If you have trouble getting started, begin with your thesis.** Forget about an introduction; you can add one later.

4. **If you get stuck for a long period, return to idea generation.** You may not have enough material for your draft, and additional idea generation can give you more material. Then, adjust your outline, and try again to draft.

5. **If you have enough ideas but cannot find a way to write them down, write your draft the way you would speak your ideas to a friend or classmate.** Later, when you revise, you can make necessary changes in word choice and sentence structure.

6. **Do not worry about your grammar at this point.** You can correct mistakes later.

7. **If necessary, start over.** If you are certain that your topic or ideas are not working, go ahead and change your topic, alter your thesis, shift your audience and purpose, or do whatever is necessary to move forward.

COMPUTER TIP

If you have trouble writing a portion of your draft, copy and paste in the relevant portion of your outline to serve as a placeholder.

3h TRY IT OUT 5

Write a First Draft

1. Using any of the outlines you developed for Try It Out 4, write as much of a first draft as you can in fifteen minutes. Be sure to follow the Strategies for Drafting.

2. Read over your draft. Does it have potential? That is, with additional drafting and careful revising, can the draft become an essay that fulfills your purpose for writing? Explain.

3i CONVENTIONS AND EXPECTATIONS AT LARGE

Agendas as Structure

Essays are not the only aspect of life that requires order. Consider business and public meetings. Without an organizational structure, little would be accomplished because those attending would not know what topics would be discussed and would speak whenever they wanted. The most forceful personalities would dominate the proceedings. To prevent such chaos, meetings are run with an **agenda,** which is a plan that sets the sequence of events. An agenda gives a meeting form because it allows for an orderly presentation of topics, so everyone knows what will be discussed and when. Often, an agenda resembles a classic essay because it sets out some activities as introductory, some as the heart of the meeting, and some as a formal wrap-up, like this:

INTRODUCTION
1. call to order
2. roll call
3. reading of minutes of the previous meeting

BODY
4. officer's reports
5. committee reports
6. important business previously designated for consideration at the meeting
7. unfinished business from previous meetings
8. new business

CONCLUSION
9. announcements
10. adjournment

Activity

What other conventions structure life and prevent confusion? List at least ten that you encounter during a typical school day. Here is one to get you started: In your campus library, books are arranged in a particular order to make it easier for you to find what you want.

Writing Topic

Discuss the role structure plays in your life. To what extent does structure help, and to what extent does it hinder? Would you benefit from more or less structure? Explain. Some structures to consider are those that emerge from class schedules, work schedules, the needs of a child, keeping a household going, and workout schedules.

CHAPTER 4

Writing Paragraphs

A chain is only as strong as its weakest link.

—Common saying

4a PARAGRAPH CONVENTIONS

As a matter of convention, brief communication can be written in a single, stand-alone paragraph. Short written communications such as examination answers, homework activities, e-mail, business memos, and thank-you notes may require nothing more than one paragraph to fulfill the writer's purpose and meet the reader's needs. Also as a matter of convention, longer communications that are written as essays are composed of several paragraphs—the introduction, the body paragraphs, and the conclusion. (If you need to review, see Chapter 1.)

THE EXPECTATION

You are probably familiar with several expectations for the paragraph. For example, you know that the first word is indented and that the paragraph is usually composed of several sentences—often about eight to twelve. In addition, both stand-alone paragraphs and body paragraphs each should focus on a single idea and fully explain or prove that idea.

MEETING THE EXPECTATION

Whether you are writing a stand-alone paragraph or a body paragraph to help develop an essay, you should meet the expectation to focus on and develop a single idea by presenting that idea in a **topic sentence** and explaining or proving the topic sentence idea with **supporting details**.

The following diagram illustrates the structure of stand-alone and body paragraphs.

TOPIC SENTENCE
(This sentence gives the focus of the paragraph.
In a body paragraph, the sentence must be related to the thesis.)

↓

SUPPORTING DETAIL
(This sentence explains or proves topic sentence.
Supporting details must relate to the topic sentence.)

↓

SUPPORTING DETAIL
(This sentence explains or proves the topic sentence.
Supporting details must relate to the topic sentence.)

↓

SUPPORTING DETAIL
(This sentence explains or proves the topic sentence.
Supporting details must relate to the topic sentence.)

↓

SUPPORTING DETAIL
(This sentence explains or proves the topic sentence.
Supporting details must relate to the topic sentence.)

Note: Continue with supporting details as needed.

4b THE TOPIC SENTENCE

Large supermarkets have signs above each aisle giving customers a general idea of what they will find there. The sign above aisle 3 might say "baking supplies," for example. Then when shoppers push their carts down aisle 3, they discover the specific baking items: cake and brownie mixes, flour, chocolate chips, sugar, coconut, and similar products. Without these signs, shoppers would have difficulty finding items. Like supermarket shoppers, readers need signs to tell them what to expect.

THE EXPECTATION

Readers do not like to be confused. In particular, they appreciate a **topic sentence** to tell them what to expect from a particular stand-alone or body paragraph—much like a sign in a supermarket aisle.

MEETING THE EXPECTATION

Open each stand-alone or body paragraph with a **topic sentence**—a sentence that indicates what point the paragraph will make.

For a stand-alone paragraph

If you are writing a stand-alone paragraph, you are writing a mini composition. For that reason, your topic sentence should have all the characteristics that the thesis of a larger composition would have. These characteristics are explained on pages 17–18. If necessary, review them now. They tell you that the topic sentence of a stand-alone paragraph should do the following, just as a thesis would:

- state your topic and viewpoint
- be limited
- be debatable or in need of explanation

In the following example of a stand-alone paragraph, the topic sentence is underlined as a study aid. Notice that it has the three characteristics in the above list.

Supporting details to explain or prove the topic sentence.

The crazed coupon clipper is a fanatic. Fired up at the prospect of saving a few quarters, this species accumulates hundreds, even thousands, of cents-off coupons. Strangely though, it does not even matter if the clipper can use the products the coupons are good for. My father has been a crazed clipper for years. His coupon envelope marked "pets" is so fat with coupons for dog biscuits, cat food, and flea collars you would think we had dozens of cats and dogs running around. The funny thing is, we have not owned a dog, cat, or any other four-legged animal since I was born. While the clipper may appear to be organized (having coupons arranged alphabetically in labeled envelopes), do not be fooled—every crazed clipper has grocery bags, shoe boxes, and crates hidden at the back of the closet with unfiled, largely expired coupons jammed in. The clipper is harmless for the most part; however, the species can be dangerous when turned loose in a market that offers double-coupon savings. Stay out of these places, for dozens of crazed clippers will be there with glazed eyes and fistful of coupons. So ecstatic are they at the prospect of doubling their savings that they race their carts frantically about, snatching products in a savings frenzy. More than once, normal shoppers have been run over by clippers crazed by the thought of saving twice as much. So beware! If ever you open your newspaper only to find rectangular holes where the news used to be, you no doubt have a crazed coupon clipper under your roof.

For a body paragraph

If you are writing a body paragraph, the point noted in your topic sentence must be clearly related to the essay's thesis. If you stray from the thesis, you create a problem with **relevance** because you introduce an unrelated idea. Have you ever listened to someone who just could not stick to the point? If so, you have experienced a problem with relevance.

Study the following body paragraph from "Banning Alcohol on College Campuses" on page 4. It supports the thesis, "Colleges must ban all alcohol consumption on college property, at off-campus housing, and in fraternity and sorority houses." Notice that the topic sentence, underlined as a study aid, presents the focus of the paragraph, is clearly related to the thesis, and presents an idea to help explain, illustrate, or prove that thesis.

<u>Colleges know that they have a responsibility to protect students.</u> That is why they have police and security forces, locks on residence halls, evening safe-escort services, and emergency call boxes. Now that they know students are dying from drinking, colleges must do what they can to prevent the deaths. In the past, schools have sponsored alcohol awareness programs and responsible drinking seminars, but these measures have not worked, since students are still dying. During my freshman orientation, the dean of students lectured us about drinking, but most of us just laughed the lecture off. No one takes the talk seriously, so tougher measures are called for. Perhaps more to the point, since colleges know their students have a drinking problem, they contribute to that problem if they do not take adequate measures to solve it.

> **Supporting details to explain, illustrate, or prove the topic sentence.**

DEPARTING FROM THE CONVENTION

Placing the Topic Sentence Last

The topic sentence does not have to come at the beginning of a paragraph, although most often it works best there. At times, you may want to place the topic sentence at the end, particularly when you want to emphasize the point it makes. Notice that in paragraph 5 of "Banning Alcohol on College Campuses" (page 4), the topic sentence comes at the end.

4c TRY IT OUT 1

Identify and Evaluate the Topic Sentence

1. Underline the topic sentence of the exemplification paragraph on page 29. Does it meet the requirements for an acceptable topic sentence? Explain. What is the topic? What is the viewpoint?
2. Underline the topic sentence of the comparison-contrast paragraph on page 30. Does it meet the requirements for an acceptable topic sentence? Explain. What is the topic? What is the viewpoint?
3. Underline the topic sentence of the cause-and-effect paragraph on page 30. Does it meet the requirements for an acceptable topic sentence? Explain. What is the topic? What is the viewpoint?

4d SUPPORTING DETAILS

Even with the signs to guide them, shoppers would become frustrated if supermarket aisles did not have the products the signs said they would, if the products were arranged on the shelves in a confusing fashion, or if there were not enough of these products. Readers are no different—they need a paragraph to include the content that the topic sentence says it will, they need the content to be logically arranged, and they need enough of that content.

THE EXPECTATION

A reader needs proof. If a political candidate wrote nothing more than "Vote for me," would you? I doubt it, because the candidate did not give you convincing reasons.

A reader also needs explanation. If I told you that to entertain twenty people for less than a hundred dollars, all you had to do was shop carefully, would you know how to do the shopping and entertaining? No, because I have not explained how. That is where supporting details come in. In both stand-alone and body paragraphs, they provide the details that explain or prove your topic sentence. In an essay, several body paragraphs with strong supporting details explain or prove your thesis.

MEETING THE EXPECTATION

To meet your readers' needs for detail and achieve your writing purpose, you can draw on your

- experience
- observation
- reading
- class work
- television viewing

Say, for example, that your thesis is that models in magazine advertisements contribute to poor body image among women. You might include these supporting details in your body paragraphs to prove that thesis:

FROM EXPERIENCE: Share your own feelings of inadequacy when you view magazine advertisements with female models.

FROM OBSERVATION: Tell about seeing thin women in the gym read magazines on the treadmill and talk about how they have to exercise more to look like the models in the ads.

FROM READING: Quote a newspaper article blaming magazine advertisements for the increase in eating disorders among women.

FROM CLASS WORK: Summarize a study you read in health class concluding that adolescent females think the women in magazine advertisements represent the standard of beauty. (For information on how to write a summary, see Guide 3.)

FROM TELEVISION VIEWING: Report the explanation a psychologist on *Oprah* gave linking body image problems with unrealistic media portrayals of women—including portrayals in magazine advertisements.

Use the Patterns of Development

Once you have your ideas—whether they come from experience, observation, reading, class work, or television viewing—you must write those ideas up. A number of strategies, called **patterns of development**, can help you do that. These patterns of development are explained next. (Patterns of development are also discussed in Guide 1.)

Description

Description paints a picture with words, so the reader can see, hear, smell, taste, or touch something in the mind's eye. The following body paragraph, developed with description, could appear in an essay with this thesis: "As a child, I always looked forward to Thanksgiving at my grandmother's house."

My grandmother's Thanksgiving table was always so inviting. Silver polished to a gleam was meticulously aligned on either side of bone china plates. The plates had traveled with Grandma from Russia, so we were all respectful of their age and difficult journey. The crystal goblets, standing as straight and tall as sentinels, sparkled in the last rays of the sun streaming through the dining room window. In the precise center of the table, orange and yellow mums were arranged around slender tapers. Just before we all sat down, the candles were lit, and the flaming tips would bend and flicker as the meal progressed. Each child vied for the honor of lighting the candles, and the lucky one got the first slice of pie. Once the candles were lit, we sat down to give thanks, with the warm aroma of cinnamon, the sweetness of vanilla, and the delicate scent of apple filling the room.

Narration

Narration is storytelling, usually to make or illustrate a point. The following body paragraph, which is developed with narration, could help explain this thesis: "Tragedies are often preventable."

The mother was asleep upstairs with her five-year-old when the smoke and heat awakened her. She screamed to the children downstairs to get out of the house, but she was trapped upstairs by the smoke. She broke a second-floor window and lowered the five-year-old as far as she could before she dropped her. The child landed on the sidewalk and suffered multiple breaks and a head injury. She has yet to regain consciousness. The mother jumped from the window after dropping her child, and she, too, broke bones. The three children downstairs never made it out. According to firefighters on the scene, the house had two smoke detectors. Neither one was working.

Exemplification

Exemplification is using examples to illustrate a point. In the following body paragraph, which is developed with exemplification, the examples help prove this thesis: "The United States is becoming an increasingly violent society."

Violence in our schools has reached alarming proportions. In 1997, three students were killed and five others were wounded at Heath High School in West Paducah, Kentucky. A 14-year-old student pleaded guilty to the shootings. In Pearl, Mississippi, a 16-year-old boy has been accused of killing his mother and then going to his high school and shooting nine students, two fatally. In May 1998, three days before his graduation, an 18-year-old opened fire in the parking lot at a high school in Fayetteville, Tennessee, killing a classmate who was dating his ex-girlfriend. In April of the same year, a science teacher was shot to death in front of students at an eighth-grade dance in Edinboro, Pennsylvania. A 14-year-old awaits trial. In March of the same year, four girls and a teacher were shot to death and ten people were wounded at a Jonesboro, Arkansas, school when two boys, 11 and 13, began shooting. In Conyers, Georgia, in 1999, a student with two guns opened fire at his high school, shooting six schoolmates. And on April 20, 1999, in the deadliest school massacre in the nation's history, two students stormed the Columbine High School in Littleton, Colorado, killing thirteen people and wounding twenty-three others.

Process Analysis

A **process analysis** explains how something is made or done. Instructions that explain how to assemble a bookshelf are a process analysis, as is the explanation in your biology book of how cells divide. The following body paragraph, which is developed with process analysis, could be part of an essay with this thesis: "Paper is expensive because going from tree to office supply store is difficult and time-consuming."

Paper is made of cellulose fibers, from the cell walls of trees. The bark of a tree log is stripped off, and the wood is turned into pulp by grinding it up or cooking it with chemicals, or both. Next, the wood pulp is washed to clean out impurities and chemicals. Often, the pulp is bleached at this point to make it whiter, so printing and writing will show up better on it. In the next step, the pulp is beaten in a large machine and mixed with water. The beating frays the fibers and mats them together. Starch or clay is often added to the water to give the paper a better surface for writing. The pulp then goes to a machine called a Jordan refiner, where the fibers are trimmed evenly. It is now ready for the paper-making machine, where water is pumped out as the pulp is vibrated to make the fibers interlock and mat together. The wet mat is passed under a roller into a smooth sheet. Then the sheet goes through a series of pressing rolls, which squeeze out remaining water and make the paper smooth and dense. Next it passes through heated drums, where a coating can be applied to make the paper slick and shiny. Finally, it comes out of the drums in rolls that can be trimmed to the desired size.

Comparison-Contrast

Comparison shows similarities between two things, **contrast** shows differences, and **comparison-contrast** shows both similarities and differences. Often comparison-contrast is used to show that one thing is superior to another, as in this body paragraph that could help prove the thesis: "Local voters have important decisions to make in the upcoming midterm elections."

Both Melanie Petrakis and Julio Torres are running for the office of township trustee, but Petrakis is the candidate who deserves our vote. Her vision for the township is more progressive than Torres's. She favors extending water lines to the northern corner of the township to allow for development of the area, but Torres opposes the water line extension, maintaining that our township is already too developed. Torres fails to take into account the fact that businesses are eager to relocate to that sector, and the tax revenue they would bring can help us enhance township services. Petrakis also supports building a new high school; however, Torres does not. He claims the existing school is good enough, despite overcrowding, plumbing problems, and the lack of an auditorium. Finally, Petrakis favors a partnership with adjoining townships to create an enterprise zone to attract new industry to the area. Torres, on the other hand, is opposed to the concept. He would prefer to maintain the status quo, refusing to acknowledge that anything that stands still eventually dies.

Cause-and-Effect Analysis

Cause-and-effect analysis gives the reasons an event occurs, the results of the event, or both the reasons and results. An explanation of why the earth's temperature is rising and what will happen if it continues to rise is a cause-and-effect analysis. Here is an example of a body paragraph developed with cause-and-effect analysis that could help prove this thesis: "Colleges should ban drinking on their campuses and in off-campus housing and facilities."

Drinking is common on college campuses, but few college students fully understand the effects of alcohol consumption. Average male students who have one drink a day see their grades drop below the C–level. Interestingly, women need to drink only half the amount as men to experience the same negative effect on their grades. Almost half of all academic problems stem from abusing alcohol. Further, alcohol abuse is responsible for about a third of all dropouts. A number of nonacademic problems also result from alcohol consumption by college students, including jail time and fines as a result of drunk driving and underage drinking. Fights, sexual assault, and injuries are more likely to occur when a student has been drinking. Finally, one-third of those who die in drunk driving crashes are under twenty-five years old. Such accidents are the leading cause of death in young people.

Definition

Definition explains the meaning of something difficult to understand (such as *fiber optics*) in order to inform the reader. Definition can also give the writer's understanding of something that means different things to different people (such as *justice*) in order to persuade the reader of the truth of that view. Here is an example of a body paragraph developed with definition. It could help explain this thesis: "Most Americans lack even the most basic understanding of economics, even though economics profoundly affects our well-being."

> We live in a capitalist economy, but many of us do not really know what that means. Capitalism is an economic system based on private property. Individuals can own things, amass wealth, and decide how to use that wealth. At the heart of capitalism is the notion that people will be motivated by self-interest, and the pursuit of self-interest benefits society as a whole. For example, individuals desire to make a profit, so they will make and sell goods that others want to buy. What will be bought and sold, how much a buyer will pay, and how much profit the seller can make are determined in the marketplace. In theory, the marketplace operates to make sure that society's needs for goods and services are met in an efficient manner.

Classification

Classification groups items according to some principle. For example, diet plans can be classified according to how easy they are to stick to or according to how healthy they are. The following body paragraph, developed with classification, could help explain this thesis: "To survive in college, students must learn how to take notes."

> Because lectures are the mainstay of the college classroom, students spend a great deal of time taking notes in class. Over the years, I have noticed three kinds of note-takers. The first is the speedwriter. Speedwriters never reflect on what their professors are saying; they never distinguish main points from secondary ones, generalizations from examples. Instead, they madly copy every word the professor utters, assuming each is equally important. By the end of an hour, these students are exhausted, and their hands are cramped. Studying their notes is difficult because they must sort through reams of paper and figure out what is important. The second note-taker, the memory whiz, is at the other extreme. Memory whizzes have an exaggerated faith in their ability to remember. They write down one or two things and assume that will remind them of everything else spoken. They are relaxed by the end of class, but studying their notes is futile because they have so little information. Memory whizzes end up borrowing someone else's notes. The best note-taker is the informal outliner. Informal outliners listen for main points, write them down, and give them a number. Below each numbered main point, they list examples, definitions, and explanatory points that clarify the main points, using abbreviations, phrases, and personal shorthand.

Argumentation

Argumentation aims to convince a reader to think a particular way or to act a particular way. The following body paragraph, which is developed with argumentation, helps prove this thesis: "Many images in our society cause even young children to develop poor self-concepts."

> People who design Barbie dolls and G.I. Joe action figures create an unrealistic sense of what the male and female bodies typically look like. Consider the Barbie doll. Girls who play with her grow into adolescence thinking they should have ridiculously small waists, alarmingly tiny hips, and large breasts, just like Barbie. If they don't have this figure—and they don't because it is an impossible shape to achieve—then they have poor body images and low self-esteem. Boys are equally burdened. Today's G.I. Joe, unlike the action figure of years back, has an unrealistically inflated chest, shoulders,

and biceps. Boys who come to view this physique as the ideal are destined to be disappointed in themselves. Today, both males and females are plagued with eating disorders and self-esteem problems. Certainly, unrealistic dolls and action figures contribute to those problems.

4f   TRY IT OUT   2

Identify the Pattern of Development

Assume that each of the following sentences opens a stand-alone or body paragraph. What pattern of development is likely to develop the ideas in that paragraph?

1. The basement of the old administration building is a very scary place.
2. A college student's life contains a great deal of stress.
3. After watching my son run track for four years, I have identified four distinct running styles.
4. To reduce the amount of poverty, we must solve the problem of teenage pregnancy.
5. For several reasons, capital punishment should be abolished.
6. As I entered the kitchen, I was reminded of the last day I spent in my childhood home.
7. To prepare a résumé guaranteed to get you a job, follow my advice.
8. The town square was devastated by the tornado.
9. Something must be done about the high dropout rate at our university.
10. Although the legislature wants to raise the speed limit on interstate highways, doing so would be a mistake.

4g   THE ORDER OF BODY PARAGRAPHS AND SUPPORTING DETAILS

What if you went to a play and tried to find your seat, which your ticket said was in row H—but the rows were not arranged alphabetically? Instead, row C came first, followed by row Z, then row M, and so forth in some random or incomprehensible order. Just imagine your frustration. Much the same is true of writing: Only with a logical, understandable order can readers find their way around.

THE EXPECTATION
Readers expect to find ideas presented in a logical, effective order that shows how each idea relates to the others. That means that paragraphs and their supporting details must be arranged in a way that makes sense.

MEETING THE EXPECTATION
The following are some of the most common ways to order paragraphs and supporting details.

1. **Chronological Order**. This is a time order that begins with the first event, moves to the second, and so on, until reaching the final event.
   - Chronological order is useful for telling stories, when it is important to tell what happened first, second, third, and so on.

     EXAMPLE: An essay or paragraph telling what happened when you drove to New Orleans could use chronological order.

   - Chronological order is also useful for explaining how to make or do something, when it is important to present the steps in the sequence they are performed.

     EXAMPLE: An essay or paragraph explaining how to hang wallpaper would use chronological order to ensure that the reader performs the steps in the right sequence.

2. **Spatial Order**. This order arranges items across space in a particular pattern—near to far, top to bottom, left to right, back to front, outside to inside, and so forth.

- Spatial order is useful to describe a place or scene.

  EXAMPLE: An essay or paragraph describing a child's playroom could begin the description at the door and move clockwise around the room.

- Spatial order can also be used to explain how something is arranged.

  EXAMPLE: An essay or paragraph explaining the most efficient way to set up a home office could explain what goes on and near the desk, where to put the photocopier, computer, and so forth.

3. **Progressive Order**. This is order by importance, whereby details are arranged from the least to most significant, or occasionally from most to least significant.

- Progressive order is useful for essays aiming to convince the reader of something. In such an essay, begin with your least convincing reason, follow with a more convincing reason, go on to the next most convincing reason, and so on. "Banning Alcohol on College Campuses" on page 4 follows a progressive order.

  EXAMPLE: An essay or paragraph that argues against censorship of the Internet could present reasons against it, moving from the least to the most convincing reason.

- Progressive order can also be used to rank details like examples, causes, and effects in ascending or descending order of importance.

  EXAMPLE: An essay or paragraph that explains the effects of affirmative action could give those effects from least to most significant.

4. **Problem-Solution Order**. With this order, a problem is stated and one or more solutions follow.

  EXAMPLE: An essay or paragraph could first describe a problem of poor academic performance in a local high school and then explain how adding community service work to the curriculum could solve the problem.

5. **Cause-and-Effect Order**. This order begins with an event and continues with the reasons for the event or the consequences of the event.

  EXAMPLE: An essay or paragraph could note the increased amount of violence among spectators at soccer games and then note that this increase stems from serving beer at games and from increased player violence on the field.

6. **Order by Categories**. With this order, related reasons, examples, or descriptions, are grouped and distinguished.

  EXAMPLE: An overview of good TV programming for families could begin with all the situation comedies, move on to the newsmagazines, and conclude with the dramas.

Coherence

To meet readers' expectations for a clear, logical ordering of ideas, writers must connect their ideas smoothly and show how they relate to each other. When they do so, they achieve **coherence**. Two strategies will help you achieve coherence:

- using transitions
- repeating key ideas and words

Transitions are connecting words and phrases that signal how ideas relate to each other. Different transitions signal different relationships, as the following chart explains.

TRANSITIONS

relationship	transitions
addition	*also, in addition, furthermore, moreover*
EXAMPLE:	Magazine ads depicting women cause low self-esteem. <u>Furthermore</u>, they are responsible for an increase in eating disorders.
time	*before, after, at the same time, suddenly, gradually, earlier, later, now*
EXAMPLE:	<u>Gradually</u>, magazine advertisements have made women feel inadequate.
space	*near, far, close by, beside, in front of, on one side, far, above, below, surrounding*
EXAMPLE:	<u>Near</u> the picture of a perfectly groomed woman, there is often a great-looking man, leading women to think that only the most beautiful women attract handsome men.
like	*similarly, likewise, in the same way, in like manner*
EXAMPLE:	Magazine ads cause women to feel that they should be able to take care of a family, work, and still be perfectly groomed. <u>Similarly</u>, they lead women to believe that they must weigh in at 120 pounds.
unlike	*however, in contrast, on the contrary, on the other hand, nevertheless*
EXAMPLE:	Women in magazines are the product of makeup artists, clothing designers, and lighting experts. Real women, <u>in contrast</u>, do not have the benefit of such professional services.
cause or effect	*because, since, as a result, consequently, therefore, thus, hence*
EXAMPLE:	Women are beginning to rebel against the image projected in magazine ads. <u>As a result</u>, more advertisers are using larger women in their ads.
illustration	*for example, for instance, as an illustration, in particular*
EXAMPLE:	Eating disorders are on the rise, and some authorities say magazine advertisements play a role. <u>For example</u>, a recent study revealed that women between 18 and 35 believe that they would be happier if they looked like women in magazine advertisements.

Another way to achieve coherence is to repeat key ideas and words.

KEY WORD REPEATED:	The Academic Senate is currently evaluating graduation *requirements*. These *requirements* have not been revised since 1980.
KEY IDEA REPEATED:	In our culture, *television and movie stars* are looked up to as heroes. These *celebrities* do not often deserve this status.

4h   TRY IT OUT   3

Order Ideas

Assume that each sentence in Try It Out 2 on page 32 is a topic sentence. In what order are the supporting details likely to be arranged? Be prepared to explain why you chose each order.

4i   TRY IT OUT   4

Identify and Write Coherence Devices

1. Turn back to "Banning Alcohol on College Campuses" on page 4 and identify the following:
   a. *two* coherence devices in paragraph 2, sentence 4
   b. the first coherence device in paragraph 3, sentence 2

c. two words repeated for coherence in paragraph 5, sentence 2

d. the first coherence device in paragraph 6, sentence 4

e. the coherence device in paragraph 6, the second-to-last sentence

2. Write sentences according to the directions given.

a. Write two sentences about examinations. In the second sentence, include a transitional word or phrase that signals addition.

b. Write two sentences about friends. In the second sentence, include a transitional word or phrase that signals "like."

c. Write two sentences about music. In the second sentence, include a transitional word or phrase that signals "unlike."

d. Write two sentences about sports. In the second sentence, achieve coherence with repetition of a key word or idea.

4j WRITING THE INTRODUCTION

When you meet someone at a party, you quickly form a first impression. You notice the person's face, manner of speech, clothes, and gestures and react positively or negatively based on this limited information. Yes, such first impressions are superficial, and true, they are often wrong. Nonetheless, they are powerful, and for that reason they are important. In writing, first impressions are also important.

THE EXPECTATION

Essay introductions create first impressions, causing readers to make quick decisions about whether they are interested in what you have to say and, hence, whether they will read further. Readers expect to learn the focus of your writing early on, and they expect to discover whether that topic will interest them.

MEETING THE EXPECTATION

To engage the reader, the introduction to an essay should do two things:

- it should spark interest
- it should give the essay's thesis

You learned about the thesis in Chapter 3. If you need to review that material, turn to pages 17–18. In addition, the strategies explained next can spark your readers' interest in your thesis and essay.

1. **Select an interesting quotation.** Use fresh quotations likely to stimulate your reader's interest rather than tired expressions.

    FRESH: "The way a person works," my father always told me, "tells what that person is like." If Dad is right, then the way my chemistry lab partner performs his experiments indicates that he has a death wish.

    TIRED: "Nice guys finish last" or "The early bird gets the worm."

2. **Create contrast.** Open by stating the opposite of your thesis. In the following example, the last sentence is the thesis; the material before that thesis is the contrast.

    Because Pittsburgh is only about 70 miles from where I live, I never considered it as a vacation site. I always thought of a cabin nestled in the mountains or a hotel at a seaside resort, not a big, busy city so close to home. Much to my surprise, I found Pittsburgh to be the ideal vacation spot.

3. **Use description.** With well-chosen description, you can paint interesting mental pictures, as in this example.

    Just in time for finals week, a late winter storm cast a bleak pall over the campus. The dingy grey sky darkened the landscape as frigid winds whipped across the greens, sending enormous snowflakes swirling in every direction at once. Students on their way to exams lowered their heads and trudged into the wind. Little did they know that the worst ice storm of the century was about to hit and paralyze the campus.

4. **Ask interesting questions.** Interesting questions can pique your reader's curiosity and get your reader thinking about your topic as in this example.

> Wouldn't you be surprised if holidays were the relaxing, enjoyable breaks that we all pretend they are? Wouldn't you love it if that Thanksgiving get-together with Mom and Dad and Great-Aunt Mabel didn't turn into a stress-filled afternoon? Most of us do not like to admit it, but too much closeness with family can be disastrous. The family dinner I gave last year to celebrate my brother's engagement proves this unfortunate fact.

5. **Tell a brief story.** Everyone enjoys good stories, so telling one can be an excellent way to spark interest, as in this example.

> Ordinarily, I would go to the drive-through window to cash my paycheck, but the line was longer than usual, so I decided to go into the bank. I took my place at the end of the shortest line and the unthinkable happened. The man at the head of the line began shouting at the teller, who shouted back. As a security guard approached, the unhappy customer pulled a gun and fired three shots into the teller and one into himself. This is yet another example of what happens when guns are too easily available.

6. **Preview the ideas you will give to explain or prove your thesis.** Doing this gives your reader an idea of what will come in your essay. Notice that in the following example, the first sentence presents the essay's thesis and the remaining sentences present the three ideas that will be developed later in the essay to support the thesis.

> Parents should limit the amount of violence their young children watch on television. Very young children become frightened by violent shows and grow up fretful and fearful. Evidence even suggests that children who watch violent programming become desensitized to violence. Worse, they may pick up violent tendencies themselves and engage in antisocial behavior.

7. **Give important background information.** If there are some things your reader should know for full understanding or appreciation of your essay, you can provide that background information, as in the following example. Notice that the last sentence states the thesis, and the sentences before that offer background information.

> Americans are attached to the nine-month school year, for the three-month vacation in summer is a long-standing tradition that will not die easily. Farmers want their children home in the summer to help with the crops; parents want a three-month opportunity for family vacations; children want camp, baseball, and lazy days that last the whole summer. However, despite opposition to an extended school year, a change to an eleven-month academic calendar has many benefits.

DEPARTING FROM THE CONVENTION

Implying the Thesis or Placing It at the End

Most readers appreciate a clearly stated thesis in the introduction. However, in some essays, the thesis is not written out; instead, it is *implied*. When a thesis is implied, the reader can figure out the central point from the clues in the essay. In other essays, the thesis does not appear early on; instead, it can appear as late as in the conclusion. In this case, the reader can usually figure out what the thesis is before getting to the stated thesis. For now, you may want to state your thesis in the introduction. Later, when you are more experienced, you can experiment with implied and delayed theses.

4k TRY IT OUT 5

Generate Ideas for Introductions

For each essay described, suggest an approach to the introduction. Be prepared to explain why you have made each choice.

> EXAMPLE: an essay about the dangers of televised violence, written for *TV Guide*
>
> *Tell a story of a ten-year-old who assaulted a six-year-old after watching a violent program.*

1. an essay about how to select the best courses, written for the campus newspaper
2. an essay describing the scenic beauty of a mountain resort, written for a travel magazine
3. an essay explaining the economic impact of Clinton administration taxing policies, written as an assignment for a political science class
4. an essay about the irresponsibility in the mayor's office, written as a letter to the editor of a local newspaper
5. an autobiographical essay, written as part of an application for a scholarship competition
6. an essay that compares and contrasts two kinds of sport utility vehicles, written for *Car and Driver* magazine
7. an essay that explains the causes of pollution of a local river, written as an assignment for a geography class

4l TRY IT OUT 6

Write Two Introductions

Write two introductions, each with a different approach, for the following thesis.

> Colleges should [or should not] abolish final examinations.

4m WRITING THE CONCLUSION

Envision the final basketball game of the season. The star player, who has performed magnificently all year, fouls out in the last few minutes, and the team loses as a result. Or think about going into a final exam with an A– average, getting a C on the final, and earning a B in the course as a result. We tend to remember the bad—the player fouling out and the C on the final—more than the good because the most memorable event is the most recent event. This psychology holds true for writing as well.

THE EXPECTATION

In an essay, the conclusion becomes the most recent event, so make it worth remembering. Although conclusions are important, they need not be long. When you have said what you need to say, exit gracefully. There is no need for a long goodbye. The conclusion should leave your reader with a positive final impression, and it should provide closure; it need not be lengthy.

MEETING THE EXPECTATION

To meet your reader's expectation for a strong conclusion, you can use any of the approaches explained below. The approaches are illustrated with conclusions that could be used for "Banning Alcohol on College Campuses" on page 4.

1. **Restate your thesis and/or supporting ideas in a new way.** Restatement is a good approach when you want to emphasize something.

> Most college students are still young people, and that means they do not always make wise choices. In the case of alcohol, too many are choosing to drink too much. They risk a lifetime of alcoholism and even death. Colleges cannot stand by and be content that "safe drinking" lectures fulfill their obligation. They need to protect students with a bold measure. They need to ban drinking altogether.

2. **Call your reader to action.** Let your readers know specifically what they can do to help implement your thesis.

> The time has come to urge the administration to ban alcohol on our campus. We must write letters to the university president and all the members of the board of trustees. If necessary, we should make the press aware of the problem to bring public pressure to bear.

3. **Explain what will happen if your thesis is rejected.** You lend importance to your thesis by noting that if the reader does not accept it, something negative will result.

> If we do not ban alcohol on college campuses, we risk the lives of our students, for surely more will die from alcohol poisoning. Those who drink excessively and live face a lifetime of alcoholism. Students should emerge from college equipped for a happy, productive life. We cannot ensure that as long as we condone alcohol consumption on campus.

4. **Use a powerful quotation, fact, or statistic.** These can emphasize your point.

> According to the Substance Abuse and Mental Health Service Administration, 2 million Americans under 21 have been binge-drinking in the last 30 days. University administrations must play their role in reducing that statistic.

5. **Combine two or more approaches.** Any approaches can be combined. In fact, for longer conclusions, writers are more likely to combine approaches than stick with just one. The following example restates the thesis and calls the reader to action.

> Thus, we must ban alcohol on campus to ensure the safety of students. The time has come to urge the administration to take the appropriate action to do so. We must write letters to the university president and all the members of the board of trustees. If necessary, we should make the press aware of the problem to bring public pressure to bear.

4n TRY IT OUT   7

Write a Conclusion

The following essay lacks a conclusion. Using one of the approaches given in this chapter, or any other that you find suitable, write a conclusion.

The Benefits of Company Day-care Centers

Every year, companies spend thousands, and in some cases millions, of dollars on their employees. These businesses provide everything from holiday parties to basic health and life insurance to retirement funding to gymnasium memberships. These services are provided to maintain a happy and healthy staff who will work more effectively. However, companies seldom provide on-site day care for their employees' children.

On-site day care would give employees more time to spend with their children. Parents and children would be able to have lunch together. Also, the time-consuming step of getting to and from day care would be eliminated, giving parents more time with their children. Obviously, any arrangement that increases the time spent between parents and children is desirable. Parents will be happier and feel less guilt about not being with their children, and this improved attitude will enhance job performance.

In addition to increasing the time parents can spend with their children, on-site day care will reduce the stress parents feel as a result of putting their children in the care of others. Because they are physically closer to their children, parents can monitor what goes on and not worry about how their children are. They also know they can get to their children quickly in the event of an emergency, which reduces their anxiety. When employees feel less stress, they perform better.

Finally, on-site day care will reduce employee absenteeism. Employees do not have to stay home to care for their children when their baby-sitters get sick or take a vacation or move away. This means increased productivity for the employer and less stress for the employee. It also means that both employee and employer do not lose money because of absenteeism.

4o CONVENTIONS AND EXPECTATIONS AT LARGE

Greetings and Leave-Takings

Just as conventions and expectations exist for essay introductions and conclusions, they exist for saying hello and goodbye. These conventions and expectations often vary from culture to culture.

- Rather than shake hands, Greeks often embrace and kiss in greeting.
- People in the Philippines shake hands upon greeting and leave-taking, but the free hand is placed on top of the handshake or used to pat the other party on the back.
- In India, a handshake is common between two men, but to greet a woman, people place their palms together and give a slight bow.
- The Japanese bow in the direction of the person being greeted— the deeper the bow, the more respect is shown.
- Handshakes mark both the beginning and ending of an encounter in France, but they are not strong handshakes. The French tend to shake hands using a light touch rather than a squeeze.
- In New Zealand, the Maori greet by rubbing noses; in East Africa, some will spit at a person's feet in greeting; in Tibet, people stick out their tongues.

Activity

Observe and consider the conventions of openings and closings in any two of the following situations: business meetings, television newscasts, first dates, campus visitations, first class sessions, job interviews. Write two lists citing the conventions, one for each situation.

Writing Topic

Think back to a time when you made a bad first impression or left a bad final impression. Explain what happened, analyze why you think it happened, and describe what the effect was on you.

CHAPTER 5

Revising and Editing

I'm not a very good writer, but I'm an excellent rewriter.
— James A. Michener (1907–1997), American author

5a REVISING AND EDITING AS CONVENTION

As a writing student, you are accustomed to submitting your work to an instructor who reads, reacts, and makes suggestions. Then you write again and try to improve as a result of the feedback. Because almost no one works in isolation, writing students are not the only ones who submit their work for "inspection" and then make changes. For example, art dealers may ask artists to depict more popular subjects; coaches may require athletes to change their technique and form; store managers may require window dressers to add more color to a display; and conductors may tell musicians to alter tempo.

Because we are not perfect and must respond to those who react to our efforts, almost everything we attempt is a work in progress. The reworking makes the difference between a twenty-yard pass and a fifty-yard pass, an average window display and a traffic-stopper, a mediocre performance and an inspired concert.

THE EXPECTATION

For writers, the reworking process involves revising and editing. **Revising** involves improving the content, organization, and expression of ideas. **Editing** is correcting mistakes in grammar, spelling, punctuation, and capitalization. Remember, when you wrote your first draft, your goal was to get your ideas down the best way you could without being too critical. With revising and editing, however, you *should* be critical so you can meet your readers' expectations for polished writing and your own expectation to entertain, express yourself, inform, or persuade.

MEETING THE EXPECTATION

Revise before you edit—that is, first rework your draft to improve content, organization, and the expression of your ideas, and then look for grammar, spelling, punctuation, and capitalization errors. This sequence is efficient because you will not spend time correcting mistakes in sentences that you later decide to rewrite or eliminate.

In addition, be aware of resources that can help you revise and edit. If you have questions or concerns, try one or more of the following.

1. **Visit your campus writing center.** There you will find sensitive readers who will describe their reactions to your draft to give you an understanding of what changes you should consider. Writing center staff will not revise and edit for you—they do not "fix" your papers—but they will help you understand what *you* need to do to improve a draft.
2. **Consult this book.** Relevant sections of this book will help you understand how to improve your writing. To find the pages you need, check the index or the revising and editing checklists on pages 45 and 50.
3. **Use a reliable reader.** Share your draft with someone who has good judgment about the qualities of effective writing—someone who will not hesitate to offer constructive criticism. For more on using a reliable reader—and being one yourself.
4. **Have a conference with your instructor.** During scheduled office hours or with an appointment, discuss your draft with your instructor. In particular, talk about what you see as its chief strengths and weaknesses and your ideas for revision.

COMPUTER TIP

Microsoft Word's Track Changes function allows you to highlight revisions. Deletions appear as crossed-out text, and additions appear in a contrasting color. With this feature, you can keep track of your revisions until you are sure which ones you want to keep. To use this feature, go to Tools, then Track Changes, and then Highlight Changes.

5b   REVISING CONTENT

Imagine a teacher explaining to first graders what they should do in the event of a fire. The teacher might say, "Open your ears, close your mouth, and listen to what your teacher tells you to do." For sixth graders, however, a teacher might say, "Stop talking immediately, and listen for instructions." Now imagine a teacher explaining how to prevent fires in the home. With this new purpose, what the teacher says to either audience changes dramatically. Like teachers, writers must suit their content to their audience and purpose.

THE EXPECTATION

For your writing to be successful, your content must meet the needs of your audience and fulfill your purpose for writing. Thus, if you want to convince college students to register to vote, everything you do must work to persuade readers with characteristics typical of college students. (To review audience and purpose, turn back to page 8.)

MEETING THE EXPECTATION

As you revise your content to meet your readers' needs and fulfill your writing purpose, remember the following:

1. **Check your thesis.** Revise as necessary to be sure your thesis
   - states a topic and viewpoint
   - is limited
   - presents something debatable or in need of explanation
   - avoids language that announces
   - avoids expressions like "I think" and "in my opinion"

   Also, if your thesis states the points you will develop in your essay, write those points in the order they are discussed.
2. **Suit your supporting details to your audience and purpose.** If you aim to convince magazine advertising executives to use photographs of average women rather than supermodels, do not mention that millions of women try unsuccessfully to look like the models. This point would not achieve your purpose with this particular audience because if millions of women are reading the ads, then advertisers will view them as successful. Instead, note that increasing numbers of women are receptive to ads with models that look like average women. (For more on supporting details, Chapter 4.)
3. **Be clear.** We know so well in our own minds what we mean that we assume our readers will understand readily, but this is not always the case. To be sure everything is clear, ask a reliable reader to review your draft and note anything that is not understandable.
4. **Explain or prove each point.** You can support each point by
   - using examples
   - telling a story
   - adding vivid description
   - defining key concepts
   - comparing and contrasting specific points
   - explaining a process (how something is made or done)
   - including quotations from your reading
   - presenting information you have learned in your classes

- citing evidence from your own observation and experience
- explaining the significance of your points

For more on now to prove or explain your points, see Chapter 4.

5. **Avoid straying from your thesis.** No matter how much you want to include a piece of information, you should not do so if it does not directly relate to your thesis. Thus, if your thesis states that magazine advertisements contribute to poor body image among women, you should not state that television commercials are also part of the problem. Nor should you note that men also lose self-esteem when they view magazine ads. Although these points are *somewhat* related to the thesis, they are not *directly* related to it.

6. **Avoid obvious statements.** When something is so obvious that it does not need to be stated, do not state it. For example, you do not need to state that magazines have advertisements, and many advertisements portray women. Obvious statements insult the reader's intelligence.

7. **Tighten your draft as needed.** If your draft is too long, try one or more of the following:
   - Narrow your thesis to cover less territory. Instead of discussing all the reasons that magazine advertisements should use models that look like average women, discuss only the most important reasons.
   - Check the relevance of all your points to be sure you are not straying from your thesis.
   - Eliminate wordiness and repetition. Instead of writing "black in color," just write "black." Also, be sure you are not repeating yourself by writing the same ideas more than once but in different ways.
   - Avoid introductions and conclusions that are too long. Review these paragraphs to be sure you are not rambling.

8. **Extend your draft as needed.** If your draft is too short, develop additional points using the patterns of development explained on page 28. If you cannot think of additional points, return to idea generation. If necessary, expand your thesis to take in more territory.

9. **Be sure your opening stimulates interest and that your conclusion ties things up in a satisfying way.** Your reader should be motivated by your opening to read on and should not feel let down by your ending. Consult pages 35 and 37–38 for strategies for your introduction and conclusion.

5c REVISING ORGANIZATION

Imagine trying to read a book with the chapters scrambled into a random order. How far do you think you would get before you put the book down and found something else to do? Or imagine trying to follow a newspaper account of a bank robbery if the events were arranged out of sequence. How long do you think you would read before you became frustrated trying to follow what happened? When elements are not arranged in an easy-to-follow order, readers have a hard time of it—and they often give up.

THE EXPECTATION

Readers expect to follow the progression of your ideas easily. No matter how good your points are, if they are not presented in an understandable order, your reader can become confused. Therefore, an important part of revising is checking organization and coherence.

MEETING THE EXPECTATION

When you revise for organization, remember the following points.

1. **Have each body paragraph make a separate, distinct point.** Avoid jamming several important points in a single paragraph. If a point is important enough to make, it is important enough to develop fully in its own paragraph.

2. **Present ideas in a logical order.** This is the time to rearrange ideas and even whole paragraphs to create a logical sequence. One of these orders, discussed on page 32 is likely to work well:
   - chronological order
   - spatial order
   - progressive order
   - problem-solution order
   - cause-and-effect order
   - order by categories

3. **Add transitions and repetition to signal how ideas are related.** One way to determine whether you need a transition or repetition of a word or idea is to read your work aloud. If you hear a gap or an abrupt shift in direction, add a transition or repeat a key word or idea. For more on transitions and repetition, see page 33 on coherence.

COMPUTER TIP

To try a different organization, use the Copy and Move functions to rearrange paragraphs and sentences.

5d　REVISING FOR EFFECTIVE EXPRESSION

One of the most famous—and ridiculed—openings ever written was penned by Victorian novelist Edward George Earl Bulwer-Lytton, who opened his 1830 novel *Paul Clifford* with "It was a dark and stormy night." Now, a contest to write the worst opening line is held every year, and that contest is named after Bulwer-Lytton. One of the 1999 winners of the Bulwer-Lytton award was David Hirsch, who wrote this opening:

> Rain—violent torrents of it, rain like fetid water from a God-sized pot of pasta strained through a sky-wide colander, rain as Noah knew it, flaying the shuddering trees, whipping the whitecapped waters, violating the sodden firmament, purging purity and filth alike from the land, rain without mercy, without surcease, incontinent rain, turning to intermittent showers overnight with partial clearing Tuesday.

Hirsch's introduction is funny because it is so intentionally poorly expressed.

THE EXPECTATION

Because readers expect to enjoy what they read, they have little patience for poorly written sentences. In fact, even if the ideas interest them, they are likely to stop reading if those ideas are expressed in wordy or hard-to-understand sentences. Thus, in addition to solid content and understandable organization, writers must revise for effective expression in order to meet their readers' needs and fulfill their own purpose for writing.

MEETING THE EXPECTATION

Keep the following points in mind.

1. **Suit your vocabulary to your audience.** You can use words like *bumptious, egregious,* and *parsimonious* if your reader is highly educated, but avoid such high-flown words for a more general reader. If you are writing for children, keep the words simple, and if you are writing a formal piece for an instructor, avoid slang.

2. **Use specific words.** To give your writing interest, replace some general nouns (like *book, car,* and *drink*) with specific ones (like Wuthering Heights, *Ford Explorer,* and *cocoa*); replace some general verbs (like *said, eat,* and *go*) with specific ones (like *shouted, devour,* and *saunter*). Also, use some specific descriptive words to give phrases life (like <u>*driving*</u> rain, <u>*brittle*</u> paper, and *running <u>in a frantic rush</u>*).

REVISING CHECKLIST

To be sure you have considered everything, be certain you can answer "yes" to every question in the following checklist. The page numbers in parentheses refer you to the appropriate sections of this book.

_____ 1. Is my introduction likely to spark my reader's interest? (page 35)
_____ 2. Does my essay have a readily identifiable thesis? (page 17)
_____   a. Does my thesis express my topic and viewpoint? (page 17)
_____   b. Is my thesis limited? (page 18)
_____   c. Does my thesis present something debatable or in need of explanation? (page 18)
_____   d. Have I avoided making an announcement? (page 18)
_____   e. Have I presented my viewpoint in specific language? (page 19)
_____   f. Have I avoided language such as "I think" and "in my opinion"? (page 19)
_____   g. If my thesis includes the points I develop in the essay, are those points in the same order they appear in the essay? (page 19)
_____ 3. Does every paragraph make a separate, distinct point? (page 43)
_____ 4. Are my details arranged in a logical, suitable order? (page 32)
_____ 5. Have I used transitions to signal how ideas are related? (page 34)
_____ 6. Are all my points backed up with specific evidence? (page 27)
_____ 7. Are all my details suitable to my audience and purpose? (page 42)
_____ 8. Is my vocabulary suited to my audience? (page 44)
_____ 9. Have I avoided details that stray from my thesis? (page 43)
_____ 10. Have I avoided stating the obvious? (page 43)
_____ 11. Have I expressed my ideas clearly? (page 42)
_____ 12. Have I avoided repetition? (page 42)
_____ 13. Have I used specific words? (page 44)
_____ 14. Is my essay the appropriate length? (page 43)
_____ 15. Does my conclusion tie things up in a satisfying way? (page 38)
_____ 16. Have I given my essay a suitable title? (page 45)

COMPUTER TIP

Save a revision checklist as a file. When you revise, you can split your screen and place the checklist in one window and your draft in the other.

5e   WRITING A TITLE

Titles are like the icing on the cake. They suggest the treat in store, and they can be put on last.

THE EXPECTATION

An essay's title is important because it gives your reader a first clue about what is coming. However, you need not compose the title first; it can be decided on at any time. In fact, many writers think of their best titles near the end of the writing process.

MEETING THE EXPECTATION

When you write your titles, remember the following guidelines.

1. **Suit your title to your content.** A serious piece should not have a humorous title.
2. **Avoid titles that tell little about the focus of your writing.** For example, the title "Advertising" tells the reader little about what to expect. However, the title "The Image of Women in Cigarette Advertisements" tells the reader a great deal.

3. **Do not use quotation marks, underlining, or italics for your own titles on the title page.** These are reserved for titles that are mentioned in the body of a paper.

4. **Capitalize correctly.** Capitalize the first word and the last word. In between, capitalize everything except articles (*a, an, the*), conjunctions (words like *and, but, or, nor, for, so, yet*), and prepositions (words like *in, at, on, near, beside, of*).

> EXAMPLES: *In the Heat of the Night*   *The Death of a Salesman*
>
> *The Once and Future King*   *Gone with the Wind*

STRATEGIES FOR REVISING

1. **Work in stages.** Revising is a gradual process. If you expect dramatic improvements in one or two quick sessions, you will become frustrated. You will be much more successful if you revise in a series of steps and think about the essay in between. One of the following approaches may work well for you:
   - Make the easy changes first, and then make the hard ones.
   - Make the hard changes first, and then make the easy ones.
   - Revise one paragraph at a time.
   - Work through the revising checklist on page 45.

2. **Give yourself time and distance.**
   - Take a break for a day or so. After generating ideas and writing your draft, you need a cooling-off period. After some time away, you will be more objective about evaluating the strengths and weaknesses of your draft.
   - Take a break between stages. To stay sharp and focused, take a break between each phase of your revising—or whenever you feel the need to refresh yourself.
   - Give yourself plenty of time. Revising is best done over a period of days—even weeks, for longer pieces. Rushing the process leads to a final version that is less than what it could or should be.

3. **Type your draft if it is handwritten or print out a computer draft and copy it in longhand.** When you type a handwritten draft, you will see weaknesses in typed or word-processed copy that you overlook in your own handwriting. Similarly, the act of hand copying a computer draft can bring improvements to mind.

4. **Listen to your draft.** Read it out loud or ask a classmate to read it to you. Many writers *hear* problems more readily than they *see* them.

5. **Trust your instincts.** Never ignore a feeling that says you have a problem. If you sense that something is wrong, the chances are excellent that a problem really exists.

COMPUTER TIP

- Revise both on the screen and on paper because each view of your draft gives you a different perspective. Triple-space drafts on paper to allow room for writing in changes.
- The computer makes your draft look neat and professional. Do not let the polished appearance mislead you into thinking the draft does not need work.
- Save deleted material in a separate file in case you change your mind and decide to use it.
- E-mail your draft to a reliable reader for reactions and suggestions.

5f   TRY IT OUT   1

Compare Paragraphs

The following paragraphs each have the same number of sentences. However, one paragraph is better than the other. Decide which paragraph is better and why.

PARAGRAPH A

When you are ill, eating chicken soup is a good idea. This simple food is a good source of two things you need when you are sick: liquids and salt. When you have a high fever or when your nose is running, your body loses water. The more liquids you take in to replace lost fluids, the better off you are because fluids help push germs through your system. Furthermore, if you lose too much fluid, you can become dehydrated. That is why salt is important; it helps your body retain its fluids. Thus, Grandma knew exactly what she was doing when she brought you that chicken soup the last time you were sick.

PARAGRAPH B

When you are ill, eating chicken soup is a good idea. If you do not feel well, try some chicken soup because you will certainly feel better. I know how comforting it is first-hand because recently I had the flu. My roommate brought me chicken soup from the dining hall, which did help me perk up a little. Apparently, researchers have discovered that liquids and salt are beneficial to sick people. The soup, which is obviously liquid, contains a considerable amount of salt. Thus, the next time you are sick, try some chicken soup.

5g   TRY IT OUT   2

Eliminate the Relevance Problem

In the following paragraph, one sentence strays from the point. Cross out that sentence.

Margo has tried the craziest diets. First, she tried a diet that consisted of eating only foods that began with the letter *A*. Next, she tried one that let her eat whatever she wanted on Mondays, Wednesdays, Fridays, and Sundays, but she could eat nothing during the rest of the week. Margo also tried a diet that required her to drink eight glasses of milk before 7:00 A.M. She did not mind this diet at all, but her little brother could never stick to it because he is allergic to dairy products. The last diet Margo tried had her eating raw fish for breakfast and eggs for dinner. If she is not careful, Margo will ruin her health with these weird diets.

5h   TRY IT OUT   3

Give Specific Evidence

Follow each statement with a specific example, explanation, or piece of evidence.

EXAMPLE: *general statement:* College students do not always eat properly.

specific statement: Because they are often rushed, college students eat high-fat fast food.

1. *general statement:* Lee is very lazy.

specific statement: _____

_____

2. *general statement:* Visiting a foreign city is a challenging experience.

specific statement: _____

_____

3. *general statement:* Good writing skills are important to success in college.

   specific statement: _____

   _____

4. *general statement:* The thought of surgery is terrifying to many people.

   specific statement: _____

   _____

5. *general statement:* Pat knows the most interesting people.

   specific statement: _____

   _____

5i TRY IT OUT   4

Evaluate a Draft

The following is a first draft of an essay by a first-year student. Although it has some strengths, it also has a number of weaknesses that could be improved with rewriting. Read the draft, and then evaluate it by answering the questions that follow it.

Buying a Stereo That Plays Compact Discs

1   Music is the greatest. The human experience would not be the same if we had to go without it. Music is the embodiment of our souls and an art form. However, to be completely enjoyed, music must be listened to correctly. An important component to this is to have the correct stereo system. When purchasing a compact disc playing stereo, there are several steps that should be followed to insure that you have made a wise selection.

2   The first step in making a wise stereo purchase is to begin your shopping at a reputable store. In a store that is not reputable you can be led astray by salespeople who are overly anxious to get a sale out of you, and not interested enough in going through the motions that are necessary in helping you choose a quality stereo.

3   Set a price range that you would like to stay within. It is not always necessary to spend a lot of money to get a quality stereo.

4   The next step in purchasing a stereo is to bring along a compact disc to test out the sound of the stereos that you are looking at. Play the CD on the disc player to test it out.

5   Be very careful to look at all the features the system has to offer. Many times a system will have gadgets, like a multiple disc changer or overly complicated graphic equalizer, that serve no useful purpose except to bump up the price. These gadgets can even compromise the sound quality. A good way to guard against this is to look for systems that have gadgets that are truly useful. Such a gadget would be a remote control.

6   Most important is judging the quality of the graphic equalizers. These are devices that allow you to adjust the bass, treble, and middle sound qualities of the stereo. Watch out for overly complicated systems because they make it hard to get the sound quality you want. A good rule to go by is the less adjustment you have to do, the better.

7   So, listen to music. However, you must remember to listen correctly by following the steps just given.

EVALUATION QUESTIONS

1. Answer the following questions about the introduction:
   a. First, what purpose does the introduction of an essay serve?
   b. Which paragraph forms the introduction of "Buying a Stereo That Plays Compact Discs"?
   c. Underline the thesis. What does the thesis present as the essay's topic and viewpoint?
   d. How well does the student's introduction spark your interest? Explain.
2. Answer the following questions about the body paragraphs:
   a. What purpose do the body paragraphs of an essay serve?
   b. Which paragraphs are the body paragraphs of the student essay?
3. Evaluate how well each of the following body paragraphs supports or explains the essay's thesis. Explain your view.
   a. paragraph 2
   b. paragraph 3
   c. paragraph 4
   d. paragraph 5
4. Answer the following questions about the conclusion:
   a. What purpose does the conclusion of an essay serve?
   b. How well does the conclusion of the student's essay fulfill that purpose? Explain your view.

5j   TRY IT OUT   5

Evaluate a Draft

Using the revising checklist on page 45, evaluate the following draft and make a list of suggestions for the author to consider during revision.

Me

From birth until I was ten, I lived in seven different places, from the slums of Squirrel Hill to the woods of Conneaut Lake, from urban North Lauderdale to suburban Cleveland. I attended five different elementary schools, which was very difficult for me. Being tossed around from school to school was very hard.

I was ridiculed and talked about because I was different from everybody else. To make matters worse, the teacher would sometimes give me special attention to help me feel comfortable. This would cause the other kids to call me the teacher's pet. It always seemed that once I did feel comfortable in my new school, we would be packing and moving again.

I wanted so badly to fit in at my new schools, but I never did. Moving from the city to the country, from the North to the South, meant that my clothes and other things about me were not quite right. I stood out for lots of reasons, so I was constantly laughed at. I was never with the rest of my class in my studies. I was either ahead or behind, labeled "Miss Brain" or "dimwit." No matter how hard I tried, I never fit in. I suppose, though, that all the rejection made me stronger.

Being a new kid in school is no fun at all. As a result of all the years of moving around and trying to fit in, I still feel insecure and unaccepted. I will never start a family until I am sure I am firmly rooted in one place.

5k EDITING

Being correct can be very important. In writing computer software, for example, a single incorrect character can cause serious problems. In one famous instance, a misplaced minus sign in a computer program caused a fighter jet's control system to flip the plane on its back whenever it crossed the equator.

THE EXPECTATION

Details count! Writers must take care with grammar, spelling, punctuation, and capitalization, or the results can be troublesome. Errors can cause miscommunication, and they can diminish the reader's respect for the writer's ability. Thus, you must check your writing carefully to find and correct mistakes in grammar, spelling, punctuation, and capitalization. The process of finding and correcting these errors is **editing.**

MEETING THE EXPECTATION

The following suggestions can help you meet your readers' expectations for error-free prose. In addition, use the resources mentioned on page 41.

1. **Learn the rules.** You cannot edit with confidence if you do not know the rules. As necessary, refer to Part 2 of this book, and learn the rules you are unsure of.

2. **Learn your pattern of error.** Pay attention to the mistakes your instructors and other readers note in your writing to discover the kinds of errors you habitually make (with fragments, with subject-verb agreement, with semicolons, and so forth). Then you can be particularly vigilant about looking for these errors when you edit.

3. **Understand the difference between editing and proofreading. Proofreading** is the final check for clerical errors made after you copy or type your essay into its final form. Proofreading is the check for mistakes like omitting words, writing the same word twice, or transposing letters. You edit for mistakes *before* copying or typing your essay into its final form; you proofread *afterward.*

4. **Turn to Application 1 at the back of this book and edit the passages that appear there.** This practice will help you identify grammar rules you currently do not know and review those you do know.

EDITING CHECKLIST

Be sure you can answer "yes" to the following questions.

_____   1. Have I eliminated any sentence fragments?
_____   2. Have I eliminated any comma splices and run-on sentences?
_____   3. Have I maintained subject-verb agreement?
_____   4. Have I maintained pronoun-antecedent agreement?
_____   5. Have I used subject, object, and possessive pronouns correctly?
_____   6. Have I used adjectives and adverbs correctly?
_____   7. Have I eliminated dangling modifiers?
_____   8. Have I eliminated misplaced modifiers?
_____   9. Have I used frequently confused words correctly?
_____   10. Have I used capital letters correctly?
_____   11. Have I used commas correctly?
_____   12. Have I used semicolons correctly?
_____   13. Have I used apostrophes correctly?
_____   14. Have I used quotation marks correctly?
_____   15. Have I used dashes and parentheses correctly?
_____   16. Have I checked all spellings that I am unsure of?
_____   17. *Personal Checklist:* I need to be careful to check _____. (Fill in the blank with the error(s) you habitually make.)

COMPUTER TIP

Save an editing checklist as a file. You can then split your screen and place the checklist in one of the windows to guide your editing.

5I   EDITING ENGLISH AS A SECOND LANGUAGE

People who know multiple languages are fortunate because they have a rich source of information about the world that others do not. Those who learn a second language as children are the most fortunate because language learning is easiest during childhood. If you are learning English as an adult, you will need time, patience, and practice.

THE EXPECTATION

If you have spoken English for many years, you may need only to pick up subtle grammar points, learn the current idioms and slang, and perhaps practice your pronunciation. If English is new to you, you will have more to learn. Either way, be realistic about what you expect of yourself. Strive for small, steady gains. Language learning always takes time.

MEETING THE EXPECTATION

Whether you are new to English or a long-time user of English as a second language, the following can help you improve your use of the language. As your English skills increase, your editing ability will improve at the same time.

1. **Listen actively.** Pay close attention to conversations you hear and listen often to radio and television broadcasts. Make note of words, usages, and sentence structures that you do not understand and ask your teacher to explain.

2. **Use a tutor.** Your school may have a tutoring center or international student association that provides tutors. Meet with that person regularly to practice English.

3. **Work in the writing center.** When you have writing tasks, the writing center staff can help you with English grammar and idiomatic usage.

4. **Interact with others often.** Even if you feel shy about your skill with the language, speak up in class, talk to other students on campus, and ask questions. The more verbal exchanges you have in English, the more fluent you will become. Do not be concerned about an accent or limited vocabulary. Most people will be patient and kind.

5. **Study Guide 7, "Writing and Speaking English as a Second Language."** This section of the book offers important information on English grammar that can be particularly helpful when you edit.

STRATEGIES FOR EDITING

1. **Revise first; then edit.** When you revise, you consider content, organization and expression of your ideas. To operate efficiently, do not check spelling, grammar, and such until you have shaped your material during revision.

2. **Take a break before editing and whenever you need to refresh yourself.** By the time you get to the editing stage, you are so familiar with your writing that you may overlook mistakes. You will have a tendency to see what you meant to write and not what you really did write. To minimize this tendency, take a break to clear your head before you begin to edit. Also, anytime you get tired, you will overlook errors, so edit when your mind is fresh to keep your focus sharp.

3. **Edit very slowly.** You will not find errors if you simply read over your draft. Slow down to study carefully every word and sentence. Try pointing to each word with a pen and lingering

over it for three seconds. Or place a ruler under each line to focus hard on just a few words at a time.

4. **Edit more than once.** Because it is so easy to overlook mistakes, you should edit two or three times. One time, look only for the kinds of errors you habitually make.

COMPUTER TIP

- Edit both on screen and on a paper copy of your draft because each view gives you a different perspective.
- Use your computer's grammar checker cautiously because it is neither foolproof nor complete.

5m TRY IT OUT   6

Consider Your Editing Needs

1. Do you have a pattern of error? That is, what mistakes do you make most often (for example, spelling, subject-verb agreement, or run-on sentences)? If so what are those errors?
2. Check the index. What pages of this book discuss the errors you make most often?
3. Read the Editing Checklist on page 50. Are any of the points mentioned there ones you think you need to learn more about? If so, which ones?
4. How do you currently edit your writing? Is that procedure successful? Explain.
5. Make an appointment at your campus writing center and learn what services the staff there provide.

5n CONVENTIONS AND EXPECTATIONS AT LARGE

Considering the Expectations of Others

Revising means taking into account the expectations of your reader. However, considering the expectations of others is not new to us; we adjust our actions to anticipate their effect on others every day. Consider gift-giving, for example. The gift we give can vary widely according to the conventions and expectations of different cultures.

- The Japanese avoid gifts with an even number of components, such as an even number of flowers in a bouquet. Presents that are white are avoided, too, as white symbolizes death.
- The Chinese avoid giving clocks, handkerchiefs, or anything white, black, or blue.
- Mexicans avoid gifts of silver, which is associated with tourist trinkets.
- Norwegians avoid carnations and bouquets of only white flowers, which are reserved for funerals. Chocolates, wine, and pastries are a better choice.

Gift-giving always involves thinking about the interests and reactions of the recipient.

Activity

To whom would you give a subscription to each of these publications: *Sports Illustrated, Seventeen,* the *New York Times, TV Guide,* and *Car and Driver*? List the characteristics of the readers of each.

Writing Topic

Select any two of the publications above and compare and contrast the expectations readers have for each. Consider topics covered, vocabulary, kinds of detail, amount of detail, sentence structure, and anything else you think is appropriate. Support your points with examples from recent issues of the publications themselves.

CHAPTER 6

The Active Reading Process

CHAPTER OBJECTIVES

In this chapter you will learn to:

- Read actively.

- Preview before reading.

- Read chapters, and student and professional essays.

- Use idea maps to understand readings.

- Handle difficult readings.

- Read critically.

- Build your vocabulary.

6a WRITE ABOUT IT!

Study the two photographs above. Write a sentence explaining how they are different. One photograph shows sports fans actively involved with the game they are watching. The second photo shows spectators who seem less involved. The first set of fans is active and involved with the events on the field. They direct the plays, criticize the calls, encourage the players, and reprimand the coaches. They care enough to get actively engaged with the game. Just like interested fans, active readers get involved. They question, challenge, and criticize, as well as understand what they are reading. As a reader, you will be more successful if you become actively involved with what you read. This chapter will give you valuable tips on how to become an active, successful reader. Active reading is important in many aspects of your life, as shown below.

Everyday Scenarios

- **Reading** your credit card statement for accuracy
- **Reading** the terms of your auto insurance policy before accepting it

Academic Scenarios

- **Reading** an assigned article in *Newsweek* on taser guns for a class discussion
- **Reading** an exam essay question to determine what to include in your answer

Workplace Scenarios

- **Reading** your yearly performance evaluation before responding to it in writing
- Reading required worker safety regulations before starting a new job

6b READING ACTIVELY

Active readers are involved with what they are reading. They interact with the author and his or her ideas. Table 6-1 contrasts the active strategies of successful readers with the passive ones of less successful readers. Throughout the remainder of this chapter and this book, you will discover specific strategies for becoming a more active reader and learner. Not all strategies work for everyone. Experiment to discover those that work for you.

Table 6-1 Active Versus Passive Reading

Active Readers . . .	Passive Readers . . .
Tailor their reading strategies to suit each assignment.	Read all assignments the same way.
Analyze the purpose of a reading assignment.	Read an assignment because it was assigned.
Adjust their reading speed to suit their purposes.	Read everything at the same speed.
Question ideas in the assignment.	Accept whatever is in print as true.
Skim the headings or introduction and conclusion to find out what an assignment is about before beginning to read.	Check the length of an assignment and then beginning to read.
Make sure they understand what they are reading as they go along.	Read until the assignment is completed.
Read with pencil in hand, highlighting, jotting notes, and marking key vocabulary.	Simply read.
Develop personalized strategies that are particularly effective.	Follow routine, standard methods.

6c EXERCISE 6-1

Directions: Rate each of the following statements as either helpful (H) or not helpful (NH) in reading actively. Then discuss how each of the statements marked NH could be changed to be more helpful.

_____   1. Beginning to write an essay without reviewing the chapter in which is it assigned

_____   2. Giving yourself a maximum of one hour to write an essay

_____   3. Using different techniques to read different types of essays

_____   4. Highlighting important new words in an essay

_____   5. Rereading an essay the same way as many times as necessary to understand it

Previewing Before Reading

Previewing is a way of learning what a reading is about before you actually read it. It is like looking at a map before driving in an unfamiliar city. By reading brief, selected portions of an essay, you can discover a great deal about its content and its organization. You become familiar with its layout so that you can understand it more easily as you read. Previewing is not time consuming.

How to Preview

You can preview a brief essay in two or three minutes by following these basic steps:

- **Read and think about the title.** What does it tell you about the subject? Does it offer any clues about how the author feels about the subject or how he or she will approach it?
- **Check out the author.** Read any biographical information about the author that is provided with the article. Is the author's name familiar? If so, what do you know about him or her?
- **Read the first paragraph.** Here the author introduces the subject. Look for a statement of the main point of the entire reading.
- **Read all bold headings.** Headings divide the reading into pieces and announce the topic of each section.
- **Read the first sentence under each heading.** This sentence often states the main point of the section.
- **Read the first sentence of each paragraph.** You will discover many of the main ideas of the article in the opening sentences of the paragraphs. If the reading consists of very short paragraphs, read the first sentence of every third or fourth paragraph.
- **Read the last paragraph.** Often this paragraph summarizes or concludes the reading.

The more you practice previewing, the more effective you will find it. You will find that an essay is easier to read if you have previewed it. You will also discover that you are able to remember more of what you read if you preview and then read. Be sure to use previewing for all of your college textbooks and assigned readings.

Demonstration of Previewing

The following essay, taken from the book titled *Never Be Lied to Again,* has been highlighted to show you what to read while previewing. Preview it now, reading only the highlighted sections.

Body Language: Never Be Lied to Again
David J. Lieberman

Our fingers, hands, arms, and legs and their movements offer a fascinating insight into our true feelings. Most people aren't aware that their body speaks a language all its own; try as they will to deceive you with their words, the truth can be always silently observed.

You may already have read or heard about some of these clues, but they are only a small portion of the tactics that you will learn.

The Language of the Eyes

No or little direct eye contact is a classic sign of deception. A person who is lying to you will do everything to avoid making eye contact. Unconsciously he feels you will be able to see through him—via his eyes. And feeling guilty, he doesn't want to face you. Instead he will glance down or his eyes may dart from side to side. Conversely, when we tell the truth or we're offended by a false accusation, we tend to give our full focus and have fixed concentration. We lock eyes with our accuser as if to say "You're not getting away until we get to the bottom of this."

The Body Never Lies
Lacking Animation

The hands and arms are excellent indicators of deceit because they are used to gesture with and are more easily visible than our feet and legs. But hands, arms, legs, and feet can *all* give us information if we're watching carefully. When someone is lying or keeping something in, he tends to be less expressive with his hands or arms. He may keep them on his lap if he's sitting, or at his side if he's standing; he may stuff his hands in his pockets or clench them. Fingers may be folded into the hands; full extension of the fingers is usually a gesture of openness.

Have you ever noticed that when you're passionate about what you're saying, your hands and arms wave all about, emphasizing your point and conveying your enthusiasm? And have you ever realized that when you don't believe in what you're saying, your body language echoes these feelings and becomes inexpressive?

Additionally, if you ask someone a question and her hands clench or go palm down, this is a sign of defensiveness and withdrawal. If she is genuinely confused at the accusations or the line of questioning, her hands turn palm-up as if to say "Give me more information; I do not understand," or "I have nothing to hide."

Keeping Something In

When a person sits with his legs and arms close to his body, perhaps crossed but not outstretched, he is evincing the thought *I'm keeping something in*. His arms and legs may be crossed because he feels he must defend himself. When we feel comfortable and confident we tend to stretch out—claim our space, as it were. When we feel less secure, we take up less physical space and fold our arms and legs into our bodies, into what is almost a fetal position.

Displaying Artificial Movements

Arm movements and gestures seem stiff and almost mechanical. This behavior can be readily observed by watching unpolished actors and politicians. They try to use gestures to convince us that they're impassioned about their beliefs, but there's no fluidity to their movements. The movements are contrived, not natural.

The Unconscious Cover-up

If her hand goes straight to her face while she is responding to a question or when she is making a statement, this is often an indication of deceit. Her hand may cover her mouth while she is speaking, indicating that she really doesn't believe what she is saying to be true; it acts as a screen, an unconscious attempt to hide her words.

When she is listening she covers or touches her face as an unconscious manifestation of the thought *I really don't want to be listening to this.* Touching the nose is also considered to be a sign of deception, as well as scratching behind or on the ear or rubbing the eyes.

This should not be confused with posture associated with deep thought, which usually conveys concentration and attention.

The Partial Shrug

The shrugging of one's shoulders is a gesture that usually indicates ignorance or indifference: "I don't know" or "I don't care." If a person makes this gesture he or she usually means to communicate that very message. However, if this gesture is fleeting—if you catch only a glimpse of it—it's a sign of something else. This person is trying to demonstrate the she is casual and relaxed about her answer, when in fact she really isn't. Because what she feels isn't a true emotion, she doesn't really shrug.

This situation is similar to that of someone who is embarrassed by a joke but wants to pretend that she thinks it's funny. What you see is a "lips only" smile, not a big grin encompassing her entire face.

Summary

- The person will make little or no eye contact.
- Physical expression will be limited, with few arm and hand movements. What arm and hand movements are present will seem stiff, and mechanical. Hands, arms, and legs pull in toward the body; the individual takes up less space.
- His hand(s) may go up to his face or throat. But contact with his body is limited to these areas. He is also unlikely to touch his chest with an open hand gesture.
- If he is trying to appear casual and relaxed about his answer, he may shrug a little.

What did you learn about the essay from your preview? To find out how valuable previewing can be, try the following quiz in Exercise 6-2. You will find that you can answer many or all of the questions, indicating that you did learn a great deal by previewing.

6d **EXERCISE 6-2**

Directions: Answer each question by marking T for True of F for False. When you have finished, check your answers on p. 62.

_____ 1. You can often spot a liar by studying his or her body language.

_____ 2. A liar will usually make direct eye contact.

_____ 3. Hand and arm gestures may reveal that someone is lying.

_____ 4. Crossed legs and folded arms suggest that a person has something to hide.

_____ 5. Touching one's face is not usually an indicator of deceit.

6e **EXERCISE 6-3**

Directions: Match the previewing step listed in Column A with the type of information it provides in Column B. Use each item only once. Write the letter of your choice in the space provided.

Column A   **Column B**

_____ 1. first paragraph   a. identifies the subject

_____ 2. bold headings   b. provides an overview

_____ 3. section headings   c. summarizes the article

_____ 4. last paragraph   d. dentify and separate main topics

_____ 5. title   e. indicate important information

6f **EXERCISE 6-4**

Reading and Writing in Progress

Directions: Choose a professional reading from Part V, "A Multicultural Reader." Preview the reading, using the steps listed above, and answer the following questions:

1. What is the topic of the reading?

2. What main point does the reading make about the topic?

3. What did you already know about the topic?

Making Predictions

After previewing a reading assignment, you can make predictions about its content and organization. Specifically, you can anticipate what topics will be covered and how they will be presented. Ask the following questions to sharpen your previewing skills and strengthen your recall of what you read:

• How difficult is the material?

• How is it organized?

- What is the overall subject and how is it approached?

- What type of material is it (instructional material, a sample student essay, a model professional essay)?

- Why was this material assigned?

6g EXERCISE 6-5

Reading and Writing in Progress

Directions: For the reading you chose in Exercise 6-4, answer the three questions above, under the heading "Making Predictions."

Reading to Learn: Chapters, Student Essays, and Professional Essays

Before you begin reading a chapter or an assigned essay, it is helpful if you decide what you want to learn from it. By determining what to look for as you read, you will find that you learn and remember more than if you just read material because it is assigned.

In this book you should read the instructional material, the sample student writing, and the model professional essays differently and with different purposes.

Reading Chapters in This Book

The instructional portion of each chapter teaches you specific writing skills. Your focus when working through each of these chapters should be to understand each skill and to find out how to apply the skill in your own writing. Use the exercises in the chapter to help you test out the skill before you use it in a new piece of writing. Here are some specific suggestions:

1. **Plan on rereading.** After previewing the chapter, read it once to get a general understanding of the skills taught. Read it again with a "how-to" focus, paying attention to how to apply the skills to your own writing.
2. **Decide what it is you want and need to learn from the chapter.**
3. **As you read each chapter, read with a highlighter in hand.** Mark useful information that you can use when you write. Use the sticky note "Important: Review This" to mark sections that you will want to refer to frequently.
4. **Pay attention to examples.** The examples show you how a skill works and how it can be applied.
5. **Use the exercises to try out or test the skill before writing a paragraph or essay in which you use the skill.**
6. **Use the "Visualize It!" sections.** These sections contain idea maps and diagrams that show you how to create a mental picture of the organization of a piece of writing. Use them as a model, and draw similar maps of ideas you plan to include in your own writing.

6h EXERCISE 6-6

Directions:

1. Preview the chapter.

2. Read the instructional portion of the chapter (everything that comes before the professional reading).

3. Identify each of the following sections:

a. "Visualize It!"

b. Workplace Scenario

c. Examples

d. Exercises

Determine what each section contributes to the chapter and how they can help you learn.

Reading Student Sample Essays

The student essays included in the Academic Scenarios are intended to be realistic models of good writing. They are not perfect, but they are acceptable. The student essays also illustrate the writing techniques taught in the chapters in which they appear. Here are some suggestions for reading and learning from the sample student essays:

1. **Read the essay first to understand the writer's message.** Then, once you understand it, focus on aspects of writing. In particular, determine how it illustrates the skills taught in the chapter in which it is included.
2. **Plan on reading the essay several times, each time for a different purpose.** For example, you might read it once noticing how the paragraphs are organized and read it again later noticing the vocabulary the writer uses.
3. **Read with this question in mind: What techniques does this writer use that I can use in my own writing?**
4. **Read with a highlighter in hand**. Mark sentences, paragraphs, words, or phrases that you want to look at again, that you think are particularly effective, or that you want to use.
5. **Study the annotations.** The marginal notes are intended to call your attention to specific techniques or writing strategies.

Here is a portion of the student essay. The annotations show some of the things you might notice as you study the essay. You will learn more about these features as you work through this book.

Author provides background on his situation

Different meaning of "road" introduced

Sentence that states what the essay will be about

Background of job

Excerpt from Education: The (Open Road)

Reference to truck driving

by Doug Mello

Coming from a working class family, the option of pursuing an education was, for me, not a choice. Going to work after high school was my only choice and also what my parents expected of me. One of the first jobs I had provided me with the opportunity to acquire a commercial driver's license, which allowed me to become a truck driver. Due to a good driving record and work history, my employment and wages always seemed to get better as I searched for the perfect truck-driving job. At the age of twenty-nine, a company hired me that I thought offered a promising career future. However, what I failed to see was where this particular (road) would take me. After several years I found that there were no opportunities for advancement within the company. I realized, at this point in my life, that an education could offer challenges, opportunities, and a career that would last a lifetime.

There was one particular event that that led to my decision to get an education. After five years with the company I was frequently asked for advice on routing schedules and was assigned the job of dispatching when the plant manager was on vacation. Being involved in the operations of the company allowed me to see the constant waste of time and money that resulted from day-to-day planning. I finally came up with a plan I thought would allow me to advance within the company and get out of my truck and off the road. I went to the president of the company with my proposal, which could have saved the company twice my wages each year in transportation costs. His response was, "our company is not large enough to have a transportation manager and you have no education." Obviously he believed that without an education driving trucks was the only job I was qualified to do. (However,) for me, driving trucks for thirty-five more years was not a career; it was only a job that was never finished. I realized that with an education, the open road could have a completely different meaning; education is a through road not a dead end.

Quotation used to make situation real

Word signals contrasting ideas will follow

Reading Professional Essays

The professional essays at the end of each chapter are models of good writing. By studying the writing of professional writers, you can improve your own writing. You will need to read the essays several times. On the first few readings, you should concentrate on understanding the message the writer is communicating. The section following each reading, titled "Examining the Reading," is intended to help you assess whether you grasp the writer's message. Then, once you are confident that you understand the reading, you are ready to examine the writing techniques used. Most importantly, look for techniques that the writer uses that you could use in your own writing. Here are a few specific suggestions:

1. **Read the "Thinking Before Reading" section that comes before the reading.** It is intended to help you get into the reading by telling you a little about the author and the reading itself. Answer the questions that ask you to connect the reading to your own experience. These will help you recall ideas and experiences that you can relate to the reading, in order to help you understand it better.
2. **Identify the writer's purpose.** Study how he or she achieves it.
3. **Study the title.** What does it reveal about the essay's content or purpose?
4. **Examine the essay's introduction.** It should do three things: 1) provide needed background information, 2) get you interested in the reading, and 3) state the essay's main point. Observe how the writer accomplishes these things.
5. **Examine the body of the essay.** Study how the writer supports his or her main points.
6. **Examine how paragraphs are organized.** How does the writer state and develop the main point of each paragraph? How are these main points explained or developed?
7. **Examine the sentences the writer creates.** How are the sentences similar to and different from those you write? Are there some sentence patterns you could model?
8. **Examine the writer's use of vocabulary.** What words/phrases seem particularly effective? How could you use them? Use the words listed in the "Strengthening Your Vocabulary" exercise that follows the reading as a guide.
9. **Examine the essay's conclusion.** Observe how the writer draws the essay to a close. Could you use this technique?

6i EXERCISE 6-7

Reading and Writing in Progress

Directions: Read the essay you chose in Exercise 6-4 using two of the suggestions given above. List the two suggestions that you have chosen here.

1. _____

2. _____

Using Idea Maps to Understand Readings

An idea map is a visual picture of the organization and content of an essay. It is a drawing that enables you to see what is included in an essay in a brief, outline form. Idea maps are used throughout this book for both reading and writing. For reading, you can use them to help you understand a reading—discover how it is organized and study how ideas relate to one another. For writing, an idea map can help you organize your own ideas and check to be sure that all the ideas you have included belong in the essay.

An idea map is shown below.

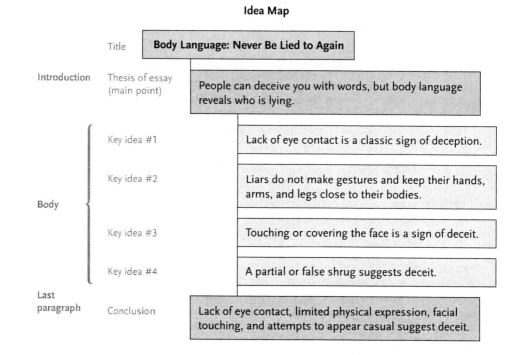

Idea Map

Title — **Body Language: Never Be Lied to Again**

Introduction — Thesis of essay (main point): People can deceive you with words, but body language reveals who is lying.

Body —
Key idea #1: Lack of eye contact is a classic sign of deception.
Key idea #2: Liars do not make gestures and keep their hands, arms, and legs close to their bodies.
Key idea #3: Touching or covering the face is a sign of deceit.
Key idea #4: A partial or false shrug suggests deceit.

Last paragraph — Conclusion: Lack of eye contact, limited physical expression, facial touching, and attempts to appear casual suggest deceit.

Notice how easily and quickly you can see what the essay is about and how it is organized. By filling in an idea map for a reading, you are reviewing the reading and analyzing its structure. Both of these activities will help you remember what you read. Though it takes time to draw, an idea map will save you time in the long run. You can avoid rereading, and the content of the essay will stick in your mind, preparing you for class discussions and writing about the reading. Use the model below to draw idea maps. (These models also appear on the book's Web site, at http://www.ablongman.com/mcwhorterexpressways1e.) You may need to add extra boxes or you may not need all the boxes included, depending on the number of ideas and details in the essay. The sample idea map above and the model on the next page show only the essay's main point (thesis) and the key ideas. You can draw idea maps that include details as well, if it suits your purpose.

6j   EXERCISE 6-8

Reading and Writing in Progress

Directions: Draw an idea map of the professional reading you chose in Exercise 6-4. Use the following model as a guide.

Model for Idea Map

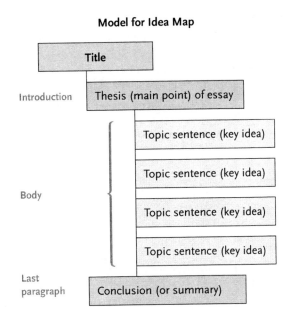

Understanding Difficult Readings

The professional readings that end each chapter are intended to be challenging as well as models of good writing. Depending on your background knowledge and experience, you may encounter one or more readings that are difficult. Use the following suggestions to help you find new strategies for approaching a difficult reading.

1. **Analyze the time and place in which you are reading.** If you've been working for several hours, mental fatigue may be the source of the problem. If you are reading in a place with distractions or interruptions, you might not be able to understand what you are reading.
2. **Rephrase each paragraph in your own words.** You might need to approach complicated material sentence by sentence, expressing each in your own words.
3. **Read aloud sentences or sections that are particularly difficult.** Reading out loud sometimes makes complicated material easier to understand.
4. **Reread difficult or complicated sections.** In fact, sometimes several readings are appropriate and necessary.
5. **Slow down your reading rate.** On occasion, simply reading more slowly and carefully will provide you with the needed boost in comprehension.
6. **Write a brief outline of major points.** This will help you see the overall organization and progression of ideas.
7. **Highlight key ideas.** After you have read a section, go back and think about and highlight what is important. Highlighting forces you to sort out what is important, and this sorting process builds comprehension and recall.

6k   EXERCISE 6-9

Reading and Writing in Progress

Directions: Consider the professional reading you read for Exercise 6-4. Write a paragraph that assesses and analyzes how using any of the above techniques could have improved your understanding of the reading.

Reading Critically

Reading critically means questioning, reacting to, and evaluating what you read. Critical reading is an essential skill because most college instructors expect you not only to understand what you read, but to be able to respond to it critically. Critical thinking is also an essential workplace skill: employers hire people who can think, solve problems, and respond to issues.

Throughout this book, you will learn a variety of critical reading skills. Each end-of-the-chapter reading has a section titled "Thinking Critically." To develop the habit of thinking critically, use the following suggestions:

1. **Read an essay more than once.** Read it several times, if necessary, to understand the author's message; then read it again to analyze and evaluate the author's ideas.
2. **Read with a pen in your hand.** Highlight important passages or particularly meaningful or insightful sentences and phrases.
3. **Make marginal notes as you read.** Write marginal notes (sometimes called annotations) that record what you are thinking as you read. These notes will be helpful as you write about the reading.
4. **Look for evidence that supports the writer's ideas.** It is not enough for a writer to state an opinion; he or she should give you reasons or evidence to support his or her ideas.
5. **Ask questions as you read.** Question and challenge the author and the ideas presented. How do the ideas mesh or fit with your own knowledge, experience, beliefs, and values? If they do not fit, ask why. Do you need to adjust your thinking or do further reading or research on the topic?

6l EXERCISE 6-10

Reading and Writing in Progress

Directions: Reread, annotate, and then write several critical questions you could ask about the reading you chose in Exercise 2-4.

Building Your Vocabulary Through Reading

Your vocabulary is an important asset, both in college and in the workplace. Words are the vehicles or building blocks with which you express ideas both in speech and in writing. A strong vocabulary identifies you as a learned, educated person as well as an effective communicator.

Figuring Out Unfamiliar Words

One of the best ways to improve your vocabulary is to read! Reading essays, by both professional and student authors, is an excellent way to build your vocabulary. As you read them, you will encounter words that you can use to expand your vocabulary. Use the "Strengthening Your Vocabulary" exercise that follows each reading to learn new words in the reading. You may also encounter other words in the reading that are unfamiliar to you or you may come upon uncommon uses for words you already know. As you find words that you want to make part of your writing vocabulary, circle or highlight them as you read, mark them with a sticky tab labeled "Vocabulary," and use the tips on page 65 to learn their meanings. Notice that the first step is not what you expect, which would be to look words up in a dictionary.

In addition to adding words to your vocabulary, you can also learn creative and interesting ways to use language. As you read, look for the following:

1. **Euphemisms** These are words that hide or disguise the importance, reality, or seriousness of something. (Ladies' room is a euphemism for toilet; "victim of friendly fire" is a euphemism for a soldier shot by his or her own troops.)
2. **Connotative meanings** Words have shades of meaning called connotations. These are the emotional associations that accompany words for some readers. The word "mother" has many connotative meanings. For some it means a warm, loving, caregiver. For others it may suggest a strict disciplinarian.

3. **Jargon** Jargon is specialized terminology used in a particular field of study. Football has its own jargon: linebackers, kick off, touchdown, etc. Academic disciplines also have their own language (psychology: drive, motivation, stressor).

HOW TO FIGURE OUT UNFAMILIAR WORDS

Use the following steps to figure out a word you do not know:

1. **Pronounce the word.** Often, by "hearing" the word, you will recall its meaning.
2. **Try to figure out the word from its context—the words and sentences around the unfamiliar word.** Often there is a clue in the context that will help you figure out a meaning.

   Example: During his lecture, the **ornithologist** described her research on western spotted owls as well as other species of birds.

   The context reveals that an ornithologist is a person who studies birds.
   Be sure to look for clues to meaning after the word, as well as before it.

   Example: The elderly man walked with the help of a **prosthesis.** He was proud that his artificial limb enabled him to walk without assistance.

   The context reveals that a prosthesis is an artificial limb.
3. **Look for parts of the word that are familiar.** You may spot a familiar root (for example, in the word "improbability" you may see a variant spelling of the word "probable"), or you may recognize a familiar beginning (for example, in the word "unconventional," knowing that un- means "not" lets you figure out that the word means not conventional).
4. **If you still cannot figure out the word, mark it using a Vocabulary sticky tab and keep reading, unless the sentence does not make sense without knowing what the word means.** If it does not, then stop and look up the word in a print or online dictionary.
5. **When you finish reading, look up all the words you have marked.**
6. **After reading be sure to record, in a vocabulary log notebook or computer file, the words you figured out or looked up so you can review and use them frequently.**

4. **Foreign words and phrases** Many Latin, French, and Spanish words have entered our language and are used as if they are part of our language. Here are a few examples:

   Aficionado (Spanish) someone enthusiastic and knowledgeable about something

   Et cetera (Latin)—and so forth

   Faux pas (French)—embarrassing social blunder

   Guerilla (Spanish)—freedom fighter

   Status quo (Latin)—the way things are, an existing state of affairs

   Tête-à-tête (French)—a private conversation between two people

- **Figurative language** Figurative language consists of words and phrases that make sense creatively or imaginatively but not literally. The expression "The exam was a piece of cake" means, creatively, that the exam was easy, as eating cake is easy. But the exam did not literally resemble a cake.
- **Neologisms** Neologisms are new words that have recently entered our language. As technology and society change, new words are created. Here are a few examples: blogs (Web logs or diaries), spamming (sending unwanted e-mail to someone), and egosurfing (searching online for information about yourself.)

6m **EXERCISE 6-11**

Reading and Writing in Progress

Directions: For the professional reading you chose in Exercise 6-4, list any words for which you did not know the meaning. For each word listed, write the meaning and indicate what method you used to figure it out (context, words parts, or dictionary).

	Word	Meaning	Method
1.	_____	_____	_____
2.	_____	_____	_____
3.	_____	_____	_____

Using Word Mapping

Word mapping is a visual method of expanding your vocabulary. It involves examining a word in detail by considering its meanings, synonyms (words similar in meaning), antonyms (words opposite in meaning), part(s) of speech, word parts, and usages. A word map is a form of word study. By the time you have completed the map, you will find that you have learned the word and are ready to use it in your speech and writing.

The following is a sample map for the word "intercepted."

Word Map

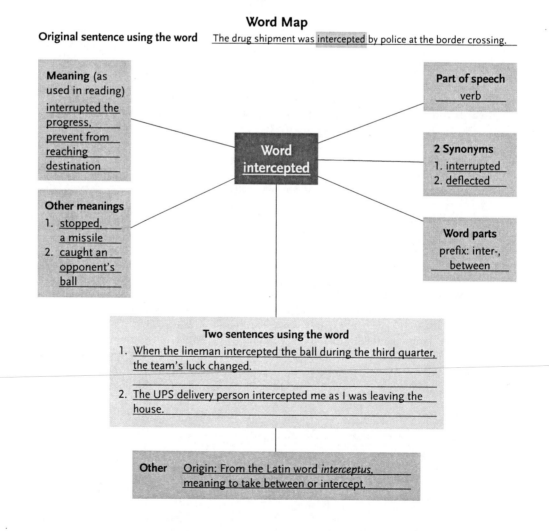

Original sentence using the word   The drug shipment was intercepted by police at the border crossing.

Word intercepted

Meaning (as used in reading) interrupted the progress, prevent from reaching destination

Other meanings
1. stopped, a missile
2. caught an opponent's ball

Part of speech verb

2 Synonyms
1. interrupted
2. deflected

Word parts prefix: inter-, between

Two sentences using the word
1. When the lineman intercepted the ball during the third quarter, the team's luck changed.
2. The UPS delivery person intercepted me as I was leaving the house.

Other   Origin: From the Latin word *interceptus*, meaning to take between or intercept.

Use the following steps in completing a word map:

1   **When you find a word you don't know, locate the entry for the word in a dictionary.** Write the sentence in which the word appeared at the top of the map. Figure out which meaning fits the context and write it in the box labeled "Meaning (as used in reading)." Fill in the word's part of speech as used in this context.

2. **Study the dictionary entry to discover other meanings of the word.** Fill those in on the map in the box labeled "Other Meanings."

3. **Find or think of two synonyms (words similar in meaning).** You might need to use a thesaurus for this.

4. **Write two sentences using the word.**

5. **Analyze the word's parts. Identify any prefixes, roots, and suffixes.** Write the word part and its meaning in the box labeled "Word Parts."

6. **In the box labeled "Other," include any other interesting information about the word.** You might include antonyms, restrictive meanings, or the word's history or derivation).

6n **EXERCISE 6-12**

Reading and Writing in Progress

Directions: Using a dictionary, complete the following word map for one word in the reading you chose for Exercise 6-4.

Word Map

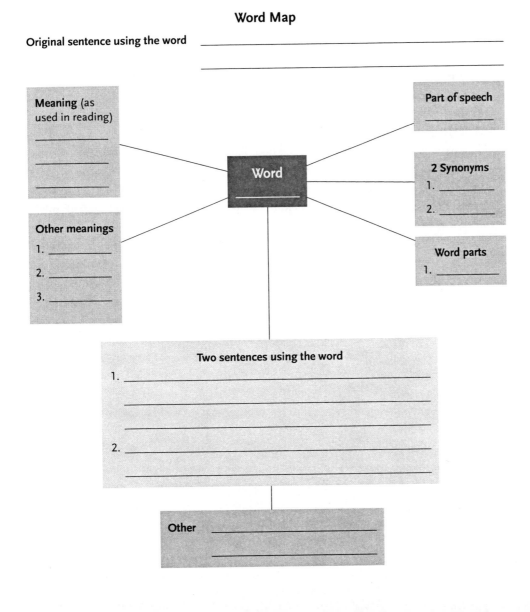

Original sentence using the word _____

Meaning (as used in reading)
_____
_____
_____

Part of speech
_____

Word
_____

2 Synonyms
1. _____
2. _____

Other meanings
1. _____
2. _____
3. _____

Word parts
1. _____

Two sentences using the word
1. _____
_____
_____
2. _____
_____

Other _____
_____

60 WRITING ABOUT A READING

Thinking Before Reading

This essay first appeared in *Newsweek* magazine in August 2004. It is a good example of the kind of professional essays you will be asked to read in this book.

1. Preview the reading.
2. Connect the reading to your own experience by:
   a. brainstorming a list of acts of kindness you have performed, received, or observed.
   b. comparing it to a serious or life-threatening illness that you, a family member, or a friend have faced. What emotions did you experience?

READING

Saved by the Kindness of a Virtual Stranger

My wife needed a kidney, but we didn't know how to ask friends for help. Turns out we didn't have to.

Mark Zelermyer

1   I grew up thinking that if miracles existed at all, they were larger than life, spectacular acts that suspended the laws of nature (think Cecil B. DeMille's "The Ten Commandments"). Even as an adult, whenever I read about some medical phenomenon that doctors were hard pressed to explain, like a late-stage tumor that disappeared long after a patient's treatment was discontinued, I chalked it up to the sort of inexplicable divine intervention that trumps macrobiotic diets and crystals. It was something to hope for in your darkest hour, perhaps, but not to expect. So when I learned that my wife would need a kidney transplant within two years, I focused on what modern medicine had to offer.

2   Her polycystic kidney disease had been controlled with medication for some 20 years, but in the spring of 2001 it began to worsen. The nephrologist explained that her best shot at regaining her health was to receive a living kidney, which would function better and longer than a cadaveric kidney. The challenge was to find a healthy person with the same type O blood who was willing to undergo a regimen of tests and ultimately donate a kidney. Otherwise, she would have to start the time-consuming, punishing process of dialysis in order to get on the five-year waiting list for a cadaveric transplant.

3   I was quickly ruled out as a donor because my blood type didn't match my wife's. Her family produced no candidates either. In fact, her mother had died from complications of the same genetic disease, and her brother had received a cadaveric transplant the year before.

4   We desperately needed help, and yet we felt uncomfortable asking for it. After all, how do you ask another person to give up a kidney? We finally turned to our friends, and one of them, our rabbi, gave an impassioned appeal during Yom Kippur services. A number of congregants agreed to be tested, but all of them were eliminated after the first stage of screening. It looked as if we had hit a wall.

5   Then one evening I rode home on the train with Carolyn Hodges, a friend of mine from work. I was feeling particularly low that day, and I told her about our situation. The next day she stopped by my office and told me that she and her husband were type O's and longtime blood and platelet donors who were listed with the bone-marrow registry. They had talked it over and decided they were willing to be tested as potential matches. Carolyn was eliminated shortly thereafter, but John, whom we barely knew, emerged as the surgeon's donor of choice.

6   John is a scientist by training, and once he got the news he began diligently researching kidney disease and transplant surgery. By the time he met with the surgeon, he had compiled a list of incredibly detailed questions, the likes of which the doctor had never seen before. Most donors are blood relations who are more likely to beg the surgeon to take their kidney than grill him on the latest studies.

7   Despite his thorough research, John encountered a fair amount of resistance from his family members and close friends. They'd ask, "Why should someone in good health put himself on the line for a person he hardly knows?" But John strongly believed that this was a way for him to actively make the world a better place. He would simply tell them he had considered every potential danger and determined that the rewards— for my wife, her family and himself—outweighed the risks. He was even more reassured after talking with his daughter's teacher, who had donated a kidney to her brother years before, and his good friend who was a transplant counselor.

8   By the beginning of this past May, my wife's condition had deteriorated to the point that she was in danger of being too sick for the transplant operation. To make matters worse, the procedure required two operating rooms and a 20-person surgical team— and both were booked solid for nearly two months. We were scared.

9   Thankfully, one week later there was a last-minute cancellation, and we received word one afternoon to go to the hospital at once for pre-op work—the surgery would begin the following morning at 6:30. Without hesitation, John dropped everything and drove over.

10   I am happy to report that the operation was a success. "Little Johnny," as my wife calls her new kidney, is working exceptionally well. After John spent a few weeks recovering at home, he was able to ease back to work and resume his normal routine.

11   Except that life will never really be the way it was before the surgery for either of our families. A tremendous bond now joins us. We will forever be connected by John's generous, selfless gift of life.

12   I've learned that miracles come in myriad forms, including human. John and Carolyn Hodges are living proof.

Getting Ready to Write

Reviewing the Reading

1. Explain why Mrs. Zelermyer's medical condition necessitated a transplant.
2. Why was it so difficult to find a donor?
3. Why was John Hodges's family opposed to his decision?
4. How have the lives of the Zelermyers and John Hodges changed as a result of the transplant?

Examining the Reading: Drawing an Idea Map

As described, an idea map can help you grasp the content and organization of an essay. Drawing an idea map is also an excellent way to check your understanding and review the reading in preparation for discussing or writing about it.

Complete the following idea map of "Saved By the Kindness of a Virtual Stranger" by filling in the missing information. Because this essay relates events in story form, this map takes the form of a time line. Time lines are used to show the sequence of events.

Format for drawing time lines:

Model for Time Line

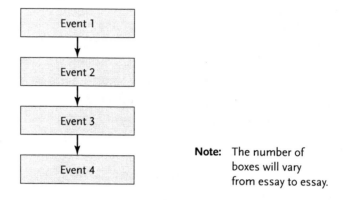

| Event 1 |
| Event 2 |
| Event 3 |
| Event 4 |

Note: The number of boxes will vary from essay to essay.

Time Line for "Saved by the Kindness of a Virtual Stranger"

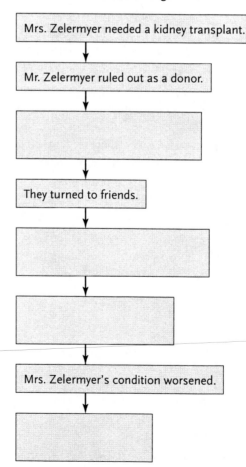

| Mrs. Zelermyer needed a kidney transplant. |

| Mr. Zelermyer ruled out as a donor. |

| |

| They turned to friends. |

| |

| |

| Mrs. Zelermyer's condition worsened. |

| |

Thinking Critically: Asking Critical Questions

An important part of thinking critically is asking questions about what you read. It is a way of expanding your thinking, as well as a way of discovering ideas to write about. Here are a few examples of critical questions you might ask about this essay. After you read and answer these, try to form a few critical questions of your own.

1. The author is writing about his wife. Do you think his perception and description of events might be colored by his emotional attachment to her? Is there evidence in the reading to suggest this?
2. What else would you like to know about John Hodges, the donor? What information might help you understand his willingness to be a donor?
3. This article was originally published in 2003. Has organ donation changed since then? That is, are people more willing to be donors, have new laws been passed to regulate organ donation, or have new cases come into the public eye?
4. Why is the author's wife, who is the donor recipient, not named?

Strengthening Your Vocabulary

Part A: Using the word's context, word parts, or a dictionary, write a brief definition of each of the following words or phrases as it is used in the reading.

1. phenomenon (paragraph 1)_____

    _____

2. inexplicable (paragraph 1) _____

    _____

3. diligently (paragraph 6)_____

    _____

4. deteriorated (paragraph 8)_____

    _____

5. congregants (paragraph 4)_____

    _____

Part B: Choose one of the above words and draw a word map of it.

Reacting to Ideas: Discussion and Journal Writing

1. Discuss John's motivation for, and his family's reaction to, his kidney donation. Should family members have any right to prevent a relative from donating a kidney?
2. Other than through organ donations, brainstorm a list of things people could do to make the world a better place.
3. Discuss the issue of organ donation. Who should and who should not be allowed to donate? Should restrictions be placed on who can receive donated organs? Should donors be paid?

Writing About the Reading
Paragraph Options

1. Write a paragraph explaining whether you think miracles actually happen.
2. Write a paragraph explaining and evaluating the reasons John Hodges gave for choosing to donate his kidney.

3. Write a paragraph giving at least three reasons why you would not consider donating a kidney to a non-family member.
4. Write a paragraph describing a situation in which you helped a stranger. Describe how the act made you feel.

Essay Options

5. Write an essay describing a situation which might be considered as a human miracle.
6. Write an essay describing help or assistance you received from someone unexpectedly. Discuss the possible motivations of the donor.
7. Write an essay discussing the issue of organ sales. Give reasons why someone should or should not be allowed to sell his or her organs.
8 Write an essay analyzing Mr. Zelermyer's attitude toward miracles and how it changed as a result of the events described in the essay.

6p CHAPTER REVIEW AND PRACTICE

Chapter Review

What is active reading?	Active reading is a method of thinking about a reading as you read it, and becoming engaged with the text.
What is previewing?	Previewing is a method of familiarizing yourself with the content and organization of a chapter or essay before you read it.
What features in this book need to be read in specific ways to get the most from them?	Chapter instructional material, student essays, and professional readings each need to be read differently.
What are idea maps?	Idea maps are diagrams that show the content and organization of an essay.
Name two techniques to use to handle difficult readings.	See numbered list under Understanding Difficult Readings heading on p. 63.
What does critical reading involve?	Critical reading involves questioning and evaluating what you read.
How can you improve your vocabulary by reading essays?	Use context, word parts, and a dictionary to figure out words you do not know. Keep track of new words in a vocabulary log or computer file.

CHAPTER 7

The Term Paper

- The Survey

- The Argument

7a THE TERM PAPER

The information discussed in this section will deal with the traditional "term paper" as opposed to the "research paper." Although the terms are sometimes interchanged, there is a substantial difference between the two types of papers. I have chosen to discuss the "term paper" because this is the type of end-of-semester paper most frequently required by instructors. I will attempt to present information about the "research paper" in a separate booklet that will be written at a later date.

The term paper is similar to other writing assignments in that students are asked to find information about a topic to fulfill a specific purpose. It is different, however, from other types of writing assignments because the major source of information for this paper is not from a student's own observations, memory, or lecture notes, but from books, articles, or other information found in a library.

There are two basic kinds of term papers: the survey and the argument.

The Survey

The survey (also called summary) is a factual review of what other people have written about a topic. When students choose a subject for this type of paper, they should select one that has created much controversy or generated extensive commentary. Their task is to examine all sides of the subject objectively and to provide accurate documentation for their sources. Their purpose *is not* to present their own argument about the subject they chose or to analyze or assess the information they gathered. Their purpose *is* to identify and summarize the major arguments that other researchers presented about the subject. Students should imagine that their readers have an interest in their subject, but have not taken a position. Students must present a survey of the major arguments to help readers determine a position. A paper that cites without comment the health hazards associated with industrial pollution of our streams and rivers is a survey paper.

The Argument

In an argument, students present an analysis of a subject that others have researched. They are expected to interpret and evaluate the information they have gathered to draw conclusions to support a position they have taken. Their purpose is to convince the reader to adopt a particular view or to take a particular action. To do this, they are expected to present a strong analysis of the subject, citing the proper authorities to support their viewpoint. Students should imagine that their readers are curious and uncommitted about the subject, but are ready to be convinced by a good argument. Students, then, can assume the role of a lawyer and make a case for their position. They *should not* simply list a neutral summary of what others have written about the subject. A paper with the title, "Heavy Fines Must Be Levied Against Industries Who Pollute Our Streams And Rivers" would be considered an argument because there is no question what the writer's position is about the topic.

Standards

Since a term paper represents a culminating activity for a course, it should reflect students' polished efforts. Not only should students prove that they have a solid grasp of the topic assigned to them, they must also show that they have consulted a wide variety of sources of information and were able to sort out, analyze, and organize this information into a written form that embodies all the elements (standards) of correct writing.

Length

Most undergraduate term papers should be between 1,500 to 3,000 words. This represents six to twelve double-spaced and typewritten or computer processed pages. This length can vary depending upon the instructor's expectations for the content of the paper and the complexity of the topic assigned.

CHAPTER 8

Cause and Effect

CHAPTER OBJECTIVES

In this chapter you will learn to:

- Understand cause-and-effect relationships.

- Write effective topic sentences.

- Develop and organize supporting details.

- Use transitions effectively.

- Write cause-and-effect essays.

8a WRITE ABOUT IT!

Study the photograph above. Write an explanation of what happened that caused the environmental damage shown. Also explain what might be done to prevent such damage.

You have just written a draft of a cause-and-effect paragraph. Cause and effect is concerned with why things happen (**cause**) and the result of an action or event (**effect**). Cause and effect is a common method of organizing and presenting information and you will encounter it frequently in everyday, academic, and workplace situations. In this chapter you will learn to use cause and effect in both paragraphs and essays.

Everyday Scenarios

- A letter to a bank explaining why a loan payment is late
- A car-accident report to your insurance company explaining how an accident occurred

Academic Scenarios

- Essay exam questions that begin with "Explain why" or "Discuss the causes of"
- An assignment that asks you to agree or disagree with a statement and explain your reasons

Workplace Scenarios

- A letter to a customer explaining why you can't reimburse her for an antique quilt damaged during dry cleaning
- A letter to a loan applicant explaining why the bank won't increase his home equity line of credit

8b   UNDERSTANDING CAUSE AND EFFECT

What Is Cause and Effect?

Each day we face situations that require cause-and-effect analysis. Some are daily events; others mark important life decisions. Why won't my car start? Why didn't I get my student loan check? What will happen if I skip class today? How will my family react if I decide to get married? We seek to make sense of and control our lives by understanding cause-and-effect relationships. **Causes** are explanations of why things happen. **Effects** are explanations of what happens as a result of an action or event.

8c   EXERCISE 8-1

Directions: Working alone or with another student, brainstorm a list of times in your own life when cause and effect played an important role.

Distinguishing Between Cause and Effect

How do we distinguish between cause and effect? To determine a cause, ask:

"Why did this happen?"

To identify an effect, ask:

"What happened because of this?"

Let's consider an everyday situation: You turn the ignition key, but your car won't start because it's out of gas. This is a simple case in which one cause produces one effect. You can diagram this situation as follows:

Here are a few other examples of one cause producing one effect:

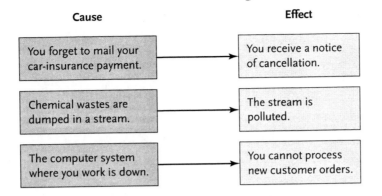

Most situations, however, are much more complicated than those shown above, and even a simple cause-and-effect sequence may contain hidden complexities. Perhaps your car was out of gas because you forgot to buy gas, and you forgot because you were making preparations for the upcoming visit of a good friend. Suppose you missed your math class because the car would not start, and an exam was scheduled for that day. Missing the exam lowered your average, and as a result, you failed the course.

You can see, then, that cause and effect often works like a chain reaction: one cause triggers an effect, which in turn becomes the cause of another effect. In a chain reaction, each event in a series influences the next, as shown in the following example:

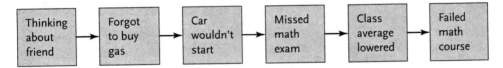

At other times, many causes may contribute to a single effect, as shown in the following diagram:

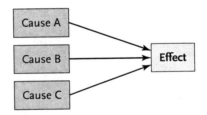

For example, there may be several reasons why you decided to major in accounting:

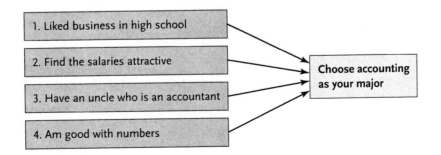

At other times, a single cause can have multiple effects, as shown below:

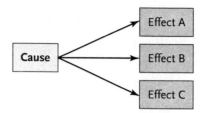

Suppose, for example, you decide to reduce your hours at your part-time job:

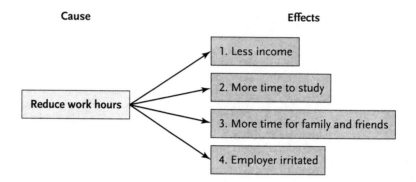

Multiple causes and multiple effects, then, are common. When analyzing a cause-and-effect situation that you plan to write about, ask yourself the following questions:

1. What are the causes? What are the effects? (To help answer these questions, draw a diagram of the situation.)
2. Which should be emphasized—cause or effect?
3. Is there a single cause or are there multiple causes? Single or multiple effects?
4. Is a chain reaction involved?

8d EXERCISE 8-2

Writing in Progress

Directions: Complete each of the following diagrams by adding a cause or an effect, as needed. The first one is done for you.

Cause and Effect

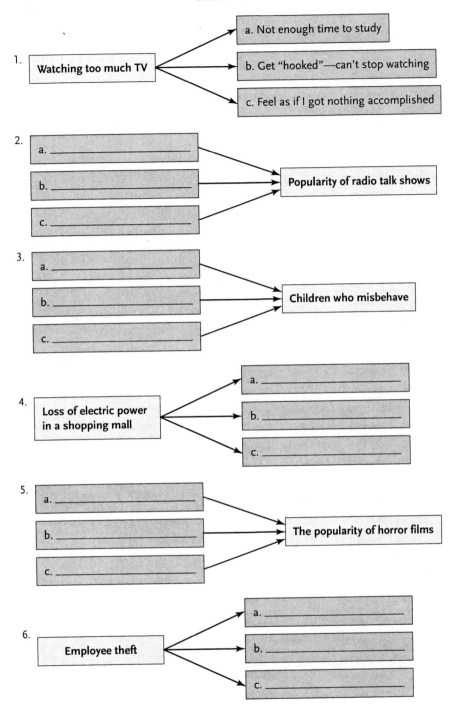

1. Watching too much TV
   - a. Not enough time to study
   - b. Get "hooked"—can't stop watching
   - c. Feel as if I got nothing accomplished

2. a. _____
   b. _____
   c. _____
   → **Popularity of radio talk shows**

3. a. _____
   b. _____
   c. _____
   → **Children who misbehave**

4. **Loss of electric power in a shopping mall**
   - a. _____
   - b. _____
   - c. _____

5. a. _____
   b. _____
   c. _____
   → **The popularity of horror films**

6. **Employee theft**
   - a. _____
   - b. _____
   - c. _____

Writing Your Topic Sentence

To write effective topic sentences for cause-and-effect paragraphs, do the following:

1. **Clarify the cause-and-effect relationship.** Before you write, carefully identify the causes and the effects. If you are uncertain, divide a sheet of paper into two columns. Label one column "Causes" and the other "Effects." Brainstorm about your topic, placing your ideas in the appropriate column.

2. **Decide whether to emphasize causes or effects.** In a single paragraph, it is best to focus on either causes or effects—not both. For example, suppose you are writing about students who drop out of college. You need to decide whether to discuss why they drop out (causes) or what happens to students who drop out (effects). Your topic sentence should indicate whether you are going to emphasize causes or effects. (In essays, you may consider both causes and effects.)

3. **Determine if the events are related or independent.** Analyze the causes or effects to discover if they occurred as part of a chain reaction or if they are not related to one another. Your topic sentence should suggest the type of relationship about which you are writing. If you are writing about a chain of events, your topic sentence should reflect this—for example, "A series of events led up to my sister's decision to drop out of college." If the causes or effects are not related to one another, then your sentence should indicate that—for example, "Students drop out of college for a number of different reasons."

Now read the following paragraph that a sales representative wrote to her regional manager to explain why she had failed to meet a monthly quota. Then study the diagram that accompanies it. Notice that the topic sentence makes it clear that she is focusing on the causes (circumstances) that led to her failure to make her sales quota for the month.

> In the past, I have always met or exceeded my monthly sales quota at Thompson's Office Furniture. This January I was $20,000 short, due to a set of unusual and uncontrollable circumstances in my territory. The month began with a severe snowstorm that closed most businesses in the area for most of the first week. Travel continued to be a problem the remainder of the week, and many purchasing agents did not report to work. Once they were back at their desks, they were not eager to meet with sales reps; instead, they wanted to catch up with their backlog of paperwork. Later that month, an ice storm resulted in power losses, again closing most plants for almost two days. Finally, some of our clients took extended weekends over the Martin Luther King holiday. Overall, my client contact days were reduced by more than 25%, yet my sales were only 15% below the quota.

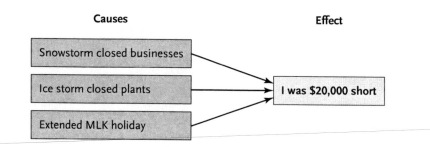

8e ## EXERCISE 8-3

Writing in Progress

Directions: Review the diagrams you made for Exercise 8-2. For each situation, write a topic sentence for a paragraph that will explain either its causes *or* effects.

Organizing Supporting Details

Providing supporting details for cause-and-effect paragraphs requires careful thought and planning. Details must be relevant, sufficient, and effectively organized.

Providing Relevant and Sufficient Details

Each cause or effect you describe must be relevant to the situation introduced in your topic sentence. Suppose you are writing a paragraph explaining why you are attending college. Each sentence must explain this topic. You could not include ideas, for example, about how college is different from what you expected.

If, while writing, you discover you have more ideas about how college is different from what you expected than you do about your reasons for attending college, you need to revise your topic sentence in order to refocus your paragraph.

Each cause or reason requires explanation, particularly if it is *not* obvious. For example, it is not sufficient to write, "One reason I decided to attend college was to advance my position in life." This sentence needs further explanation. For example, you could discuss the types of advancement (financial, job security, job satisfaction) you hope to attain.

Jot down a list of the causes or reasons you plan to include. This process may help you think of additional causes and will give you a chance to consider how to explain or support each one. You might decide to eliminate one or to combine several. Here is one student's list of reasons for attending college.

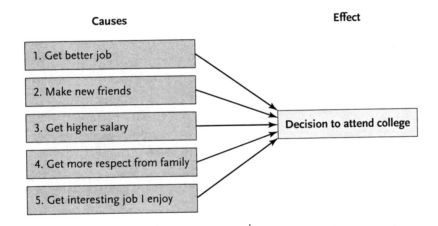

By listing his reasons, this student realized that the first one—to get a better job—was too general and was covered more specifically later in the list, so he eliminated it. He also realized that "get higher salary" and "get interesting job" could be combined. He then wrote the following paragraph:

There are three main reasons I decided to attend Ambrose Community College. First, and most important to me, I want to get a high-paying, interesting job that I will enjoy. Right now, the only jobs I can get pay minimum wage, and as a result, I'm working in a fast-food restaurant. This kind of job doesn't make me proud of myself, and I get bored with routine tasks. Second, my parents have always wanted me to have a better job than they do, and I know my father will not respect me until I do. A college degree would make them proud of me. A third reason for attending college is to make new friends. It is hard to meet people, and everyone in my neighborhood seems stuck in a rut. I want to meet other people who are interested in improving themselves like I am.

Organizing Your Details

There are several ways to arrange the details in a cause-and-effect paragraph. The method you choose depends on your purpose in writing, as well as your topic. Suppose you are writing a paragraph about the effects of a hurricane on a coastal town. Several different arrangements of details are possible:

1. **Chronological** A chronological organization arranges your details in the order in which situations or events happened. The order in which the hurricane damage occurred becomes the order for your details. A chronological arrangement works for situations and events that occurred in a specific order.

2. **Order of importance** In an order-of-importance organization, the details are arranged from least to most important or from most to least important. In describing the effects of the hurricane, you could discuss the most severe damage first and then describe lesser damage. Alternatively, you could build up from the least to the most important damage for dramatic effect.

3. **Spatial** Spatial arrangement of details uses physical or geographical position as a means of organization. In describing the hurricane damage, you could start by describing damage to the beach and work toward the center of town.

4. **Categorical** This form of arrangement divides the topic into parts or categories. Using this arrangement to describe hurricane damage, you could recount what the storm did to businesses, roads, city services, and homes.

As the hurricane example shows, there are many ways to organize cause-and-effect details. Each has a different emphasis and achieves a different purpose. The organization you choose, then, depends on the point you want to make.

Once you decide on a method of organization, return to your preliminary list of effects. Study your list again, make changes, eliminate, or combine. Then rearrange or number the items on your list to indicate the order in which you will include them.

8f   EXERCISE 8-4

Directions: Choose one of the following topic sentences and develop a paragraph using it. Organize your paragraph by using one of the methods described above.

1. Exercise has several positive (or negative) effects on the body.
2. Professional athletes deserve (or do not deserve) the high salaries they are paid.
3. There are several reasons why parents should reserve time each day to spend with their children.
4. Many students work two or even three part-time jobs; the results are often disastrous.

8g   EXERCISE 8-5

Writing in Progress

Directions: Write a paragraph developing one of the topic sentences you wrote for Exercise 8-3. Be sure to include relevant and sufficient details. Organize your paragraph according to one of the methods described above.

Useful Transitions

To blend your details smoothly, use the transitional words and phrases listed below.

Table 8-1 Transitions for Cause-and-Effect Paragraphs	
For causes	**For effects**
because, due to, one cause is . . . , another is . . . , since, for, first, second	consequently, as a result, thus, resulted in, one result is . . . , another is . . . , therefore

8h EXERCISE 8-6

Directions: In each blank provided, supply a transitional word or phrase that strengthens the connection between the two ideas.

1. Many companies have day care centers for children. _____ employees are able to manage child care problems easily.

2. Computers provide an easy way to store and process information quickly. _____ computers have become an integral part of most businesses.

3. Animal skins are warm and very durable; _____ almost every culture has made use of them for clothing or shelter.

4. _____ some people refused to accept his views and beliefs, Martin Luther King, Jr., was brutally murdered.

8i EXERCISE 8-7

Writing in Progress

Directions: Reread the paragraphs you wrote for Exercises 8-4 and 8-5. Add transitional words and phrases, if needed, to connect your details.

Applying Your Skills to Essay Writing: Cause and Effect

When writing cause-and-effect essays, keep the following suggestions in mind:

1. **Write an effective thesis statement.** Be sure that your thesis statement states the cause-and-effect relationship clearly and directly. Do not leave it for your reader to figure out what the relationship is. Here is an example:

   WEAK, INDIRECT THESIS   Temperatures can be dangerous for animals. Many suffer from heat stroke or dehydration.

   CLEAR, DIRECT THESIS   High summer temperatures can be dangerous for household pets because they can cause heat stroke or dehydration.

2. **Remember your purpose for writing as you plan your essay.** There are two main purposes for writing cause-and-effect essays:

   • to inform

   • to persuade

   For example, you may be writing to explain the effects of cigarette smoking or to convince your reader that the effects of smoking are harmful. Focus your essay to suit your purpose and choose details accordingly.

3. **Focus on primary—immediate and direct—causes or effects.** Unless you are writing a lengthy paper, it is best to limit yourself to primary causes or effects. Secondary causes or effects—those that occur later or are indirectly related—may confuse and distract your reader. For example, the immediate effects of cigarette smoking would include physical effects on smokers and those around them. The secondary effects might include higher medical insurance rates due to the costs of treating smoking-related illnesses.

4. **Strengthen your essay by using supporting evidence.** In explaining causes and/or effects, you may need to define terms, offer facts and statistics, or provide examples, anecdotes, or personal observations that support your ideas.

5. **Be cautious in determining cause-and-effect relationships.** Many errors in logic can occur in regard to cause-and-effect relationships. Do not assume that because one event occurs close in time to another, it caused the other or that they are even related.

6. **Qualify or limit your statements about cause-and-effect relationships.** Unless there is clear, indisputable evidence that one event is related to another, qualify your statements by using such wording as "It appears that the cause was . . ." or "Available evidence suggests. . . ."

NEED TO KNOW

Avoiding Errors in Logical Reasoning

Cause-and-effect relationships are often complex and it is easy to make errors when thinking and writing about them. Here are three ways to avoid common errors:

1. **Do not overlook underlying causes.** While it may appear that one thing causes another, it is possible that what you perceive as a cause may be only a symptom. For example, if a person complains of abdominal pain and is vomiting, you may think he or she just has a stomachache. However, it is possible the person has appendicitis, the pain and vomiting are actually symptoms, and an infected appendix is the true cause of the discomfort. To avoid this type of error, be sure to look for hidden, underlying causes rather than simply accepting an obvious explanation of an event.

2. **Do not assume that things that follow one another cause one another.** Just because Event Y follows Event X, it is not necessarily true that one caused the other. For example, an advertisement shows a family eating a particular brand of breakfast cereal and then shows everyone having a successful day at school and at work. The ad suggests that eating the cereal caused everyone to have a good day. To avoid this error, be sure to look for evidence that establishes the cause-and-effect relationship.

3. **Do not make the mistake of thinking things that happen at the same time are automatically related.** Because two events happen at once does not necessarily mean that one caused the other. For example, increased sales in beach umbrellas could occur at the same time that sales of portable fans increase. It is not logical to assume that the sale of beach umbrellas caused the increased sales of fans. More likely, both were caused by a heat wave. To avoid this error, check for evidence that connects the two events.

8j   EXERCISE 8-8

Directions: Suppose you are taking a course in education and have been assigned a paper. Select one of the following topics and write a one-page paper on it.

1. Watch a television show or movie that contains violence, and consider what it might teach a young child watching it alone about what is right and wrong, and about how people behave and should behave. Summarize your findings.

2. Talk to or think of someone who has dropped out of high school. What problems facing that person seem to be related to dropping out? Summarize your findings.

3. What are the effects of the course registration system used at your school? As you answer this question, use examples to support your points.

AN ACADEMIC SCENARIO

A Student Essay

The Academic Writer and the Writing Task

Veronica Evans-Johnson is a student at Durham Technical College where she is studying criminal justice. For her writing class, Veronica was asked to write a cause-and-effect essay; she chose to write about the causes of procrastination. As you read, notice that she devotes one paragraph to each cause of procrastination.

Causes of Procrastination
Veronica Evans-Johnson

Do you put off difficult or unpleasant tasks until tomorrow? If so, you are guilty of procrastination. Procrastination is the habit of putting off work or tasks that you are responsible for doing. It is a habit many people have and one they find it hard to break. There are a variety of reasons why people procrastinate, and whatever the cause, the results of procrastination are always the same—frustration.

Procrastination is common among students. Some students may lack the skills needed to complete an assignment and would rather put off doing the work than risk feeling "stupid." For instance, if a student does not know how to locate sources to complete a research paper, he or she, instead of facing this problem, may postpone writing the research paper until the night before it is due. By not facing his or her inability to conduct research and by not getting help from a college librarian, this student runs the risks of getting a poor grade, failing a course, or worse.

Other students put off doing homework because it's just not fun. They would rather have a good time than tackle the work in front of them. They may think they can leave their assignments until the last minute and still get them done on time, but usually the work suffers. The result may be a bad grade and the frustration of knowing that they would have received a much better grade if they'd spent more time preparing.

Another common cause behind many people's tendency to put things off is poor work habits. Many students have trouble organizing, prioritizing tasks, and scheduling time. This problem is complicated by the fact that many students are so busy, working full-time or multiple jobs, caring for family, doing housework and going to school that they're exhausted and can't *make* the time to get organized.

There are also many emotional and psychological causes for procrastinating. Fear of failure and fear of success are opposite sides of the same coin, but equally troubling. One person may believe that no matter what he or she does, failure is inevitable. Another person may be afraid of the attention or added responsibilities that success would bring. Still someone else may feel overwhelmed by the size of a project and not know where to start. And then there are the perfectionists. These people set unrealistic goals and hold themselves to impossible standards. They feel they have no choice but to put off doing things until conditions are just right—which, if you're a perfectionist, is never.

Unfortunately, we all face doing things at some time in our lives that we dislike. It could be housework, balancing a checkbook, or writing a report. Rather than wishing away unpleasant tasks, try to identify the reason you don't want to do them. Preparation is also a good cure for procrastination. Identify the task, make a list of what needs to get done and in what order, and set priorities. If a task seems huge and overwhelming, try breaking it down into separate parts and set aside a small amount of time for each. Every time one small part is completed, the overall task becomes smaller. This can make a big project more manageable.

Finally, whatever your reason for procrastinating, take a good, hard look at it. If you stop putting off the things that need to be done today, you'll be taking a big step toward a life of fewer frustrations tomorrow.

Straightforward title that identifies the subject of the essay

Definition of the term

Thesis statement

Cause 1

Example
Effect

Cause 2

Effect

Cause 3

Cause 4

Addresses cures for procrastination

Conclusion: refers back to the frustration mentioned in the first paragraph

Examining Academic Writing

1. How does Evans-Johnson personally engage the reader?
2. Do you think more examples would have improved the essay?
3. Evans-Johnson presents effects for causes annotated as 1 and 2, but does not do so for 3 and 4. Should she have done so?
4. Suggest ways Evans-Johnson could make the introduction more lively and interesting.
5. Are there causes of procrastination that the author did not address?

Academic Writing Assignments

1. You are taking a course in computer basics. Your instructor has asked the class to write a paragraph explaining why spamming—the process of sending advertisements to a large number of e-mail addresses—is a wasteful practice.
2. For a health and wellness class, you have been asked to choose an unhealthy practice or habit and to write an essay explaining why it is unhealthy. (You might choose smoking, binge drinking, or overeating, for example.)
3. In your criminal justice class you are studying white collar crimes—non-violent crimes that are carried out in one's place of employment. Write a paragraph exploring reasons why an employee might commit a crime against his or her company.

A WORKPLACE SCENARIO

Writing a Speech

The Workplace Writer and the Writing Task

Glen Corma is the owner of Glennie's Restaurant. As a small business owner, he was asked to give a speech at a meeting of the American Express Establishment Services convention. The text of his speech, which is shown below, explains the reasons he chose to accept the American Express credit card at his restaurant. As you read, identify and highlight each reason.

Text of the Speech:

You know the old saying "never say never"? It's true. My being here is proof that you shouldn't ever say never.

When I opened my restaurant Glennie's back in 2002, I said I would never take the American Express card. At the time, American Express rates were high and MasterCard and Visa's were low. I thought the extra expense wasn't worth it. AmEx tried to persuade me of the value of taking the card; that card holders spend more on eating out and that I'd pick up a lot more corporate business. But it would have cost me over $10,000.00 a year to accept the card and at the time I didn't think I needed it. Glennie's was constantly booked and, in fact, I joked that we didn't have room to seat American Express card holders! So I said "never" to AmEx and forgot about it.

As time went on, other restaurants opened in the area. Suddenly I had competition I'd never had before. And I noticed that some customers would leave when they found out I didn't take AmEx, choosing to eat at one of the competitors who did. Still, business was good and I figured I didn't need them.

Then, three things happened in rapid succession. First, American Express rolled back its rates. Second, one day a new customer came into the restaurant. When it came time to pay and he found out we didn't take American Express, he went ballistic. He stood there, in front of all my regulars, yelling that he couldn't believe a restaurant of this stature wouldn't take American Express. Now, I assume that if someone's got an American Express card, they've got other cards. And he did—but he wouldn't use them. All of his other cards were personal accounts and this was a business lunch. No way was he going to spend his own money and do all the paperwork to get reimbursed when he had a company AmEx card.

> The third thing was the final straw. One of my regular customers ate at one of the new restaurants that had opened near me. He came into Glennie's the next day and gave his report: the food wasn't as good, the décor was boring—and he planned to go back. Why? You guessed it; they took his American Express card.
>
> I realized that in today's competitive environment, I couldn't afford to keep saying "Never!" to American Express. So I signed up. And six months later, I know what an important decision it was. Forty-four percent of the American Express charges coming in are from corporate clients. And they do spend more.
>
> Here's even more proof; even though we didn't do any advertising, within one week 50 percent of the charges at Glennie's went to American Express. And customers I hadn't seen in months started coming back on a regular basis.
>
> Last week, an account rep from American Express came in for lunch. He wanted to make sure there weren't any problems and he wanted to try Glennie's for himself. He asked my wife and me to join him, ordered enough food for ten people, and picked up the check.
>
> How did he pay? With his American Express card, of course!
>
> And so, ladies and gentlemen, I leave you with a promise: I will never say never again.

Examining Workplace Writing

1. Was Glen's speech informative or persuasive (intended to get listeners to agree with him)?
2. Was Glen's speech interesting and engaging? If so, why?
3. Evaluate Glen's introduction and conclusion. Why are they effective?
4. In what ways does speech writing differ from traditional essays written to be read in print?

Workplace Writing Assignments

1. You work for your town's summer recreation department as a lifeguard at the local pool. There have been several accidents, all minor, but people were injured. Your supervisor has asked you to write a notice about pool safety to post at the entrance. Write a list of do's and don'ts (causes) that will result in pool safety and reduce accidents (effects).
2. You have a part-time job as a sales clerk in a candy shop. Customers often ask you for samples, but company policy does not allow you to give them out. Write a memo to your boss explaining the advantages (effects) of giving free samples to serious customers.
3. You own a local car wash and have received a number of customer complaints about your employees' attitude toward and treatment of them. Write a memo to your employees suggesting behaviors (causes) that will promote customer satisfaction (effects).

8k WRITING ABOUT A READING

Thinking Before Reading

The following article, "Why We Love Bad News," first appeared in *Psychology Today Magazine*. In it, the writer Hara Marano reports on the research of two scientists that explains why negative information has a stronger impact than positive information and shows how this affects our lives. As you read, identify both causes and effects.

1. Preview the reading.
2. Activate your thinking by answering the following questions:
   a. When someone says, "I have good news and bad news . . . ," which do you usually ask to hear first? Why?
   b. Imagine you have a job that pays well, but a boss who never has anything positive to say about your work. Would you continue in that job or look elsewhere?

READING

Why We Love Bad News
Hara Marano

1   Why do insults once hurled at us stick inside our skull, sometimes for decades? Why do political smear campaigns outpull positive ones?

2   The answer is, nastiness makes a bigger impact on your brain.

3   And that, says Ohio State University psychologist John T. Cacioppo, Ph.D., is due to the brain's "negativity bias": your brain is simply built with a greater sensitivity to unpleasant news. The bias is so automatic that it can be detected at the earliest stage of the brain's information processing.

4   In studies he has done, Cacioppo showed people pictures known to arouse positive feelings (such as a Ferrari or a pizza), those certain to stir up negative feelings (like a mutilated face or dead cat) and those known to produce neutral feelings (a plate, a hair dryer). Meanwhile, he recorded electrical activity of the brain's **cerebral cortex** that reflects the magnitude of information processing taking place.

5   The brain, Cacioppo demonstrated, reacts more strongly to stimuli it deems negative. That is, there is a greater surge in electrical activity. Thus, our attitudes are more heavily influenced by downbeat news than good news.

6   Our capacity to weigh negative input so heavily evolved for a good reason—to keep us out of harm's way. From the dawn of human history our very survival depended on our skill at dodging danger. The brain developed systems that would make it unavoidable for us not to notice danger and thus, hopefully, respond to it.

7   All well and good. Having the built-in brain apparatus supersensitive to negativity means that the same bias also is at work in every sphere of our lives at all times.

8   So it should come as no surprise to learn that it plays an especially powerful role in our most intimate relationships. Numerous researchers have found that there is "an ecology of marriage," an ideal balance between negativity and positivity in the atmosphere between partners.

9   Psychologist John Gottman, Ph.D., at the University of Washington is one. He finds that there seems to be some kind of thermostat operating in healthy marriages that regulates the balance between positive and negative. For example, when partners get contemptuous—that is, when they fight by hurling criticism with the intent to insult the partner, which the partner rightly perceives as especially hurtful—they correct it with lots of positivity—touching, smiling, paying compliments, laughing, and other such acts. They don't correct necessarily right away, but they definitely do it sometime soon.

10   What really separates contented couples from those in deep marital misery is a healthy balance between their positive and negative feelings and actions toward each other. Even couples who are volatile and argue a lot stick together by balancing their frequent arguments with a lot of demonstrations of love and passion.

11   Because of the disproportionate weight of the negative, balance does not mean a 50-50 **equilibrium**. Gottman, for example, as part of his research carefully charted the amount of time couples spent fighting versus interacting positively. Across the board he found that a very specific ratio exists between the amount of positivity and negativity required to make a marriage satisfying.

cerebral cortex
a layer of gray matter that covers the brain and coordinates sensory and motor information

equilibrium
balance

12   That magic ratio is 5 to 1. As long as there is five times as much positive feeling and interaction between husband and wife as there is negative, the marriage was likely to be stable over time. In contrast, those couples who were heading for divorce were doing far too little on the positive side to compensate for the growing negativity between them.

13   Other researchers have found the same thing. It is the frequency of small positive acts that matters most, in a ratio of about 5 to 1.

14   Interestingly, occasional large positive experiences—say, a big birthday bash—are nice, but they don't make the necessary impact on our brain to override the tilt to negativity. It takes frequent small positive experiences to tip the scales toward happiness.

Getting Ready to Write

Reviewing the Reading

1. State the author's thesis in your own words.
2. Why do candidates who run negative campaign ads get more votes than other politicians?
3. How did Dr. Cacioppo prove his theory about the brain's reaction to positive and negative stimuli?
4. What group of people did John Gottman study?
5. Explain what a 5-to-1 ratio means.

Examining the Reading: Using an Idea Map to Grasp Cause-and-Effect Relationships

"Why We Love Bad News" explores why the brain instinctively reacts to negative information and how this can affect our lives, particularly our personal relationships. Complete the map of the reading on the following page. You will notice that it first examines causes and then moves to effects:

Thinking Critically: Evaluating Cause-and-Effect Relationships

Even though scientific research is usually accepted as sound, different influences can affect the outcome of an experiment. These influences are called "variables." For example, suppose a researcher gives a group of people a dose of vitamins and find that the group is healthier than a group of people who did not take the vitamins. What factors (variables) other than the vitamins could account for the differences? If the non-vitamin group ate a healthier diet than the vitamin-taking group, diet is a variable that could account for the differences.

Think of some variables that might have caused Dr. Cacioppo and Dr. Gottman's experiments to have different outcomes. Answer the following questions to help you analyze variables that affect cause-and-effect relationships.

1. How could gender (using only men or only women) affect the outcome of the studies?
2. How might age affect the outcome of the studies? Would children and adults have the same or different responses?
3. How might educational level affect the outcome of the studies? Would people with graduate degrees respond differently than people who did not go to college?

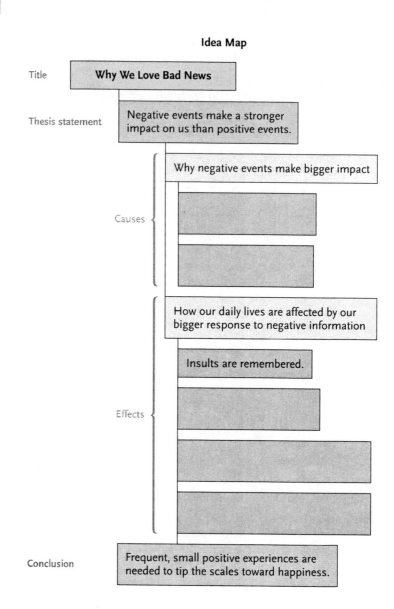

Idea Map

Title — **Why We Love Bad News**

Thesis statement — Negative events make a stronger impact on us than positive events.

Causes {

Why negative events make bigger impact

Effects {

How our daily lives are affected by our bigger response to negative information

Insults are remembered.

Conclusion — Frequent, small positive experiences are needed to tip the scales toward happiness.

Strengthening Your Vocabulary

Part A: Using the word's context, word parts, or a dictionary, write a brief definition of each of the following words or phrases as it is used in the reading.

1. bias (paragraph 3) _____

_____

2. stimuli (paragraph 5) _____

_____

3. input (paragraph 6) _____

_____

4. sphere (paragraph 7) _____

_____

5. volatile (paragraph 10) _____

_____

6. disproportionate (paragraph 11) _____

_____

7. compensate (paragraph 12) _____

_____

Part B: Draw a word map of one of the words above.

Reacting to Ideas: Discussion and Journal Writing

1. Knowing that the brain reacts more strongly to negative stimuli, can you think of places you would never want to work or jobs you would never consider taking?
2. Do you think a test could be developed to determine what kind of relationship couples will have *before* they get married? If so, would you take the test?
3. Based on the 5-to-1 ratio, what could a boss do to make a workplace better? Give some examples.
4. If a teacher corrected you in front of the whole class one day, then brought in a cake the next day, which do you think you would remember longer? Why?

Writing About the Reading

Paragraph Options

1. Think about something that happened in your life that seemed big at the time, but really didn't have much effect on the rest of your life. Write a paragraph that describes what happened, how you felt about it then, and how you feel about it now.
2. Imagine you are doing the same research as Dr. Cacioppo and Dr. Gottman. You have to pick three pictures to show your subjects. Describe your pictures in detail. Predict which picture will cause the most brain activity in your subjects and which the least.
3. Write a paragraph about a partner, spouse, or friend who once insulted you or did something nasty to you. How did it affect your relationship with that person?

Essay Options

4. Choose a small experience that had a big effect on your life (see paragraph 14 of the reading). Write an essay about this experience and why you think it made such an impact.
5. Besides a 5-to-1 ratio of positive to negative input, what are some other factors that make a good relationship? List some of these factors and use examples to show how they might make a couple happy.

Revision Checklist

1. Is your paragraph or essay appropriate for your audience? Does it give them the background information they need? Will it interest them?
2. Will your paragraph or essay accomplish your purpose?
3. Is your main point clearly expressed?
4. Is each detail relevant? Does each explain or support your main point?

5. Have you supported your main point with sufficient detail to make it understandable and believable?
6. Do you use specific and vivid words to explain each detail?

For Cause-and-Effect Writing

7. Does your topic sentence or thesis statement indicate whether you will emphasize causes or effects?
8. Does your topic sentence or thesis statement indicate whether the events you are describing are related or independent?
9. Are your details presented in one of the following arrangements: chronological, order of importance, spatial, or categorical?
10. Have you used transitional words and phrases to blend your details smoothly?
11. Have you proofread?

8I CHAPTER REVIEW AND PRACTICE

Chapter Review

What is cause and effect?	**Cause** focuses on the reasons an event or behavior happened. **Effect** is the explanation of what happens as a result of an action or event.
What should your topic sentence contain	It should identify the cause-and-effect relationship, and focus on either causes or effects.
How should the details be organized?	Three common choices are chronological, order of importance, spatial, and categorical.
What are the guidelines for writing cause-and-effect essays?	Write a strong thesis, focus on primary causes or effects, provide adequate supporting evidence, avoid logical errors, and qualify or limit the cause-and-effect relationship.

STUDENT ESSAY

The following student essay was written by Carl Novack in response to this assignment:

In "Our Schedules, Our Selves," Jay Walljasper examines the way Palm Pilots, cell phones, e-mail, and other technologies have resulted in our "overbooking" our daily lives. Think of another aspect of everyday life that has changed recently, and discuss those factors that you believe are responsible for the change.

While reading Carl's paper, try to determine how well it applies the principles of causal analysis. The annotations on Carl's paper and the commentary following it will help you look at the essay more closely.

Americans and Food

by Carl Novack

Introduction

1   An offbeat but timely cartoon recently appeared in the local newspaper. The single panel showed a gravel-pit operation with piles of raw earth and large cranes. Next to one of the cranes stood the owner of the gravel pit—a grizzled, tough-looking character, hammer in hand, pointing proudly to the new sign he had just tacked up. The sign

read, "Fred's Fill Dirt and Croissants." The cartoon illustrates an interesting phenome-non: the changing food habits of Americans. Our meals used to consist of something like home-cooked pot roast, mashed potatoes laced with butter and salt, a thick slice of apple pie topped with a healthy scoop of vanilla ice cream--plain, heavy meals, cooked from scratch, and eaten leisurely at home. But America has changed, and as it has, so have what we Americans eat and how we eat it.   — Thesis

2   We used to have simple, unsophisticated tastes and looked with suspicion at any-thing more exotic than hamburger. Admittedly, we did adopt some foods from the vari-ous immigrant groups who flocked to our shores. We learned to eat Chinese food, pizza, and bagels. But in the last few years, the international character of our diet has   — Topic sentence: Background paragraph
grown tremendously. We can walk into any mall in Middle America and buy pita sand-wiches, quiche, and tacos. Such foods are often changed on their journey from exotic imports to ordinary "American" meals (no Pakistani, for example, eats frozen-on-a-stick   — Topic sentence: Three causes answer the question
boysenberry-flavored yogurt), but the imports are still a long way from hamburger on a bun.

3   Why have we become more worldly in our tastes? For one thing, television blankets   — First cause
the country with information about new food products and trends. Viewers in rural Montana know that the latest craving in Washington, D.C., is Cajun cooking or that something called tofu is now available in the local supermarket. Another reason for the   — Second cause
growing international flavor of our food is that many young Americans have traveled abroad and gotten hooked on new tastes and flavors. Backpacking students and young professionals vacationing in Europe come home with cravings for authentic French bread or German beer. Finally, continuing waves of immigrants settle in the cities where   — Third cause
many of us live, causing significant changes in what we eat. Vietnamese, Haitians, and Thais, for instance, bring their native foods and cooking styles with them and eventu-ally open small markets or restaurants. In time, the new food will become American-ized enough to take its place in our national diet.

4   Our growing concern with health has also affected the way we eat. For the last few   — Topic sentence: Another cause
years, the media have warned us about the dangers of our traditional diet, high in salt and fat, low in fiber. The media also began to educate us about the dangers of processed foods pumped full of chemical additives. As a result, consumers began to   — Start of a causal chain
demand healthier foods, and manufacturers started to change some of their products. Many foods, such as lunch meat, canned vegetables, and soups, were made available in low-fat, low-sodium versions. Whole-grain cereals and higher-fiber breads also be-gan to appear on the grocery shelves. Moreover, the food industry started to produce all-natural products—everything from potato chips to ice cream—without additives and preservatives. Not surprisingly, the restaurant industry responded to this switch to healthier foods, luring customers with salad bars, broiled fish, and steamed vegetables.

5   Our food habits are being affected, too, by the rapid increase in the number of women   — Topic sentence: Another cause
working outside the home. Sociologists and other experts believe that two important fac-tors triggered this phenomenon: the women's movement and a changing economic cli-mate. Women were assured that it was acceptable, even rewarding, to work outside the home; many women also discovered that they had to work just to keep up with the cost of living. As the traditional role of homemaker changed, so did the way families ate. With Mom working, there wasn't time for her to prepare the traditional three square meals a day. In-stead, families began looking for alternatives to provide quick meals. What was the result?   — Start of a causal chain
For one thing, there was a boom in fast-food restaurants. The suburban or downtown strip

that once contained a lone McDonald's now features Wendy's, Roy Rogers, Taco Bell, Burger King, and Pizza Hut. Families also began to depend on frozen foods as another time-saving alternative. Once again, though, demand changed the kind of frozen food available. Frozen foods no longer consist of foil trays divided into greasy fried chicken, watery corn niblets, and lumpy mashed potatoes. Supermarkets now stock a range of supposedly gourmet frozen dinners—from fettucini in cream sauce to braised beef en brochette.

Conclusion

6   It may not be possible to pick up a ton of fill dirt and a half-dozen croissants at the same place, but America's food habits are definitely changing. If it is true that "you are what you eat," then America's identity is evolving along with its diet.

COMMENTARY

Title and Introduction

Asked to prepare a paper analyzing the reasons behind a change in our lives, Carl decided to write about a shift he had noticed in Americans' eating habits. The title of the essay, "Americans and Food," identifies Carl's subject but could be livelier and more interesting.

Despite his rather uninspired title, Carl starts his *causal analysis* in an engaging way—with the vivid description of a cartoon. He then connects the cartoon to his subject with the following sentence: "The cartoon illustrates an interesting phenomenon: the changing food habits of Americans." To back up his belief that there has been a revolution in our eating habits, Carl uses the first paragraph to summarize the kind of meal that people used to eat. He then moves into his *thesis:* "But America has changed, and as it has, so have what Americans eat and how we eat it." The thesis implies that Carl's paper will focus on both causes and effects.

Purpose

Carl's *purpose* was to write an *informative* causal analysis. But before he could present the causes of the change in eating habits, he needed to show that such a change had, in fact, taken place. He therefore uses the second paragraph to document one aspect of this change—the internationalization of our eating habits.

Topic Sentences

At the beginning of the third paragraph, Carl uses a question—"Why have we become more worldly in our tastes?"—to signal that his discussion of causes is about to begin. This question also serves as the paragraph's *topic sentence,* indicating that the paragraph will focus on reasons for the increasingly international flavor of our food. The next two paragraphs, also focused by topic sentences, identify two other major reasons for the change in eating habits: "Our growing concern with health has also affected the way we eat" (paragraph 4), and "Our food habits are being affected, too, by the rapid increase in the number of women working outside the home" (5).

Combining Patterns of Development

Carl draws on two patterns—comparison-contrast and exemplification—to develop his causal analysis. At the heart of the essay is a basic *contrast* between the way we used to eat and the way we eat now. And throughout his essay, Carl provides convincing *examples* to demonstrate the validity of his points. Consider for a moment the third paragraph. Here Carl asserts that one reason for our new eating habits is our growing exposure to international foods. He then presents concrete evidence to show that we have indeed become more familiar with international cuisine: Television exposes rural Montana to Cajun cooking; students traveling abroad take a liking to French bread; urban dwellers enjoy the exotic fare served by numerous immigrant groups. The fourth and fifth paragraphs use similarly specific evidence (for example, "low-fat, low-sodium versions" of "lunch meat, canned vegetables, and soups") to illustrate the soundness of key ideas.

Causal Chains

Let's look more closely at the evidence in the essay. Not satisfied with obvious explanations, Carl thought through his ideas carefully and even brainstormed with friends to arrive at as comprehensive an analysis as possible. Not surprisingly, much of the evidence Carl uncovered took the form of *causal chains*. In the fourth paragraph, Carl writes, "The media also began to educate us about the dangers of processed foods pumped full of chemical additives. As a result, consumers began to demand healthier foods, and manufacturers started to change some of their products." And the next paragraph shows how the changing role of American women caused families to search for alternative ways of eating. This shift, in turn, caused the restaurant and food industries to respond with a wide range of food alternatives.

Making the Paper Easy to Follow

Although Carl's analysis digs beneath the surface and reveals complex cause-effect relationships, he wisely limits his pursuit of causal chains to *primary causes and effects*. He doesn't let the complexities distract him from his main purpose: to show why and how the American diet is changing. Carl is also careful to provide his essay with abundant *connecting devices,* making it easy for readers to see the links between points. Consider the use of *transitions* (signaled by italics) in the following sentences: "*Another* reason for the growing international flavor of our food is that many young Americans have traveled abroad" (paragraph 3); "*As a result,* consumers began to demand healthier foods" (4); and "*As* the traditional role of homemaker changed, so did the way families ate" (5).

A Problem with the Essay's Close

When reading the essay, you probably noticed that Carl's conclusion is a bit weak. Although his reference to the cartoon works well, the rest of the paragraph limps to a tired close. Ending an otherwise vigorous essay with such a slight conclusion undercuts the effectiveness of the whole paper. Carl spent so much energy developing the body of his essay that he ran out of the stamina needed to conclude the piece more forcefully. Careful budgeting of his time would have allowed him to prepare a stronger concluding paragraph.

Revising the First Draft

When Carl was ready to revise, he showed the first draft of his essay to several classmates during a peer review session. Listening carefully to what they said, he jotted down their most helpful comments and eventually transferred them, numbered in order of importance, to his draft. Comparing Carl's original version of his fourth paragraph (shown here) with his final version in the essay will show you how he went about revising.

Original Version of the Fourth Paragraph

A growing concern with health has also affected the way we eat, especially because the media have sent us warnings the last few years about the dangers of salt, sugar, food additives, high-fat and low-fiber diets. We have started to worry that our traditional meals may have been shortening our lives. As a result, consumers demanded healthier foods and manufacturers started taking some of the salt and sugar out of canned foods. "All-natural" became an effective selling point, leading to many preservative-free products. Restaurants, too, adapted their menus, luring customers with light meals. Because we now know about the link between overweight and a variety of health problems, including heart attacks, we are counting calories. In turn, food companies made fortunes on diet beer and diet cola. Sometimes, though, we seem a bit confused about the health issue; we drink soda that is sugar-free but loaded with chemical sweeteners. Still, we believe we are lengthening our lives through changing our diets.

On the advice of his classmates, Carl decided to omit all references to the way our concern with weight has affected our eating habits. It's true, of course, that calorie-counting has changed how we eat. But as soon as Carl started to discuss this point, he got involved in a causal chain that undercut the paragraph's unity. He ended up describing the paradoxical situation in which we find ourselves. In an attempt to eat healthy, we stay away from sugar and use instead artificial sweeteners that probably aren't very good for us. This is an interesting issue, but it detracts from the point Carl wants to make: that our concern with health has affected our eating habits in a *positive* way.

Carl's peer reviewers also pointed out that the fourth paragraph's first sentence contained too much material to be an effective topic sentence. Carl corrected the problem by breaking the overlong sentence into two short ones: "Our growing concern with health has also affected the way we eat. For the last few years, the media have warned us about the dangers of our traditional diet, high in salt and fat, low in fiber." The first of these sentences serves as a crisp topic sentence that focuses the rest of the paragraph.

Finally, Carl agreed with his classmates that the fourth paragraph lacked convincing specifics. When revising, he changed "manufacturers started taking some of the salt and sugar out of canned foods" to the more specific "Many foods, such as lunch meats, canned vegetables, and soups, were made available in low-fat, low-sodium versions." Similarly, generalizations about "light meals" and "all-natural products" gained life through the addition of concrete examples: restaurants lured "customers with salad bars, broiled fish, and steamed vegetables," and the food industry produced "everything from potato chips to ice cream—without additives and preservatives."

Carl did an equally good job revising other sections of his paper. With the exception of the weak spots already discussed, he made the changes needed to craft a well-reasoned essay, one that demonstrates his ability to analyze a complex phenomenon.

ACTIVITIES: CAUSE-EFFECT

Prewriting Activities

1. Imagine you're writing two essays: One *argues* the need for high school courses in personal finance (how to budget money, balance a checkbook, and the like); the other explains a *process* for showing appreciation. Jot down ways you might use cause-effect in each essay.

2. Use mapping, collaborative brainstorming, or another prewriting technique to generate possible causes and/or effects for *one* of the topics below. Be sure to keep in mind the audience indicated in parentheses. Next, devise a thesis and decide whether your purpose would be informative, persuasive, speculative, or some combination of these. Finally, organize your raw material into a brief outline, with related causes and effects grouped in the same section.

   a. Pressure on students to do well (*high school students*)
   b. Children's access to pornography on the Internet (*parents*)
   c. Being physically fit (*those who are out of shape*)
   d. Spiraling costs of a college education (*college officials*)

Revising Activities

3. Explain how the following statements demonstrate *post hoc* thinking and confuse correlation and cause-effect.

   a. Our city now has many immigrants from Latin American countries. The crime rate in our city has increased. Latin American immigrants are the cause of the crime wave.
   b. The divorce rate has skyrocketed. More women are working outside the home than ever before. Working outside the home destroys marriages.
   c. A high percentage of people in Dixville have developed cancer. The landfill, used by XYZ Industries, has been located in Dixville for twenty years. The XYZ landfill has caused cancer in Dixville residents.

4. The following paragraph is from the first draft of an essay arguing that technological advances can diminish the quality of life. How solid is the paragraph's causal analysis? Which causes and/or effects should be eliminated? Where is the analysis simplistic? Where does the writer make absolute claims even though cause-effect relationships are no more than a possibility? Keeping these questions in mind, revise the paragraph.

How did the banking industry respond to inflation? It simply introduced a new technology—the automated teller machine (ATM). By making money more available to the average person, the ATM gives people the cash to buy inflated goods—whether or not they can afford them. Not surprisingly, automated teller machines have had a number of negative consequences for the average individual. Since people know they can get cash at any time, they use their lunch hours for something other than going to the bank. How do they spend this newfound time? They go shopping, and machine-vended money means more impulse buying, even more than with a credit card. Also, because people don't need their checkbooks to withdraw money, they can't keep track of their accounts and therefore develop a casual attitude toward financial matters. It's no wonder children don't appreciate the value of money. Another problem is that people who would never dream of robbing a bank try to trick the machine into dispensing money "for free." There's no doubt that this kind of fraud contributes to the immoral climate in the country.

READING

Stephen King

Probably the best-known living horror writer, Stephen King (1947–) is the author of more than thirty books. Before earning fame through his vastly popular books, including *Carrie* (1974), *The Shining* (1977), *Cujo* (1981), and *Tommyknockers* (1987), King worked as a high school English teacher and an industrial laundry worker. Much of King's prolific output has been adapted for the screen; movies based on King's work include *Misery* (1990), *Stand By Me* (1986), and *The Green Mile* (1999). More recent works include *Dreamcatcher* (2001), *Everything's Eventual* (2002), *From a Buick 8* (2002), and Volumes V, VI, and VII in the *Dark Tower* series (published in 2003, 2004, and 2004, respectively). His book *On Writing: A Memoir of the Craft* (2000) offers insight into the writing process and examines the role that writing has played in King's own life—especially following a near-fatal accident in 1999. King lives with his wife in Bangor, Maine, and has three adult children. The following essay first appeared in *Playboy* in 1982.

Pre-Reading Journal Entry

Several forms of entertainment, besides horror movies, are highly popular despite what many consider a low level of quality. In your journal, list as many "low-brow" forms of entertainment as you can. Possibilities include professional wrestling, aggressive video games, Internet chat rooms, and so on. Review your list, and respond to the following question in your journal: What is it about each form of entertainment that attracts such popularity—and inspires such criticism?

Why We Crave Horror Movies

1   I think that we're all mentally ill: those of us outside the asylums only hide it a little better—and maybe not all that much better, after all. We've all known people who talk to themselves, people who sometimes squinch their faces into horrible grimaces when they believe no one is watching, people who have some hysterical fear—of snakes, the

dark, the tight place, the long drop . . . and, of course, those final worms and grubs that are waiting so patiently underground.

2   When we pay our four or five bucks and seat ourselves at tenth-row center in a theater showing a horror movie, we are daring the nightmare.

3   Why? Some of the reasons are simple and obvious. To show that we can, that we are not afraid, that we can ride this roller coaster. Which is not to say that a really good horror movie may not surprise a scream out of us at some point, the way we may scream when the roller coaster twists through a complete 360 or plows through a lake at the bottom of the drop. And horror movies, like roller coasters, have always been the special province of the young; by the time one turns 40 or 50, one's appetite for double twists or 360-degree loops may be considerably depleted.

4   We also go to re-establish our feelings of essential normality; the horror movie is innately conservative, even reactionary. Freda Jackson as the horrible melting woman in *Die, Monster, Die!* confirms for us that no matter how far we may be removed from the beauty of a Robert Redford or a Diana Ross, we are still light-years from true ugliness.

5   And we go to have fun.

6   Ah, but this is where the ground starts to slope away, isn't it? Because this is a very peculiar sort of fun indeed. The fun comes from seeing others menaced—sometimes killed. One critic has suggested that if pro football has become the voyeur's version of combat, then the horror film has become the modern version of the public lynching.

7   It is true that the mythic, "fairytale" horror film intends to take away the shades of gray. . . . It urges us to put away our more civilized and adult penchant for analysis and to become children again, seeing things in pure blacks and whites. It may be that horror movies provide psychic relief on this level because this invitation to lapse into simplicity, irrationality and even outright madness is extended so rarely. We are told we may allow our emotions a free rein . . . or no rein at all.

8   If we are all insane, then sanity becomes a matter of degree. If your insanity leads you to carve up women like Jack the Ripper or the Cleveland Torso Murderer, we clap you away in the funny farm (but neither of those two amateur-night surgeons was ever caught, heh-heh-heh); if, on the other hand your insanity leads you only to talk to yourself when you're under stress or to pick your nose on the morning bus, then you are left alone to go about your business . . . though it is doubtful that you will ever be invited to the best parties.

9   The potential lyncher is in almost all of us (excluding saints, past and present; but then, most saints have been crazy in their own ways), and every now and then, he has to be let loose to scream and roll around in the grass. Our emotions and our fears form their own body, and we recognize that it demands its own exercise to maintain proper muscle tone. Certain of these emotional muscles are accepted—even exalted—in civilized society; they are, of course, the emotions that tend to maintain the status quo of civilization itself. Love, friendship, loyalty, kindness—these are all the emotions that we applaud, emotions that have been immortalized in the couplets of Hallmark cards. . . .

10   When we exhibit these emotions, society showers us with positive reinforcement; we learn this even before we get out of diapers. When, as children, we hug our rotten little puke of a sister and give her a kiss, all the aunts and uncles smile and twit and cry, "Isn't he the sweetest little thing?" Such coveted treats as chocolate-covered graham crackers often follow. But if we deliberately slam the rotten little puke of a sister's fin-

gers in the door, sanctions follow—angry remonstrance from parents, aunts and uncles; instead of a chocolate-covered graham cracker, a spanking.

11   But anticivilization emotions don't go away, and they demand periodic exercise. We have such "sick" jokes as, "What's the difference between a truckload of bowling balls and a truckload of dead babies?" (You can't unload a truckload of bowling balls with a pitchfork . . . a joke, by the way, that I heard originally from a ten-year-old.) Such a joke may surprise a laugh or a grin out of us even as we recoil, a possibility that confirms the thesis: If we share a brotherhood of man, then we also share an insanity of man. None of which is intended as a defense of either the sick joke or insanity but merely as an explanation of why the best horror films, like the best fairy tales, manage to be reactionary, anarchistic, and revolutionary all at the same time.

12   The mythic horror movie, like the sick joke, has a dirty job to do. It deliberately appeals to all that is worst in us. It is morbidity unchained, our most base instincts let free, our nastiest fantasies realized . . . and it all happens, fittingly enough, in the dark. For those reasons, good liberals often shy away from horror films. For myself, I like to see the most aggressive of them—*Dawn of the Dead,* for instance—as lifting a trap door in the civilized forebrain and throwing a basket of raw meat to the hungry alligators swimming around in that subterranean river beneath.

13   Why bother? Because it keeps them from getting out, man. It keeps them down there and me up here. It was Lennon and McCartney who said that all you need is love, and I would agree with that.

14   As long as you keep the gators fed.

Questions for Close Reading

1. What is the selection's thesis? Locate the sentence(s) in which King states his main idea. If he doesn't state the thesis explicitly, express it in your own words.

2. In what ways do King's references to "Jack the Ripper" and the "Cleveland Torso Murderer" (paragraph 8) support his thesis?

3. What does King mean in paragraph 4 when he says that horror movies are "innately conservative, even reactionary"? What does he mean in paragraph 11 when he calls them "anarchistic, and revolutionary"?

4. In paragraphs 12 and 14, King refers to "alligators" and "gators." What does the alligator represent? What does King mean when he says that all the world needs is love—"[a]s long as you keep the gators fed"?

5. Refer to your dictionary as needed to define the following words used in the selection: *hysterical* (paragraph 1), *reactionary* (4), *voyeur's* (6), *lynching* (6), *penchant* (7), *immortalized* (9), *anarchistic* (11), and *morbidity* (12).

Questions About the Writer's Craft

1. **The pattern.** Does King's causal analysis have an essentially informative, speculative, or persuasive purpose? What makes you think so? How might King's profession as a horror writer have influenced his purpose?

2. **Other patterns.** King *compares* and *contrasts* horror movies to roller coasters (3), public lynchings (6), and sick jokes (11–12). How do these comparisons and contrasts reinforce King's thesis about horror movies?

3. **Other patterns.** Throughout the essay, King uses several *examples* involving children. Identify these instances. How do these examples help King develop his thesis?

4. What is unusual about paragraphs 2, 5, and 14? Why do you think King might have designed these paragraphs in this way?

Writing Assignments Using Cause-Effect as a Pattern of Development

1. King argues that horror movies have "a dirty job to do": they feed the hungry monsters in our psyche. Write an essay in which you put King's thesis to the test. Briefly describe the first horror movie you ever saw; then explain its effect on you. Like King, speculate about the nature of your response—your feelings and fantasies—while watching the movie.

2. Many movie critics claim that horror movies nowadays are more violent and bloody than they used to be. Write an essay about *one* other medium of popular culture that you think has changed for the worse. You might consider action movies, televised coverage of sports, men's or women's magazines, radio talk shows, TV sitcoms, and so on. Briefly describe key differences between the medium's past and present forms. Analyze the reasons for the change, and, at the end of the essay, examine the effects of the change.

Writing Assignments Combining Patterns of Development

3. King advocates the horror movie precisely because "It deliberately appeals to all that is worst in us." Write an essay in which you rebut King. *Argue* instead that horror movies should be avoided precisely *because* they satisfy monstrous feelings in us. To refute King, provide strong *examples* drawn from your own and other people's experience. Consider supplementing your informal research with material gathered in the library and/or on the Internet.

4. Write an essay in which you *illustrate,* contrary to King, that humans are by nature essentially benevolent and kind. Brainstorm with others to generate vivid *examples* in support of your thesis.

Writing Assignment Using a Journal Entry as a Starting Point

5. King believes that horror movies involve "a very peculiar sort of fun." Review your pre-reading journal entry, and select *one* other form of popular entertainment that you think provides its own strange kind of enjoyment. Like King, write an essay in which you analyze the causes of people's enjoyment of this type of entertainment. Brainstorm with others to identify convincing examples. You may, like King, endorse the phenomenon you examine—or you may condemn it.

READING

Jacques D'Amboise

When Jacques D'Amboise (1934–) was growing up in a tough, gang-infested New York City neighborhood, his French-Canadian mother wanted to give her children a glimpse into a world of beauty. She enrolled D'Amboise's sister in a ballet class and, hoping to protect her son from the dangers of street life, insisted that her son take the class, too. It was there that D'Amboise discovered his love of dance. While still in his teens, D'Amboise joined the New York City Ballet and became one of the foremost dancers of his day. He appeared in several films, including *Seven Brides for Seven Brothers* (1954) and *Carousel* (1956). In 1976, he founded the National Dance Institute (NDI), which offers dance classes to public school students, most from underprivileged backgrounds. Through NDI, hundreds of children have experienced the joy and discipline of dance. D'Amboise's NDI experience provided the basis of a book he coauthored, *Teaching the Magic of Dance* (1983), and his contributions to the arts led to his being honored at the Kennedy Center in 1995. The following selection originally appeared in *Parade* magazine in 1989.

Pre-Reading Journal Entry

While you were growing up, to what extent were you exposed to the arts: music, dance, drawing, painting, and so forth? Looking back, do you think that this exposure—or lack of exposure—worked to your advantage or to your disadvantage? Use your journal to respond to these questions.

Showing What Is Possible

1   When I was 7 years old, I was forced to watch my sister's ballet classes. This was to keep me off the street and away from my pals, who ran with gangs like the ones in *West Side Story*. The class was taught by Madame Seda, a Georgian-Armenian[1] who had a school at 181st Street and St. Nicholas Avenue in New York City. As she taught the little girls, I would sit, fidget and diabolically try to disrupt the class by making irritating little noises.

2   But she was very wise, Madame Seda. She let me get away with it, ignoring me until the end of the class, when everybody did the big jumps, a series of leaps in place, called *changements*.

3   At that point, Madame Seda turned and, stabbing a finger at me, said, "All right, little brother, if you've got so much energy, get up and do these jumps. See if you can jump as high as the girls." So I jumped. And loved it. I felt like I was flying. And she said, "Oh, that was wonderful! From now on, if you are quiet during the class, I'll let you join in the *changements*."

4   After that, I'd sit quietly in the class and wait for the jumps. A few classes later, she said, "You've got to learn how to jump and not make any noise when you come down. You should learn to do the *pliés* [graceful knee bends] that come at the beginning of the class." So I would do *pliés,* then wait respectfully for the end of class to do the jumps.

5   Finally she said, "You jump high, and you are landing beautifully, but you look awful in the air, flaying your arms about. You've got to take the rest of the class and learn how to do beautiful hands and arms."

6   I was hooked.

7   An exceptional teacher got a bored little kid, me, interested in ballet. How? She challenged me to a test, complimented me on my effort and then immediately gave me a new challenge. She set up an environment for the achievement of excellence and cared enough to invite me to be part of it. And, without realizing it fully at the time, I made an important discovery.

8   Dance is the most immediate and accessible of the arts because it involves your own body. When you learn to move your body on a note of music, it's exciting. You have taken control of your body and, by learning to do that, you discover that you can take control of your life.

9   I took classes with Madame Seda for six months, once a week, but at the end of spring, in June 1942, she called over my mother, my sister and me and did an unbelievably modest and generous thing. She said, "You and your sister are very talented. You should go to a better teacher." She sent us to George Balanchine's school—the School of American Ballet.

---

[1]A person from the neighboring republics of Georgia and Armenia, formerly of the Soviet Union (editors' note).

10   Within a few years, I was performing children's roles. At 15, I became part of a classical ballet company. What an extraordinary thing for a street boy from Washington Heights, with friends in gangs. Half grew up to become policemen and the other half gangsters—and I became a ballet dancer!

11   I had dreamed of being a doctor or an archaeologist or a priest. But by the time I was 17, I was a principal dancer performing major roles in the ballets, and by the time I was 21, I was doing movies, Broadway shows and choreography. I then married a ballerina from New York City Ballet, Carolyn George, and we were (and still are) blessed with two boys and twin daughters.

12   It was a joyful career that lasted four decades. That's a long time to be dancing and, inevitably, a time came when I realized that there were not many years left for me as a performer. I wasn't sure what to do next, but then I thought about how I had become a dancer, and the teachers who had graced my life. Perhaps I could engage young children, especially boys, in the magic of the arts—in dance in particular. Not necessarily to prepare them to be professional performers, but to create an awareness by giving them a chance to experience the arts. So I started National Dance Institute.

13   That was 13 years ago. Since then, with the help of fellow teachers and staff at NDI, I have taught dance to thousands of inner-city children. And in each class, I rediscover why teaching dance to children is so important.

14   Each time I can use dance to help a child discover that he can control the way he moves, I am filled with joy. At a class I recently taught at P.S. 59 in Brooklyn, there was one boy who couldn't get from his right foot to his left. He was terrified. Everyone was watching. And what he had to do was so simple: take a step with his left foot on a note of music. All his classmates could do it, but he couldn't.

15   He kept trying, but he kept doing it wrong until finally he was frozen, unable to move at all. I put my arm around him and said, "Let's do it together. We'll do it in slow motion." We did it. I stepped back and said, "Now do it alone, and fast." With his face twisted in concentration, he slammed his left foot down correctly on the note. He did it!

16   The whole class applauded. He was so excited. But I think I was even happier, because I knew what had taken place. He had discovered he could take control of his body, and from that he can learn to take control of his life. If I can open the door to show a child that that is possible, it is wonderful.

17   Dance is the art to express time and space. That is what our universe is about. We can hardly make a sentence without signifying some expression of distance, place or time: "See you later." "Meet you at the corner in five minutes."

18   Dance is the art that human beings have developed to express that we live, right now, in a world of movement and varying tempos.

19   Dance, as an art, has to be taught. However, when teaching, it's important to set up an environment where both the student and teacher can discover together. Never teach something you don't love and believe in. But how to set up that environment?

20   When I have a new group of young students and I'm starting a class, I use Madame Seda's technique. I say, "Can you do this test? I'm going to give all 100 of you exactly 10 seconds to get off your seats and be standing and spread out all over the stage floor. And do it silently. Go!" And I start a countdown. Naturally, they run, yelling and screaming, and somehow arrive with several seconds to spare. I say, "Freeze. You all failed. You made noise, and you got there too soon. I said 'exactly 10 seconds'—not 6 or 8 or 11. Go back to your seats, and we'll do it again. And if you don't get it, we'll go back and do

it again until you do. And if, at the end of the hour, you still haven't gotten it, I'm not going to teach you."

21   They usually get it the second time. Never have I had to do it more than three.

22   Demand precision, be clear and absolutely truthful. When they respond—and they will—congratulate them on the extraordinary control they have just exhibited. Why is that important? Because it's the beginning of knowing yourself, knowing that you can manage yourself if you want. And it's the beginning of dance. Once the children see that we are having a class of precision, order and respect, they are relieved, and we have a great class.

23   I've taught dance to Russian children, Australian children, Indian children, Chinese children, fat children, skinny children, handicapped children, groups of Australian triathletes, New York City police, senior citizens and 3-year-olds. The technique is the same everywhere, although there are cultural differences.

24   For example, when I was in China, I would say to the children, "I want everybody to come close and watch what I am going to do." But in China they have had to deal with following a teacher when there are masses of them. And they discovered that the way to see what the teacher does is not to move close but to move away. So 100 people moved back to watch the one—me.

25   I realized they were right. How did they learn that? Thousands of years of masses of people having to follow one teacher.

26   There are cultural differences and there are differences among people. In any group of dancers, there are some who are ready and excel more than others. There are many reasons—genetic, environment, the teachers they had. People blossom at different times.

27   But whatever the differences, someone admiring you, encouraging you works so much better than the reverse. "You can do it, you are wonderful," works so much better than, "You're no good, the others are better than you, you've got to try harder." That never works.

28   I don't think there are any untalented children. But I think there are those whose talents never get the chance to flower. Perhaps they were never encouraged. Perhaps no one took the time to find out how to teach them. That is a tragedy.

29   However, the single most terrible thing we are doing to our children, I believe, is polluting them. I don't mean just with smog and crack, but by not teaching them the civilizing things we have taken millions of years to develop. But you cannot have a dance class without having good manners, without having respect. Dance can teach those things.

30   I think of each person as a trunk that's up in the attic. What are you going to put in the trunk? Are you going to put in machine guns, loud noises, foul language, dirty books and ignorance? Because if you do, that's what is going to be left after you, that's what your children are going to have, and that will determine the world of the future. Or are you going to fill that trunk with music, dance, poetry, literature, good manners and loving friends?

31   I say, fill your trunk with the best that is available to you from the wealth of human culture. Those things will nourish you and your children. You can clean up your own environment and pass it on to the next generation. That's why I teach dance.

Questions for Close Reading

1. What is the selection's thesis? Locate the sentence(s) in which D'Amboise states his main idea. If he doesn't state the thesis explicitly, express it in your own words.
2. In paragraph 2, D'Amboise says that Madame Seda "was very wise." In what ways was she wise?
3. D'Amboise believes that dance has to be taught in a particular kind of environment. What, according to D'Amboise, are the most important qualities of that environment?
4. What does D'Amboise mean in paragraph 29 when he says that we pollute our children? What does D'Amboise consider the possible consequences of such pollution?
5. Refer to your dictionary as needed to define the following words used in the selection: *diabolically* (paragraph 1), *flaying* (5), *accessible* (8), *choreography* (11), *inevitably* (12), and *triathletes* (23).

Questions About the Writer's Craft

1. **The pattern.** Writers often organize cause-effect pieces using either a chronological or an emphatic sequence—or perhaps a combination of the two. Identify the organizational pattern that D'Amboise uses.
2. **Other patterns.** D'Amboise begins his essay with a *narrative* that tells the story of his first experience with Madame Seda. What is the purpose of this opening narrative? How does it prepare readers for what follows?
3. Reread paragraphs 20–21. The two short sentences in paragraph 21 could have concluded paragraph 20. Why do you think D'Amboise placed these two sentences in a separate paragraph?
4. In the last two paragraphs, D'Amboise uses an *analogy* (a comparison between two objects or people that seem to have little in common). Identify the analogy, and explain its relevance to the essay's central idea.

Writing Assignments Using Cause-Effect as a Pattern of Development

1. According to D'Amboise, a good teacher is one who provides a classroom of precision and order. Without structure and clear expectations, D'Amboise suggests, children will not flourish in the classroom. Do you think the same might be said of children in the home? Write a paper analyzing the effect on children of *one* of the following: a parenting style that imposes a reasonable number of boundaries, one that imposes too many limits, one that imposes too few restrictions. When writing, draw upon your own experiences and observations as well as those of friends, classmates, and family members.
2. D'Amboise asserts that "the single most terrible thing we are doing to our children . . . is polluting them . . . by not teaching them the civilizing things we have taken millions of years to develop." Among the pollutants he lists are drugs, violence, and pornography. Select one of these negative influences (or another you consider important), and write an essay analyzing how it pollutes children. You might show how this factor affects children's behavior, self-concept, and attitudes toward others. Before preparing your paper, interview classmates, friends, and family members to learn in what ways they think this factor influences children.

Writing Assignments Combining Patterns of Development

3. D'Amboise attributes his love of dance to Madame Seda, whom he calls an "exceptional teacher." Very likely, you too at some point in your life experienced the influence of a special adult—perhaps a teacher, coach, parent, grandparent, neighbor, or religious instructor. Using one extended *example* or a series of shorter examples, write an essay showing how your interaction with this person taught you important lessons that had a larger *impact* on your life.
4. D'Amboise's opening narrative *illustrates* how he became interested in dance. Consider the career path you have chosen or are thinking about choosing. What experiences pointed you in that direction? Write an essay in which you explain why you are interested in that particular career. *Recount* at least two experiences that helped you feel this work would be interesting and rewarding. Use vivid dialogue to dramatize the intensity of the experiences.

Writing Assignment Using a Journal Entry as a Starting Point

5. Write an essay arguing that it is *or* is not important for schools to expose children to the arts. The material you generated in your pre-reading journal entry will help you develop your position. You'll probably also find it helpful to talk to others about their experiences with the arts. Since the issue of arts-education funding is currently being debated, you should have little trouble researching this topic in the library and/or on the Internet. No matter which position you take, be sure to acknowledge opposing viewpoints, such as the one Clifford Stoll parodies in "Cyberschool".

READING

Alice Walker

The eighth child of Georgia sharecroppers, Alice Walker (1944–) has built a reputation as a sensitive chronicler of the Black experience in America. After studying at Spelman College in Atlanta, Walker graduated from Sarah Lawrence College in New York. Soon after that, she worked in the civil rights movement helping to register Black voters and teaching in Mississippi's Head Start program. The recipient of numerous writing fellowships and the founder of her own publishing company, Walker has written extensively: a biography, *Langston Hughes, American Poet* (1973); poetry, *Revolutionary Petunias and Other Poems* (1973); short stories, collected in *In Love & Trouble* (1973) and *You Can't Keep a Good Woman Down* (1981); essays, gathered in *Living by the Word* (1988) and *Alice Walker Banned* (1996); children's fiction, *To Hell with Dying* (1991); and novels for adults, including *Meridian* (1976), *The Color Purple* (1982), *The Temple of My Familiar* (1989), *By the Light of My Father's Smile* (1998), and *The Way Forward Is With a Broken Heart* (2000). *The Color Purple* won both the Pulitzer Prize and the American Book Award and was made into a feature film. The following selection comes from Walker's 1983 collection of essays, *In Search of Our Mothers' Gardens*.

Pre-Reading Journal Entry

It's easy to become discouraged when we're told we can't have—or be—something we want. That's when we most need the support of others. Who are the people in your life who have helped you focus not on your limitations but on your strengths? What specifically did each person do to encourage you? Use your journal to respond to these questions.

Beauty: When the Other Dancer Is the Self

1   It is a bright summer day in 1947. My father, a fat, funny man with beautiful eyes and a subversive wit, is trying to decide which of his eight children he will take with him to the county fair. My mother, of course, will not go. She is knocked out from getting most of us ready: I hold my neck stiff against the pressure of her knuckles as she hastily completes the braiding and then beribboning of my hair.

2   My father is the driver for the rich old white lady up the road. Her name is Miss Mey. She owns all the land for miles around, as well as the house in which we live. All I remember about her is that she once offered to pay my mother thirty-five cents for cleaning her house, raking up piles of her magnolia leaves, and washing her family's clothes, and that my mother—she of no money, eight children, and a chronic earache—refused it. But I do not think of this in 1947. I am two and a half years old. I want to go everywhere my daddy goes. I am excited at the prospect of riding in a car. Someone has

told me fairs are fun. That there is room in the car for only three of us doesn't faze me at all. Whirling happily in my starchy frock, showing off my biscuit-polished patent-leather shoes and lavender socks, tossing my head in a way that makes my ribbons bounce, I stand, hands on hips, before my father. "Take me, Daddy," I say with assurance; "I'm the prettiest!"

3   Later, it does not surprise me to find myself in Miss Mey's shiny black car, sharing the back seat with the other lucky ones. Does not surprise me that I thoroughly enjoy the fair. At home that night I tell the unlucky ones all I can remember about the merry-go-round, the man who eats live chickens, and the teddy bears, until they say: that's enough baby Alice. Shut up now, and go to sleep.

4   It is Easter Sunday, 1950. I am dressed in a green, flocked, scalloped-hem dress (handmade by my adoring sister, Ruth) that has its own smooth satin petticoat and tiny hot-pink roses tucked into each scallop. My shoes, new T-strap patent leather, again highly biscuit-polished. I am six years old and have learned one of the longest Easter speeches to be heard that day, totally unlike the speech I said when I was two: "Easter lilies / pure and white / blossom in / the morning light." When I rise to give my speech I do so on a great wave of love and pride and expectation. People in the church stop rustling their new crinolines. They seem to hold their breath. I can tell they admire my dress, but it is my spirit, bordering on sassiness (womanishness), they secretly applaud.

5   "That girl's a little *mess*," they whisper to each other, pleased.

6   Naturally I say my speech without stammer or pause, unlike those who stutter, stammer, or, worst of all, forget. This is before the word "beautiful" exists in people's vocabulary, but "Oh, isn't she the *cutest* thing?" frequently floats my way. "And got so much sense!" they gratefully add . . . for which thoughtful addition I thank them to this day.

7   *It was great fun being cute. But then, one day, it ended.*

8   I am eight years old and a tomboy. I have a cowboy hat, cowboy boots, checkered shirt and pants, all red. My playmates are my brothers, two and four years older than I. Their colors are black and green, the only difference in the way we are dressed. On Saturday nights we all go to the picture show, even my mother; Westerns are her favorite kind of movie. Back home, "on the ranch," we pretend we are Tom Mix, Hopalong Cassidy, Lash LaRue (we've even named one of our dogs Lash LaRue); we chase each other for hours rustling cattle, being outlaws, delivering damsels from distress. Then my parents decide to buy my brothers guns. These are not "real" guns. They shoot "BBs," copper pellets my brothers say will kill birds. Because I am a girl, I do not get a gun. Instantly I am relegated to the position of Indian. Now there appears a great distance between us. They shoot and shoot at everything with their new guns. I try to keep up with my bow and arrows.

9   One day while I am standing on top of our makeshift "garage"—pieces of tin nailed across some poles—holding my bow and arrow and looking out toward the fields, I feel an incredible blow in my right eye. I look down just in time to see my brother lower his gun.

10   Both brothers rush to my side. My eye stings, and I cover it with my hand. "If you tell," they say, "we will get a whipping. You don't want that to happen, do you?" I do not. "Here is a piece of wire," says the older brother, picking it up from the roof; "say you stepped on one end of it and the other flew up and hit you." The pain is beginning to start. "Yes," I say. "Yes, I will say that is what happened." If I do not say this is what hap-

pened, I know my brothers will find ways to make me wish I had. But now I will say anything that gets me to my mother.

11   Confronted by our parents we stick to the lie agreed upon. They place me on a bench on the porch and I close my left eye while they examine the right. There is a tree growing from underneath the porch that climbs past the railing to the roof. It is the last thing my right eye sees. I watch as its trunk, its branches, and then its leaves are blotted out by the rising blood.

12   I am in shock. First there is intense fever, which my father tries to break using lily leaves bound around my head. Then there are chills: my mother tries to get me to eat soup. Eventually, I do not know how, my parents learn what has happened. A week after the "accident" they take me to see a doctor. "Why did you wait so long to come?" he asks, looking into my eye and shaking his head. "Eyes are sympathetic," he says. "If one is blind, the other will likely become blind too."

13   This comment of the doctor's terrifies me. But it is really how I look that bothers me most. Where the BB pellet struck there is a glob of whitish scar tissue, a hideous cataract, on my eye. Now when I stare at people—a favorite pastime, up to now—they will stare back. Not at the "cute" little girl, but at her scar. For six years I do not stare at anyone, because I do not raise my head.

14   Years later, in the throes of a mid-life crisis, I ask my mother and sister whether I changed after the "accident." "No," they say, puzzled. "What do you mean?"

15   *What do I mean?*

16   I am eight, and, for the first time, doing poorly in school, where I have been something of a whiz since I was four. We have just moved to the place where the "accident" occurred. We do not know any of the people around us because this is a different county. The only time I see the friends I knew is when we go back to our old church. The new school is the former state penitentiary. It is a large stone building, cold and drafty, crammed to overflowing with boisterous, ill-disciplined children. On the third floor there is a huge circular imprint of some partition that has been torn out.

17   "What used to be here?" I ask a sullen girl next to me on our way past it to lunch.

18   "The electric chair," says she.

19   At night I have nightmares about the electric chair; and about all the people reputedly "fried" in it. I am afraid of the school, where all the students seem to be budding criminals.

20   "What's the matter with your eye?" they ask, critically.

21   When I don't answer (I cannot decide whether it was an "accident" or not), they shove me, insist on a fight.

22   My brother, the one who created the story about the wire, comes to my rescue. But then brags so much about "protecting" me, I become sick.

23   After months of torture at the school, my parents decide to send me back to our old community, to my old school. I live with my grandparents and the teacher they board. But there is no room for Phoebe, my cat. By the time my grandparents decide there *is* room, and I ask for my cat, she cannot be found. Miss Yarborough, the boarding teacher, takes me under her wing, and begins to teach me to play the piano. But soon she marries an African—a "prince," she says—and is whisked away to his continent.

24   At my old school there is at least one teacher who loves me. She is the teacher who "knew me before I was born" and bought my first baby clothes. It is she who makes life

bearable. It is her presence that finally helps me turn on the one child at the school who continually calls me "one-eyed bitch." One day I simply grab him by his coat and beat him until I am satisfied. It is my teacher who tells me my mother is ill.

25   My mother is lying in bed in the middle of the day, something I have never seen. She is in too much pain to speak. She has an abscess in her ear. I stand looking down on her, knowing that if she dies, I cannot live. She is being treated with warm oils and hot bricks held against her cheeks. Finally a doctor comes. But I must go back to my grandparents' house. The weeks pass but I am hardly aware of it. All I know is that my mother might die, my father is not so jolly, my brothers still have their guns, and I am the one sent away from home.

26   "You did not change," they say.

27   *Did I imagine the anguish of never looking up?*

28   I am twelve. When relatives come to visit I hide in my room. My cousin Brenda, just my age, whose father works in the post office and whose mother is a nurse, comes to find me. "Hello," she says. And then she asks, looking at my recent school picture, which I did not want taken, and on which the "glob," as I think of it, is clearly visible, "You still can't see out of that eye?"

29   "No," I say, and flop back on the bed over my book.

30   That night, as I do almost every night, I abuse my eye. I rant and rave at it, in front of the mirror. I plead with it to clear up before morning. I tell it I hate and despise it. I do not pray for sight. I pray for beauty.

31   "You did not change," they say.

32   I am fourteen and baby-sitting for my brother Bill, who lives in Boston. He is my favorite brother and there is a strong bond between us. Understanding my feelings of shame and ugliness he and his wife take me to a local hospital, where the "glob" is removed by a doctor named O. Henry. There is still a small bluish crater where the scar tissue was, but the ugly white stuff is gone. Almost immediately I become a different person from the girl who does not raise her head. Or so I think. Now that I've raised my head I win the boyfriend of my dreams. Now that I've raised my head I have plenty of friends. Now that I've raised my head classwork comes from my lips as faultlessly as Easter speeches did, and I leave high school as valedictorian, most popular student, and *queen,* hardly believing my luck. Ironically, the girl who was voted most beautiful in our class (and was) was later shot twice through the chest by a male companion, using a "real" gun, while she was pregnant. But that's another story in itself. Or is it?

33   "You did not change," they say.

34   It is now thirty years since the "accident." A beautiful journalist comes to visit and to interview me. She is going to write a cover story for her magazine that focuses on my latest book. "Decide how you want to look on the cover," she says. "Glamorous, or whatever."

35   Never mind "glamorous," it is the "whatever" that I hear. Suddenly all I can think of is whether I will get enough sleep the night before the photography session: if I don't, my eye will be tired and wander, as blind eyes will.

36   At night in bed with my lover I think up reasons why I should not appear on the cover of a magazine. "My meanest critics will say I've sold out," I say. "My family will now realize I write scandalous books."

37   "But what's the real reason you don't want to do this?" he asks.

38   "Because in all probability," I say in a rush, "my eye won't be straight."

39   "It will be straight enough," he says. Then, "Besides, I thought you'd made your peace with that."

40   And I suddenly remember that I have.

41   *I remember:*

42   I am talking to my brother Jimmy, asking if he remembers anything unusual about the day I was shot. He does not know I consider that day the last time my father, with his sweet home remedy of cool lily leaves, chose me, and that I suffered and raged inside because of this. "Well," he says, "all I remember is standing by the side of the highway with Daddy, trying to flag down a car. A white man stopped, but when Daddy said he needed somebody to take his little girl to the doctor, he drove off."

43   *I remember:*

44   I am in the desert for the first time. I fall totally in love with it. I am so overwhelmed by its beauty, I confront for the first time, consciously, the meaning of the doctor's words years ago: "Eyes are sympathetic. If one is blind, the other will likely become blind too." I realize I have dashed about the world madly, looking at this, looking at that, storing up images against the fading of the light. *But I might have missed seeing the desert!* The shock of that possibility—and gratitude for over twenty-five years of sight—sends me literally to my knees. Poem after poem comes—which is perhaps how poets pray.

45

On Sight

I am so thankful I have seen
The Desert
And the creatures in the desert
And the desert Itself.
The desert has its own moon
Which I have seen
With my own eye.
There is no flag on it.
Trees of the desert have arms
All of which are always up
That is because the moon is up
The sun is up
Also the sky
The stars
Clouds
None with flags.
If there were flags, I doubt
the trees would point.
Would you?

46   *But mostly, I remember this:*

47   I am twenty-seven, and my baby daughter is almost three. Since her birth I have worried about her discovery that her mother's eyes are different from other people's. Will she be embarrassed? I think. What will she say? Every day she watches a television program called "Big Blue Marble." It begins with a picture of the earth as it appears from the moon. It is bluish, a little battered-looking, but full of light, with whitish clouds

swirling around it. Every time I see it I weep with love, as if it is a picture of Grandma's house. One day when I am putting Rebecca down for her nap, she suddenly focuses on my eye. Something inside me cringes, gets ready to try to protect myself. All children are cruel about physical differences, I know from experience, and that they don't always mean to be is another matter. I assume Rebecca will be the same.

48   But no-o-o-o. She studies my face intently as we stand, her inside and me outside the crib. She even holds my face maternally between her dimpled little hands. Then, looking every bit as serious and lawyerlike as her father, she says, as if it may just possibly have slipped my attention: "Mommy, there's a *world* in your eye." (As in, "Don't be alarmed, or do anything crazy.") And then, gently, but with great interest: "Mommy, where did you *get* that world in your eye?"

49   For the most part, the pain left then. (So what, if my brothers grew up to buy even more powerful pellet guns for their sons and to carry real guns themselves. So what, if a young "Morehouse man" once nearly fell off the steps of Trevor Arnett Library because he thought my eyes were blue.) Crying and laughing I ran to the bathroom, while Rebecca mumbled and sang herself off to sleep. Yes indeed, I realized, looking into the mirror. There *was* a world in my eye. And I saw that it was possible to love it: that in fact, for all it had taught me of shame and anger and inner vision, I *did* love it. Even to see it drifting out of orbit in boredom, or rolling up out of fatigue, not to mention floating back at attention in excitement (bearing witness, a friend has called it), deeply suitable to my personality, and even characteristic of me.

50   That night I dream I am dancing to Stevie Wonder's song "Always" (the name of the song is really "As," but I hear it as "Always"). As I dance, whirling and joyous, happier than I've ever been in my life, another bright-faced dancer joins me. We dance and kiss each other and hold each other through the night. The other dancer has obviously come through all right, as I have done. She is beautiful, whole and free. And she is also me.

Questions for Close Reading

1. What is the selection's thesis? Locate the sentence(s) in which Walker states her main idea. If she doesn't state the thesis explicitly, express it in your own words.
2. How does Walker's injury affect her ability to express herself and relate to others?
3. What is the connection between the loss of young Alice's cat and her teacher's marriage (paragraph 23)?
4. How do you interpret the essay's title—"Beauty: When the Other Dancer Is the Self"? How does the title reinforce Walker's thesis?
5. Refer to your dictionary as needed to define the following words used in the selection: *subversive* (paragraph 1), *chronic* (2), *flocked* (4), *crinolines* (4), *cataract* (13), and *abscess* (25).

Questions About the Writer's Craft

1. **The pattern.** Walker's essay is structured around a causal chain that shows the interaction between the external and the internal. Explain how Walker develops this chain throughout the essay.
2. **Other patterns.** Although Walker *narrates* incidents occurring from infancy to midlife, she writes in the present tense. Why do you think she does this?
3. How does Walker signal the ages at which she experiences a crisis or some other major event? What technique does she use?
4. The refrain "You did not change" occurs in differing contexts throughout Walker's essay. What is the effect of this repetition?

Writing Assignments Using Cause-Effect as a Pattern of Development

1. An event initially viewed as handicapping can prove, as Walker shows, to be a blessing. Write a paper showing the effect on your life of an experience that at first seemed negative but turned out for the best.

2. Walker expects her daughter to react with revulsion to her eye injury. To her surprise, her daughter's reaction is tender and gentle. Think of a time you expected someone to treat you with kindness, but instead you were treated harshly, or, conversely, you expected severity but were met with generosity. In an essay, trace the causes of your faulty expectation as well as the possible reasons for the other person's unexpected behavior. Draw some conclusions about human nature.

Writing Assignments Combining Patterns of Development

3. Walker writes of an experience in which joyful, exuberant play turned—in an instant—to terror. Write an essay in which you *narrate* a time in your own or in someone else's life when there was a sudden reversal of events—a positive experience that became negative or vice versa. Use vivid images, varied sentence structure, and dialogue to capture what happened. Did the event leave a lasting impression? If so, end by writing briefly about this *effect*.

4. Walker mentions two elementary school teachers who responded to her in a loving, supportive way. Write a letter to beginning grade school teachers outlining the *steps* they should (and should not) take to make their students' school experience a positive one. Be sure to provide vivid *examples* to illustrate your points. For additional views on what truly matters in education, consider reading Clifford Stoll's "Cyberschool" and James Barszcz's "Can You Be Educated From a Distance?"

Writing Assignment Using a Journal Entry as a Starting Point

5. Review your pre-reading journal entry and select *one* person who encouraged you to believe in yourself. Then write an essay showing how this individual helped you shift your focus from what you couldn't do to what you could do. Start by describing briefly how you thought and felt before this person influenced you. Then use several dramatic examples to show how this person helped you develop a more optimistic and affirming mind-set.

READING

John M. Darley and Bibb Latané

Harvard graduate John M. Darley (1938–) is professor of psychology at Princeton University, where he studies the principles of moral judgment in children and adults. Bibb Latané (1937–), the former director of the Behavioral Sciences Laboratory at Ohio State University, is professor of psychology at Florida Atlantic University. A doctoral graduate of the University of Minnesota, Latané is interested in social impact and group influence theory. Darley and Latané are coauthors of *The Unresponsive Bystander: Why Doesn't He Help* (1970) and *Help in a Crisis: Bystander Response to an Emergency* (1976). Based on their research into the origins of noninvolvement, "Why People Don't Help in a Crisis? (1968) was awarded an essay prize from the American Association for the Advancement of Science.

Pre-Reading Journal Entry

Faced with a challenging or difficult situation, people sometimes choose *not* to get involved—and then later regret this decision. Such situations might include, for example, helping an injured stranger, standing up for someone being bullied, and letting in a stray animal on a cold day. In your journal, write about one or more times when you faced a difficult situation and failed to respond in a way that you now believe you should have.

Why People Don't Help in a Crisis

1   Kitty Genovese is set upon by a maniac as she returns home from work at 3 A.M. Thirty-eight of her neighbors in Kew Gardens, N.Y., come to their windows when she cries out in terror; not one comes to her assistance, even though her assailant takes half an hour to murder her. No one so much as calls the police. She dies.

2   Andrew Mormille is stabbed in the head and neck as he rides in a New York City subway train. Eleven other riders flee to another car as the 17-year-old boy bleeds to death; not one comes to his assistance, even though his attackers have left the car. He dies.

3   Eleanor Bradley trips and breaks her leg while shopping on New York City's Fifth Avenue. Dazed and in shock, she calls for help, but the hurrying stream of people simply parts and flows past. Finally, after 40 minutes, a taxi driver stops and helps her to a doctor.

4   How can so many people watch another human being in distress and do nothing? Why don't they help?

5   Since we started research on bystander responses to emergencies, we have heard many explanations for the lack of intervention in such cases. "The megalopolis in which we live makes closeness difficult and leads to the alienation of the individual from the group," says the psychoanalyst. "This sort of disaster," says the sociologist, "shakes the sense of safety and sureness of the individuals involved and causes psychological withdrawal." "Apathy," says others. "Indifference."

6   All of these analyses share one characteristic: they set the indifferent witness apart from the rest of us. Certainly not one of us who reads about these incidents in horror is apathetic, alienated or depersonalized. Certainly these terrifying cases have no personal implications for us. We needn't feel guilty, or re-examine ourselves, or anything like that. Or should we?

7   If we look closely at the behavior of witnesses to these incidents, the people involved begin to seem less inhuman and a lot more like the rest of us. They were not indifferent. The 38 witnesses of Kitty Genovese's murder, for example, did not merely look at the scene once and then ignore it. They continued to stare out of their windows, caught, fascinated, distressed, unwilling to act but unable to turn away.

8   Why, then, didn't they act?

9   There are three things the bystander must do if he is to intervene in an emergency: *notice* that something is happening; *interpret* that event as an emergency; and decide that he has *personal responsibility* for intervention. As we shall show, the presence of other bystanders may at each stage inhibit his action.

The Unseeing Eye

10   Suppose that a man has a heart attack. He clutches his chest, staggers to the nearest building and slumps sitting to the sidewalk. Will a passerby come to his assistance? First, the bystander has to notice that something is happening. He must tear himself away from his private thoughts and pay attention. But Americans consider it bad manners to look closely at other people in public. We are taught to respect the privacy of

others, and when among strangers we close our ears and avoid staring. In a crowd, then, each person is less likely to notice a potential emergency than when alone.

11   Experimental evidence corroborates this. We asked college students to an interview about their reactions to urban living. As the students waited to see the interviewer, either by themselves or with two other students, they filled out a questionnaire. Solitary students often glanced idly about while filling out their questionnaires: those in groups kept their eyes on their own papers.

12   As part of the study, we staged an emergency: smoke was released into the waiting room through a vent. Two thirds of the subjects who were alone noticed the smoke immediately, but only 25 percent of those waiting in groups saw it as quickly. Although eventually all the subjects did become aware of the smoke—when the atmosphere grew so smoky as to make them cough and rub their eyes—this study indicates that the more people present, the slower an individual may be to perceive an emergency and the more likely he is not to see it at all.

Seeing Is Not Necessarily Believing

13   Once an event is noticed, an onlooker must decide if it is truly an emergency. Emergencies are not always clearly labeled as such; "smoke" pouring into a waiting room may be caused by fire, or it may merely indicate a leak in a steam pipe. Screams in the street may signal an assault or a family quarrel. A man lying in a doorway may be having a coronary—or he may simply be sleeping off a drunk.

14   A person trying to interpret a situation often looks at those around him to see how he should react. If everyone else is calm and indifferent, he will tend to remain so; if everyone else is reacting strongly, he is likely to become aroused. This tendency is not merely slavish conformity; ordinarily we derive much valuable information about new situations from how others around us behave. It's a rare traveler who, in picking a roadside restaurant, chooses to stop at one where no other cars appear in the parking lot.

15   But occasionally the reactions of others provide false information. The studied nonchalance of patients in a dentist's waiting room is a poor indication of their inner anxiety. It is considered embarrassing to "lose your cool" in public. In a potentially acute situation, then, everyone present will appear more unconcerned that he is in fact. A crowd can thus force inaction on its members by implying, through its passivity, that an event is not an emergency. Any individual in such a crowd fears that he may appear a fool if he behaves as though it were.

16   To determine how the presence of other people affects a person's interpretation of an emergency, Latané and Judith Rodin set up another experiment. Subjects were paid $2 to participate in a survey of game and puzzle preferences conducted at Columbia University by the Consumer Testing Bureau. An attractive young market researcher met them at the door and took them to the testing room, where they were given questionnaires to fill out. Before leaving, she told them that she would be working next door in her office, which was separated from the room by a folding room-divider. She then entered her office, where she shuffled papers, opened drawers and made enough noise to remind the subjects of her presence. After four minutes she turned on a high-fidelity tape recorder.

17   On it, the subjects heard the researcher climb up on a chair, perhaps to reach for a stack of papers on the bookcase. They heard a loud crash and a scream as the chair collapsed and she fell, and they heard her moan, "Oh, my foot . . . I . . . I . . . can't move it

Oh, I . . . can't get this . . . thing off me." Her cries gradually got more subdued and controlled.

18   Twenty-six people were alone in the waiting room when the "accident" occurred. Seventy percent of them offered to help the victim. Many pushed back the divider to offer their assistance; others called out to offer their help.

19   Among those waiting in pairs, only 20 percent—8 out of 40—offered to help. The other 32 remained unresponsive. In defining the situation as a nonemergency, they explained to themselves why the other member of the pair did not leave the room; they also removed any reason for action themselves. Whatever had happened, it was believed to be not serious. "A mild sprain," some said. "I didn't want to embarrass her." In a "real" emergency, they assured us, they would be among the first to help.

The Lonely Crowd

20   Even if a person defines an event as an emergency, the presence of other bystanders may still make him less likely to intervene. He feels that his responsibility is diffused and diluted. Thus, if your car breaks down on a busy highway, hundreds of drivers whiz by without anyone's stopping to help—but if you are stuck on a nearly deserted country road, whoever passes you first is likely to stop.

21   To test this diffusion-of-responsibility theory, we simulated an emergency in which people overheard a victim calling for help. Some thought they were the only person to hear the cries; the rest believed that others heard them, too. As with the witnesses to Kitty Genovese's murder, the subjects could not *see* one another or know what others were doing. The kind of direct group inhibition found in the other two studies could not operate.

22   For the simulation, we recruited 72 students at New York University to participate in what was referred to as a "group discussion" of personal problems in an urban university. Each student was put in an individual room equipped with a set of headphones and a microphone. It was explained that this precaution had been taken because participants might feel embarrassed about discussing their problems publicly. Also, the experimenter said that he would not listen to the initial discussion, but would only ask for reactions later. Each person was to talk in turn.

23   The first to talk reported that he found it difficult to adjust to New York and his studies. Then, hesitantly and with obvious embarrassment, he mentioned that he was prone to nervous seizures when he was under stress. Other students then talked about their own problems in turn. The number of people in the "discussion" varied. But whatever the apparent size of the group—two, three or six people—only the subject was actually present; the others, as well as the instructions and the speeches of the victim-to-be, were present only on a pre-recorded tape.

24   When it was the first person's turn to talk again, he launched into the following performance, becoming louder and having increasing speech difficulties: "I can see a lot of er of er how other people's problems are similar to mine because er I mean er they're not er e-easy to handle sometimes and er I er um I think I I need er if if could er er somebody er er er give me give me a little er give me a little help here because er I er *uh* I've got a a one of the er seiz-er er things coming *on* and and er uh uh (choking sounds) . . ."

25   Eighty-five percent of the people who believed themselves to be alone with the vic-tim came out of their room to help. Sixty-two percent of the people who believed there was *one* other bystander did so. Of those who believed there were four other by-standers, only 31 percent reported the fit. The responsibility-diluting effect of other peo-ple was so strong that single individuals were more than twice as likely to report the emergency as those who thought other people also knew about it.

The Lesson Learned

26   People who failed to report the emergency showed few signs of the apathy and in-difference thought to characterize "unresponsive bystanders." When the experimenter entered the room to end the situation, the subject often asked if the victim was "all right." Many of them showed physical signs of nervousness; they often had trembling hands and sweating palms. If anything, they seemed more emotionally aroused than did those who reported the emergency. Their emotional behavior was a sign of their continuing conflict concerning whether to respond or not.

27   Thus, the stereotype of the unconcerned, depersonalized *homo urbanus*, blandly watching the misfortunes of others, proves inaccurate. Instead, we find that a bystander to an emergency is an anguished individual in genuine doubt, wanting to do the right thing but compelled to make complex decisions under pressure of stress and fear. His reactions are shaped by the actions of others—all too frequently by their inaction.

28   And we are that bystander. Caught up by the apparent indifference of others, we may pass by an emergency without helping or even realizing that help is needed. Once we are aware of the influence of those around us, however, we can resist it. We can choose to see distress and step forward to relieve it.

Questions for Close Reading

1. What is the selection's thesis? Locate the sentence(s) in which Darley and Latané state their main idea. If they don't state the thesis explicitly, express it in your own words.
2. According to the authors, what three factors prevent people in a crowd from helping victims during an emergency?
3. Why did Darley and Latané isolate the subjects in separate rooms during the staged emergency described in paragraphs 21–26?
4. What kind of person, according to the authors, would tend to ignore or bypass a person experiencing a problem? What might encourage this person to act more responsibly?
5. Refer to your dictionary as needed to define the following words used in the selection: *megalopolis* (paragraph 5), *apathy* (5), *indifference* (5), *alienated* (6), *depersonalized* (6), *inhibit* (9), *corroborates* (11), *coronary* (13), *slavish* (14), *nonchalance* (15), *diffused* (20), and *blandly* (27).

Questions About the Writer's Craft

1. **The pattern.** What techniques do Darley and Latané use to help readers focus on the causes of people's inaction during an emergency?
2. **Other patterns.** The three brief *narratives* that open the essay depict events that happened well before Darley and Latané wrote their essay. Why might the authors have chosen to recount these events in the present tense rather than in the past tense?
3. Locate places where Darley and Latané describe the experiments investigating bystander behavior. How do the authors show readers the steps—and the implications—of each experiment?
4. What purpose do you think the authors had in mind when writing the selection? How do you know?

Writing Assignments Using Cause-Effect as a Pattern of Development

1. Write an essay showing the "responsibility-diluting effect" that can occur when several people witness a critical event. Brainstorm with others to gather examples of this effect; then select two or three dramatic situations as the basis of your essay. Be sure to acknowledge other factors that may have played a role in inhibiting people's ability to act responsibly.

2. Although Darley and Latané focus on times when individuals fail to act responsibly, people often respond with moral heroism during difficult situations. Brainstorm with others to identify occasions in which people have taken the initiative to avert a crisis. Focusing on two or three compelling instances, write an essay in which you analyze the possible motives for people's responsible behavior. Also show how their actions affected the other individuals involved.

Writing Assignments Combining Patterns of Development

3. How could families or schools or communities or religious organizations encourage children to act rather than withdraw when confronted by someone in difficulty? Focusing on *one* of these situations, talk with friends, classmates, and family members to gather their experiences and recommendations. Then consider doing some research on this subject in the library and/or on the Internet. Select the most provocative ideas, and write an essay explaining the *steps* that this particular institution could take to help develop children's sense of responsibility to others. Develop your points with specific *examples* of what has been done and what could be done.

4. Darley and Latané cite social critics who believe that the United States has become a nation of strangers, alienated and withdrawn from one another. Write an essay *refuting* this claim by presenting several vivid *instances* of small acts of everyday kindness—examples in which people demonstrate their sense of connectedness to those around them. Generate examples by drawing on your own and other people's experiences.

Writing Assignment Using a Journal Entry as a Starting Point

5. Though the authors don't state so directly, they suggest that unresponsive bystanders often may regret their inaction later on. Reviewing the material you generated in your journal entry, select the most compelling or profound of the incidents you described. Then write an essay in which you narrate *one* situation in which you chose not to get involved but now realize you should have. Be sure to provide dialog and vivid descriptive details to bring the incident to life for your readers. Conclude your essay with a brief reflection on what you wish you had done and how your failure to respond properly has affected you.

READING

Gina Greenlee

Just four years after the events described in this essay, at the age of fourteen, Gina Greenlee became afflicted with wanderlust. At that time she spent the summer in Karishrue, Germany, her first time overseas. Three years later she packed up all her belongings and spent three weeks in the Caribbean. Since then she has traveled widely, visiting and living in such disparate places as Costa Rica, Singapore, Malaysia, Thailand, India, Greece, Turkey, Egypt, and much of the United States. In 2000, she took a four-month trip around the world. She is an artist and freelance writer who currently lives in Connecticut.

No Tears for Frankie

This essay was first published in *The New York Times*. Although Gina Greenlee addresses only her own childhood experience with sexual harassment in the essay, that experience is poignant enough to have wide appeal for a national newspaper readership.

As an adult, Greenlee looks back on a series of traumatic experiences that shaped her attitude towards a schoolmate's death. Notice how she carefully chooses both specific and general examples to explain her reaction to the boy's death.

1   I was in the fifth grade when Frankie died. It was 1971. My whole class planned to attend the funeral, since we knew him. My father thought going might give me nightmares, but I insisted. I had never seen a dead person before. Most of all, I wanted to be sure that the little creep would never touch me again.

2   Frankie lived in Lower Manhattan, where run-down tenements along Avenues A, B and C were on the verge of becoming the crack houses of the 80s. At the time, I lived nearby. Then in 1970 my family moved into an apartment in Co-op Village on Grand Street and F.D.R. Drive. It was only three blocks—and a world—away from the projects to a predominantly white middle-class community on the East River. Overnight at school, I became "that black girl who lives in the rich Jew buildings." Or at least that's what Frankie and my other African-American classmates thought I was. It became a familiar chant of theirs as I made my way through my old neighborhood to get to school.

3   Frankie and I were in the same grade, but I was 10 and he was 12 because he had been left back twice. He tormented all of the girls in our class. But Frankie relished singling me out . . . and he had done so since I first arrived from another school in third grade.

4   He never did any schoolwork. Instead, for the first three periods Frankie's curriculum was mayhem; by fourth period he was usually in the principal's office; and by the fifth, he was back in class unremorseful and pumped to do it again. He only got worse in that working-class, urban-blight panacea, the after-school program. It was a nice idea: children whose parents were unavailable at 3 o'clock because they were working stayed after school to study, improve skills and tackle extra-credit projects. I spent those afternoons trying to stay alive.

5   Frankie and his crew would grab my breasts, genitals and buttocks when the teachers weren't looking. Their hands, quick as filthy street rats, darted across my private parts in assembly line, during dance rehearsals and yard processions. They would leave scrawled notes in my book bag that read, "I'm gonna beat you up after school," or "I'll get you in the stairwell."

6   One spring afternoon, I had made it through another harrowing two hours after school, only to be cornered on the stairs by the whole nasty lot. They taunted me to walk down ahead of them. I managed each step as if it were my first, balancing myself on the chalk-blue shellacked handrail as I peered through the landing divider reminiscent of a wire cage, hoping to see another student, teacher, anyone. Frankie shoved me, and I tumbled one full flight, landing on my knees, my favorite brown plaid dress above my ears, easy pickings for the tiny vultures who cackled obscenities while snatching at my body, punching and kicking me. That day, I understood the depth of Frankie's perversity.

7   When I told a friend that our classroom emptied out at 3 p.m., leaving me alone with Frankie's boys, without having to share another detail, she said, "Come to my house after school." I had enjoyed two afternoons of baking cookies and doll playing when I let slip that my parents thought I was in class. My friend's mother welcomed me to play at her home anytime as long as my parents knew. "Why were you at Amy's and not in the after-school program?" my father asked me later that night. I didn't tell him because I didn't think he could help me. His interventions would only inspire retaliations and spiral me deeper into the mess.

8   I did try to tell my teachers, but nobody believed me. They chuckled and said, "Frankie just has a crush on you." That's what I told my father 15 years after the attacks, when he asked me if I had told my teachers. I guess in their world, 12-year-old boys don't sexually attack 10-year-old girls. What world did they come from, anyway? What world was I in, and how could I fix it so Frankie would disappear?

9   One morning when my teachers had stepped away from the classroom, Frankie and his boys shoved me into the coat closet and held the door shut while I was alone with Frankie. It was dark. As he kept touching me, I tried to push him away and screamed to be let out. But Frankie's friends held steadfast until the teachers arrived; then they scrambled to their seats. None of the other kids said a word. But in front of them all, I told Frankie that I hated his guts and hoped he would die.

10   Quite accommodating, he lay in a casket later that year. I didn't shed a tear. My heart was hardened, though. As usual, Frankie was up to no good—tampering with public property with the boys—when he got himself electrocuted. I was 10, and I was glad.

Meaning and Purpose

1. For what reasons did Greenlee insist on going to Frankie's funeral?
2. How did Greenlee become alienated from her fellow African-American classmates?
3. Why didn't Greenlee tell her father about her problems at school?
4. At the end of the essay, Greenlee says only that she was "glad" that Frankie had died. What other emotions do you think she felt? Why?

Strategy

1. Conventional morality tells us we should feel at least a degree of sorrow for the death of someone we know. But Greenlee uses her essay to explain and justify feeling "glad" for the death of Frankie. Does she make her case convincingly? Explain.
2. Greenlee cites typical examples of sexual harassment in paragraph 5. What is her purpose of using typical examples here?
3. She uses specific examples of harassment in paragraphs 6 and 9. Why does she use specific examples here?

Style

1. Look up the term "the projects" (paragraph 2) in a good dictionary. What is its meaning in context? Its derivation?
2. Explain what Greenlee means by "urban-blight panacea" in paragraph 4.
3. Greenlee's simile "quick as filthy street rats" (paragraph 5) describes two totally different things at the same time. What?
4. Why is Greenlee's description of a stairway landing divider as "reminiscent of a wire cage" (paragraph 6) particularly appropriate?

WRITING TASKS

1. Greenlee portrays herself as an outsider to her school in a double sense: she first transferred from another school, and then she moved out of her black neighborhood to a white neighborhood but remained at that same school. These events are, at least partially, the ultimate causes of the sexual harassment she describes. Using Greenlee's essay as a model, write an essay in which you analyze an experience you have had as an outsider, or the experience of another you have observed. Consider both the immediate and ultimate causes and/or effects of that experience.

2. Greenlee describes the causes of her sexual harassment at school and the effects those events had on her. Choose any event inside or outside your personal experience that has obvious causes and effects and write a paper that traces the development of those events. Any subject is fair game: being the member of any minority (ethnic, religious, sexual, etc.); the reluctance of many men to accept women as equals; the disintegration of a marriage or family; a candidate's success or loss of a national election. Anything.

READING

Michael Moore

Born in 1954 in Flint, Michigan, Michael Moore is an author, award-winning documentary filmmaker, and provocateur. Both his books and films unapologetically attack what he considers corrupt corporate practices and opportunistic right-wing politicians. His films include Roger & Me, Bowling for Columbine, *and* Fahrenheit 911. *His books include* Dude, Where's My Country?, Downsize This!, *and* Adventures in a TV Nation.

Why Doesn't GM Sell Crack?

In this essay, Michael Moore challenges the widely held belief that the corporate pursuit of profits at any cost is both the right and obligation of business and that government has no right to regulate that pursuit. Pay attention to the way Moore establishes cause-and-effect relationships, what happens when business profits are unregulated, and what would happen if they were regulated.

1   People in the business world like to say, "Profit is supreme." They like chanting that. "Profit is king." That's another one they like to repeat. They don't like to say, "I'll pick up the check." That means less profit. Profit is what it's all about. When they say "the bottom line," they mean their *profit*. They like that bottom line to contain a number followed by a lot of zeroes.

2   If I had a nickel for every time I heard some guy in a suit tell me that "a company must do whatever is necessary to create the biggest profit possible," I would have a very big bottom line right now. Here's another popular mantra: "The responsibility of the CEO is to make his shareholders as much money as he can."

3   Are you enjoying this lesson in capitalism? I get it every time I fly on a plane. The bottom-line feeders have all seen *Roger & Me*, yet they often mistake the fuselage of a DC-9 for the Oxford Debating Society. So I have to sit through lectures ad nauseam about the beauties of our free market system. Today the guy in the seat next to me is the owner of an American company that makes office supplies—in Taiwan. I ask the executive, "How much is 'enough'?"

4   "Enough what?" he replies.

5   How much is 'enough' profit?

6   He laughs and says, "There's no such thing as 'enough'!"

7   "So, General Motors made nearly $7 billion in profit last year—but they could make $7.1 billion by closing a factory in Parma, Ohio, and moving it to Mexico—that would be okay?"

8   "Not only okay," he responds, "it is their duty to close that plant and make the extra $.1 billion."

9   "Even if it destroys Parma, Ohio? Why can't $7 billion be enough and spare the community? Why ruin thousands of families for the sake of $.1 billion? Do you think this is *moral*?"

10   "Moral?" he asks, as if this is the first time he's heard that word since First Communion class. "This is not an issue of morality. It is purely a matter of economics. A company must be able to do whatever it wants to make a profit." Then he leans over as if to make a revelation I've never heard before.

11   "Profit, you know, is supreme."

12   So here's what I don't understand: if profit is supreme, why doesn't a company like General Motors sell crack? Crack is a *very* profitable commodity. For every pound of cocaine that is transformed into crack, a dealer stands to make a profit of $45,000. The dealer profit on a two-thousand-pound car is less than $2,000. Crack is also safer to use than automobiles. Each year, 40,000 people die in car accidents. Crack, on the other hand, kills only a few hundred people a year. And it doesn't pollute.

13   So why doesn't GM sell crack? If profit is supreme, why not sell crack?

14   GM doesn't sell crack because it is illegal. Why is it illegal? Because we, as a society, have determined that crack destroys people's lives. It ruins entire communities. It tears apart the very backbone of our country. That's why we wouldn't let a company like GM sell it, no matter what kind of profit they could make.

15   If we wouldn't let GM sell crack because it destroys our communities, then why do we let them close factories? *That, too,* destroys our communities.

16   As my frequent-flier friend would say, "We can't prevent them from closing factories because they have a right to do whatever they want to in order to make a profit."

17   No, they don't. They don't have a "right" to do a lot of things: sell child pornography, manufacture chemical weapons, or create hazardous products that could conceivably make them a profit. We can enact laws to prevent companies from doing anything to hurt us.

18   And downsizing is one of those things that is hurting us. I'm not talking about legitimate layoffs, when a company is losing money and simply doesn't have the cash reserves to pay its workers. I'm talking about companies like GM, AT&T, and GE, which fire people at a time when the company is making record profits in the billions of dollars. Executives who do this are not scorned, picketed, or arrested—they are hailed as heroes! They make the covers of *Fortune* and *Forbes*. They lecture at the Harvard Business School about their success. They throw big campaign fund-raisers and sit next to the President of the United States. They are the Masters of the Universe simply because they make huge profits regardless of the consequences to our society.

19   Are we insane or what? Why do we allow this to happen? It is *wrong* to make money off people's labor and then fire them after you've made it. It is *immoral* for a CEO to

make millions of dollars when he has just destroyed the livelihood of 40,000 families. And it's just plain *nuts* to allow American companies to move factories overseas at the expense of our own people.

20 When a company fires thousands of people, what happens to the community? Crime goes up, suicide goes up, drug abuse, alcoholism, spousal abuse, divorce—everything bad spirals dangerously upward. The same thing happens with crack. Only crack is illegal, and downsizing is not. If there was a crack house in your neighborhood, what would you do? You would try to get rid of it!

21 I think it's time we applied the same attitudes we have about crack to corporate downsizing. It's simple: if it hurts our citizens, it should be illegal. We live in a democracy. We enact laws based on what we believe is right and wrong. Murder? Wrong, so we pass a law making it illegal. Burglary? Wrong, and we attempt to prosecute those who commit it. Two really big hairy guys from Gingrich's office pummel me after they read this book? Five to ten in Sing Sing.

22 As a society, we have a right to protect ourselves from harm. As a democracy, we have a responsibility to legislate measures to protect us from harm.

23 Here's what I think we should do to protect ourselves:

1. Prohibit corporations from closing a profitable factory or business and moving it overseas. If they close a business and move it within the U.S., they must pay reparations to the community they are leaving behind. We've passed divorce laws that say that if a woman works hard to put her husband through school, and he later decides to leave her after he has become successful, he has a responsibility to compensate her for her sacrifices that allowed him to go on to acquire his wealth. The "marriage" between a company and a community should be no different. If a corporation packs up and leaves, it should have some serious alimony to pay.

2. Prohibit companies from pitting one state or city against another. We are all Americans. It is no victory for our society when one town wins at another's expense. Texas should not be able to raid Massachusetts for jobs. It is debilitating and, frankly, legal extortion.

3. Institute a 100 percent tax on any profits gained by shareholders when the company's stock goes up due to an announcement of firings. No one should be allowed to profit from such bad news.

4. Prohibit executives' salaries from being more than thirty times greater than an average employee's pay. When workers have to take a wage cut because of hard times, so, too, should the CEO. If a CEO fires a large number of employees, it should be illegal for him to collect a bonus that year.

5. Require boards of directors of publicly owned corporations to have representation from both workers and consumers. A company will run better if it has to listen to the people who have to build and/or use the products the company makes.

24 For those of you free-marketers who disagree with these modest suggestions and may end up on a plane sitting next to me, screaming, "You can't tell a business how it can operate!"—I have this to say: Oh, yes, we can! We legally require companies to build safe products, to ensure safe workplaces, to pay employees a minimum wage, to contribute to their Social Security, and to follow a host of other rules that we, as a

society, have deemed necessary for our well-being. And we can legally require each of the steps I've outlined above.

25   GM can't sell crack. Soon, I predict, they and other companies will not be able to sell us out. Just keep firing more workers, my friends, and see what happens.

Meaning and Purpose

1. What value does Moore place higher than business profits?
2. Moore claims there are two reasons for companies to downsize—one legitimate, one not. What are the differences between the two?
3. What is the reason Moore's "frequent-flier friend" says government cannot prevent companies from closing down their factories (paragraph 16)? What is Moore's reason for saying that government not only has the right to do so, but has the moral obligation to do so?
4. What do you think Moore's purpose is in writing this essay?

Strategy

1. Moore uses typical examples in paragraphs 1–3 and a specific example in the form of an anecdote in paragraphs 3–11. What is the purpose of these examples?
2. Moore specifically compares and contrasts corporate downsizing and selling crack cocaine in paragraph 20. How are the two similar? How are they different?
3. What is the function of paragraph 22?
4. Considering everything Moore has to say in paragraphs 1–22, how logical are his five proposals for social reform in paragraph 23?

Style

1. Why does Moore italicize some words? What kind of tone does he create in doing so?
2. Moore's language is sometimes satirical and derisive. Pick out the words, phrases, or passages that you find less than neutral in tone. Is his language appropriate to his purpose? Why or why not?
3. If necessary, look up the meanings of the following words: *mantra* (paragraph 2); *fuselage, ad nauseam* (3); *debilitating, extortion* (23); *deemed* (24).

WRITING TASKS

1. Write a cause-and-effect essay in which you argue against Michael Moore's position that government must regulate corporate downsizing. Do so by illustrating the deleterious effects that would result from such regulation.
2. Moore structures his argument around a syllogism—a form of deductive reasoning: Communities have the right to protect themselves by outlawing harmful behavior. Illegitimate corporate downsizing harms communities. Therefore, communities have the right to outlaw or regulate illegitimate corporate downsizing. Using Moore's essay as a model, construct your own cause-and-effect essay by structuring it around your own syllogism.

CHAPTER 9

Process

CHAPTER OBJECTIVES

In this chapter you will learn to:

- Explain processes and procedures.

- Write "how-to" paragraphs and essays.

- Write "how-it-works" paragraphs and essays.

- Use transitions to guide your readers.

- Write an effective topic sentence.

9a   WRITE ABOUT IT!

Write a paragraph explaining how to complete the task shown in the above photo. Organize your paragraph so someone who is unfamiliar with video stores and video rentals could complete the task easily.

The paragraph you have just written is a process paragraph—a paragraph that explains how to do something. In this chapter you will learn more about how to write process paragraphs and essays to fulfill both everyday, academic, and workplace tasks.

Everyday Scenarios

- Giving directions to a shopping mall
- Explaining how to file a health insurance claim

Academic Scenarios

- Explaining how to do an experiment
- Explaining how to solve a math problem

Workplace Scenarios

- Explaining how to operate a drill press
- Explaining a diet plan to a new diabetes patient

9b UNDERSTANDING PROCESS WRITING

What Is Process Writing?

A **process** is a series of steps or actions one follows in a particular order to accomplish something. When you assemble a toy, bake a cake, rebuild an engine, or put up a tent, you do things in a specific order. A **process paragraph** explains the steps to follow in completing a process. The steps are given in the order in which they are done. You can visualize a process as follows:

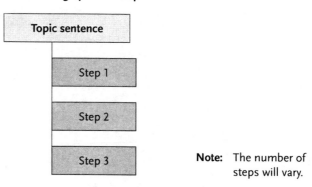

Process Paragraph Idea Map

Topic sentence

Step 1

Step 2

Step 3

Note: The number of steps will vary.

There are two types of process paragraphs—a "how-to paragraph" and a "how-it-works" paragraph.

- **"How-to" paragraphs explain how something is done.** For example, they may explain how to change a flat tire, aid a choking victim, or locate a reference source in the library.
- **"How-it-works" paragraphs explain how something operates or happens.** For example, they may explain the operation of a pump, how the human body regulates temperature, or how children acquire speech.

Here are examples of both types of paragraphs. The first explains how to wash your hands in a medical environment. The second describes how hibernation works. Be sure to study the idea map for each.

"How-to" Paragraph

Washing your hands may seem a simple task, but in a medical environment it is your first defense against the spread of disease and infection, and must be done properly.

Begin by removing all jewelry. Turn on the water using a paper towel, thus avoiding contact with contaminated faucets. Next, wet your hands under running water and squirt a dollop of liquid soap in the palm of your hand. Lather the soap, and work it over your hands for two minutes. Use a circular motion, since it creates friction that removes dirt and organisms. Keep your hands pointed downward, so water will not run onto your arms, creating further contamination. Use a brush to clean under your fingernails. Then rinse your hands, reapply soap, scrub for one minute, and rinse again thoroughly. Dry your hands using a paper towel. Finally, use a new dry paper towel to turn off the faucet, protecting your hands from contamination.

Idea Map

Washing hands must be done properly to control disease and infection.

Remove jewelry.

Use towel to turn on faucet.

Squirt dollop of soap, lather, and scrub.

Use brush for fingernails.

Rinse, reapply soap, scrub, and rinse again.

Dry hands with paper towel.

Use new paper towel to shut off faucet.

"How-It-Works" Paragraph

Hibernation is a biological process that occurs most frequently in small animals. The process enables animals to adjust to a diminishing food supply. When the outdoor temperature drops, the animal's internal thermostat senses the change. Then bodily changes begin to occur. First, the animal's heartbeat slows, and oxygen intake is reduced by slowed breathing. Metabolism is then reduced. Food intake becomes minimal. Finally, the animal falls into a sleeplike state during which it relies on stored body fat to support life functions.

Idea Map

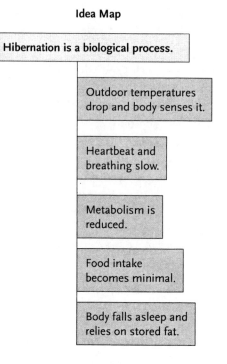

Hibernation is a biological process.

Outdoor temperatures drop and body senses it.

Heartbeat and breathing slow.

Metabolism is reduced.

Food intake becomes minimal.

Body falls asleep and relies on stored fat.

Selecting a Topic and Generating Ideas

Before you can describe a process, you must be very familiar with it. You should have done it often or have a complete understanding of how it works. Both "how-to" and "how-it-works" paragraphs describe steps that occur *only* in a specified order. Begin developing your paragraph by listing these steps in the order in which they must occur. It is helpful to visualize the process.

For "how-to" paragraphs, imagine yourself actually performing the task. For complicated "how-it-works" descriptions, draw diagrams and use them as guides in identifying the steps and putting them in the proper order.

9c   EXERCISE 9-1

Writing in Progress

Directions: Think of a process or procedure you are familiar with, or select one from the following list, and make a list of the steps involved:

1. How to find a worthwhile part-time job.

2. How to waste time.

3. How to learn to like _____.

4. How the NFL football draft works.

5. How to win at _____.

6. How to make a marriage or relationship work.

7. How to protect your right to privacy.

8. How to improve your skill at _____.

9. How to make your boss want to promote you.

Writing Your Topic Sentence

For a process paragraph, your topic sentence should accomplish two things:

- **It should identify the process or procedure.**
- **It should explain to your reader why familiarity with the process is useful or important** (*why* **he or she should learn about the process**). Your topic sentence should state a goal, offer a reason, or indicate what can be accomplished by using the process.

Here are a few examples of topic sentences that contain both of these important elements.

> Reading maps, a vital skill if you are taking vacations by car, is a simple process, except for the final refolding.

> Because leisure reading encourages a positive attitude toward reading in general, every parent should know how to select worthwhile children's books.

> To locate books in the library, you must know how to use the computerized catalog.

9d EXERCISE 9-2

Directions: Revise these topic sentences to make clear why the reader should learn the process.

1. Making pizza at home involves five steps.

2. Making a sales presentation requires good listening and speaking skills.

3. Bloodhounds that can locate criminals are remarkable creatures.

4. The dental hygienist shows patients how to use dental floss.

5. Here's how to use a search engine.

9e EXERCISE 9-3

Writing in Progress

Directions: Write a topic sentence for the process you selected in Exercise 9-1.

NEED TO KNOW

Including Helpful Information

Because your readers may be unfamiliar with your topic, try to include helpful information that will enable them to understand (for how-it-works paragraphs) and follow or complete the process (for how-to paragraphs). Consider including the following:

- **Definitions** Explain terms that may be unfamiliar. For example, explain the term "bindings" when writing about skiing.

- **Needed equipment** For how-to paragraphs, tell your readers what tools or supplies they will need to complete the process. For a how-to paragraph on making chili, list the ingredients, for example.

- **Pitfalls and problems** Alert your reader about potential problems and places where confusion or error may occur. Warn your chili-making readers to add chili peppers gradually and to taste along the way.

Sequencing and Developing Your Ideas

Use the following tips to develop an effective process paragraph:

1. **Place your topic sentence first.** This position provides your reader with a purpose for reading.
2. **Present the steps in a process in the order in which they happen.**
3. **Include only essential, necessary steps.** Avoid comments, opinions, or unnecessary information because it may confuse your reader.
4. **Assume that your reader is unfamiliar with your topic** (unless you know otherwise). Be sure to define unfamiliar terms and describe clearly any technical or specialized tools, procedures, or objects.
5. **Use a consistent point of view.** Use either the first person ("I") or the second person ("you") throughout. Don't switch between them.

9f   EXERCISE 9-4

Writing in Progress

Directions: Draft a paragraph for the process you chose in Exercise 9-1.

Useful Transitions

Transitions are particularly important in process paragraphs because they lead your reader from one step to the next. Specifically, they signal to your reader that the next step is about to begin. In the following paragraph, notice how each of the highlighted transitions signal that a new step is to follow.

Do you want to teach your children something about their background, help develop their language skills, *and* have fun at the same time? Make a family album together! First, gather the necessary supplies: family photos, sheets of colored construction paper, yarn and glue. Next, fold four sheets of paper in half; this will give you an eight-page album. Unfold the pages and lay them flat, one on top of the other. After you've evened them up, punch holes at the top and bottom of the fold, making sure you get through all four sheets. Next, thread the yarn through the holes. Now tie the yarn securely and crease the paper along the fold. Finally, glue a photo to each page. After the glue has dried, have your child write the names of the people in the pictures on each page and decorate the cover. Remember to talk to your children about the people you are including in your album. Not only will they learn about their extended family, they will have great memories of doing this creative project with you.

Table 9-1 lists commonly used transitional words and phrases that are useful in process paragraphs.

Table 9-1	Transitions for Process Paragraphs	
after	first	second
after that	following	then
afterwards	later	third
before	next	while
finally		

9g EXERCISE 9-5

Writing in Progress

Directions: Revise the draft you wrote for Exercise 9-4. Check transitional words and phrases and add them, as necessary, to make your ideas clearer.

Applying Your Skills to Essay Writing: Process

Although this chapter has focused on writing process paragraphs, you can use many of the same skills for writing process essays.

Guidelines for Writing Process Essays

Use the following guidelines for writing process essays:

1. **Before writing, list or outline the steps.** Decide how to arrange the steps and how to group them logically into paragraphs. For example, if you were writing about how to plan a wedding, you might group your steps into things to do many months ahead, things to do several weeks ahead, and things to do several days ahead.
2. **Give an overview.** If the process is long, complicated, or unfamiliar to your audience, describe that process in general terms before describing specific steps.
3. **For a difficult process, devote one paragraph to each step.** Help your reader by giving a thorough, detailed explanation of each step. By separating them into individual paragraphs, you will also help your reader distinguish one step from another.
4. **For a difficult or unfamiliar process, offer examples and make comparisons to a simpler or more familiar process.** For example, if you are writing about rugby, you might compare it to the similar and more familiar sport of football.
5. **Use the same verb tense throughout your essay.** Generally, processes are described in the present tense. There may be times, however, when you want to use the past tense; for instance, you may want to use the past tense to describe how you fixed your car this morning before leaving for school.

9h EXERCISE 9-6

Directions: Write an essay describing one of the following processes:

1. You have inherited a large sum of money, but are required to award $5,000 to each of five homeless people. Explain how you would go about choosing those five people.
2. Suppose you learn you have a serious disease, but one that with the proper treatment is completely curable. Without proper treatment, it could be fatal. Write an essay describing the process of finding the right doctor to treat you.
3. Suppose you are shopping for a used car. You find two cars in the same price range with almost the same mileage on them. How would you decide which one to buy? Write an essay describing your decision-making process.

AN ACADEMIC SCENARIO

A Student Essay

The Academic Writer and the Writing Task

Dawn Trippie is a student at Niagara County Community College where she is studying horticulture and floral design. In the course Introduction to Horticulture, her instructor assigned a paper on composting—the process of using decayed plant matter to enrich the soil. Trippie decided to explain how to create a compost pile. Her audience is the home gardener. As you read her essay, pay attention to the sequence of events and the transitions she uses to guide her reader.

Home Composting
Dawn Trippie

Title: suggests the audience for which the essay is intended

Introduction: addresses misconceptions

Definition of the term

Explanation of why the process is worth knowing about

When you hear that someone is composting, the first thing that jumps in your mind is that he or she must be some weird organic gardener. Or you may think of someone who piles up junk and garbage and tosses it into the garden. Actually, composting is the scientific process of combining plant materials so that the original raw ingredients are turned into new soil. Composting is beneficial to home gardeners because plants grow much better in a garden to which compost has been added. It can also help reduce environmental waste since more than one-half of a household's waste is actually compostable. Using compost can also reduce the amount of commercial fertilizers used in your yard. Making and using compost is a long-term and worthwhile investment to your garden because it contains almost all the nutrients needed for plants to grow and thrive.

Topic sentence identifies Step 1

Begin by deciding what size pile you want to have. A compost pile should be at least 3 feet by 3 feet by 3 feet (3 feet square). This will allow the pile to heat up to the correct temperature so you can regulate the speed of decomposition. A pile smaller than 3 feet square may not heat up sufficiently. A pile larger than 3 feet square will need to be turned frequently to provide proper aeration during the composting process. Factors to consider in deciding the size of your pile include available space for the compost pile and the amount of household and garden material available to put in the pile.

Helpful information

Topic sentence identifies Step 2

Once you know the size, you are ready to purchase a compost container. You may build your own composting bin out of wood and wire or purchase a bin from a local garden store or municipality. A container is desirable because it keeps small animals out of the compost area.

Step 3

Examples used to explain unfamiliar terms

Now you are ready to start creating your compost pile by stockpiling ingredients. You will need both carbon based and nitrogen based materials. Carbon based materials include dried leaves, straw, and sawdust. Nitrogen based materials are things that are green and/or moist. This includes plants, weeds, vegetables, and table scraps. You can also add egg shells, nutshells, coffee grounds, fruit peels, and corn cobs.

Step 4

Warning about potential problem

Then, when they have enough leaves, grass clippings and other matter saved up, you are ready build your pile. Start with a layer of dried leaves, and alternate with layers of green matter. You will want to make sure that the ingredients that you are adding to the pile are wet, but not to the point of being soggy. While building your pile, you will want to have about thirty times as much nitrogen-based as carbon-based material. If you have too much nitrogen in your pile, your will notice a sharp, foul smell.

Step 5

Once the pile is built, you will need to keep track of its temperature. Your pile will start to heat up a few days after it is built. You may use a compost thermometer to measure the temperature inside the pile. You need to reach a temperature of at least 120–130 degrees for the material to begin to decompose. When the pile starts to cool down, it will need to be turned so that the outer layer is moved to the inside of the pile. The pile will start to heat again after several days. Your compost is complete when, after turning, the pile fails to heat up anymore. This composting process can take from three months to six months or more depending on weather conditions and the season of the year. Many people keep two piles, one that is actively working and one that is ready for garden use.

Finally, you have compost, so now what? Different people have different uses for their compost. It can be worked into your soil as an amendment, used as a top dressing on your gardens, or used as a mulch to help with water retention and weed suppression. Only you can decide what use is right for you. But be certain, everyone can benefit in some way from composting.

More helpful information

Conclusion: reaffirms the value of composting

Examining Academic Writing

1. Trippie wrote a "how-to" process essay. How could this essay be revised to become a "how-it-works" essay?
2. In what ways does Trippie reveal that she is writing for a home gardener, rather than a professional in her field?
3. Highlight the transitions she uses to make it clear she is moving from one step to another.
4. Did she provide sufficient explanation and detail when writing about a technical process? Highlight places where she was particularly effective in helping you understand the composting process.

Academic Writing Assignments

1. Write a paragraph explaining one of the following processes:
   a. How to use the electronic card catalog in your campus library.
   b. How to obtain a campus ID card.
   c. How to apply for a student loan.
   d. How to get a tutor for a course in which you are having difficulty.
2. Write a paragraph explaining to a high school senior planning to attend college how to take notes in a college class or how to study for an exam in a specific subject.
3. Draw a map showing how to get to a particular place on campus from your writing classroom. Write a paragraph that explains this process. Test out the effectiveness of your paragraph by giving your paragraph to a classmate and asking him or her to reconstruct your map without seeing it.
4. Write a paragraph explaining how to use a software package with which you are familiar.
5. You are taking a first aid class and your instructor has asked you to write a brief essay on the rescue procedures for one of the following emergency situations. (You may need to use the Internet or print sources in your library to obtain basic information.)
   a. Choking
   b. Breathing stopped
   c. Poisoning
   d. External bleeding

A WORKPLACE SCENARIO

A Hiring Policies Document

The Workplace Writer and the Writing Task

The following example of workplace writing explains the hiring process for new teachers in the Leverett Elementary School in Leverett, MA, part of the Erving Union 28 Superintendency. As you read, notice that the process is detailed along with the responsibilities of the screening committee, the principal, and the superintendent of schools.

LEVERETT SCHOOL COMMITTEE

HIRING POLICY

A Screening Committee composed ordinarily of one School Committee member, two teachers, two parents, and the Principal will be formed by the Principal for the purpose of assisting in the selection of all teachers. The responsibility of the Screening Committee will be to review applications, select applicants to be interviewed, and interview as many candidates as necessary to ensure, whenever possible, that three final candidates may be selected.

The Principal will serve as Chairperson of the Screening Committee and will be authorized to interview prospective candidates in order to assist in the decision about which candidates are to be interviewed by the Committee. The Committee will decide which candidates to interview, except that the Committee will interview any candidate recommended to it by the Principal.

Selection of three final candidates for interview by the Superintendent will be the responsibility of the Screening Committee, except that the Principal may select additional final candidates. For positions which are exclusively housed in the Leverett Elementary School, the Principal will be responsible for the appointment of a candidate, subject to approval by the Superintendent. The Superintendent of Schools will inform the School Committee about any appointment.

It is understood that the hiring process be open until the Principal's appointment is approved by the Superintendent of Schools.

Examining Workplace Writing

1. Draw a process map showing how teachers are hired in the Leverett School District.
2. If you were a member of the Screening Committee, what further information would you ask about the hiring process?
3. Who is the intended audience for this document?
4. By whom do you think this policy was written?

Workplace Writing Assignments

1. Assume you are the superintendent of a school district. What process would you use to select new teachers? Write a paragraph describing the process.

2. Write a paragraph describing a process you are or were responsible for at a place where you worked. (Or, write a paragraph describing a process you have observed others performing at a local business.)

3. Based on your experience in the workplace, write a short process essay explaining how to get and keep a job.

9i WRITING ABOUT A READING

Thinking Before Reading

The following reading, "How Tattoos Work," appears on this Web site: http://www.howstuffworks.com This is an example of a "how-to" process essay. As you read, notice how the author details the steps in the process and uses illustrations to make certain processes clear.

1. Preview the reading.
2. Connect the reading to your own experience by answering the following questions:
    a. Do you have a tattoo or would you like to get one? Why?
    b. What risks or dangers are involved in tattooing?

READING

How Tattoos Work

1   It's virtually impossible to walk through a mall without spotting people of all ages with tattoos. Tattoos come in all shapes and sizes, and they can appear almost anywhere on someone's body. Permanent cosmetic studios also tattoo on eyebrows, eyeliner, and lip liner for those who want their makeup to be permanent. In these cases, you may not even know that you are looking at a tattoo! Tattoos have steadily gained popularity in the last decade—a trend that shows little sign of slowing down. In this article, we'll look at several aspects of tattooing and focus on how the tattooing process works.

Origins

2   Believe it or not, some scientists say that certain marks on the skin of the *Iceman,* a **mummified** human body dating from about 3300 B.C., are tattoos. If that's true, these markings represent the earliest known evidence of the practice. Tattooing was rediscovered by Europeans when exploration brought them into contact with **Polynesians** and American Indians. The word tattoo comes from the **Tahitian** word tattau, which means "to mark," and was first mentioned in explorer James Cook's records from his 1769 expedition to the South Pacific.

Meaning

3   The practice of tattooing means different things in different cultures. In early practice, decoration appears to have been the most common motive for tattooing, and that still holds true today. In some cultures, tattoos served as identification of the wearer's rank or status in a group. For example, the early Romans tattooed slaves and criminals.

mummified
prepared for burial, like a mummy; shriveled and dried up

Polynesians
people living in a widely scattered group of islands in the Pacific that together form Polynesia

Tahitian
someone from Tahiti, one of the Polynesian islands

rites of passage
events or acts that
mark an important
transition in a person's
life (from child to
adult, or unmarried to
married, for instance)

Tahitian tattoos served as **rites of passage**, telling the history of the wearer's life. Boys reaching manhood received one tattoo to mark the occasion, while men had another style done when they married. Sailors traveling to exotic foreign lands began to collect tattoos as souvenirs of their journeys (a dragon showed that the seaman had served on a China station), and tattoo parlors sprang up in port cities around the globe.

Modern Tattooing

4   Today, tattoos are created by injecting ink into the skin. Injection is done by a needle attached to a hand-held tool. The tool moves the needle up and down at a rate of several hundred vibrations per minute and penetrates the skin by about one millimeter. What you see when you look at a tattoo is the ink that's left in the skin after the tattooing. The ink is not in the **epidermis**, which is the layer of skin that we see and the skin that gets replaced constantly, but instead intermingles with *cells* in the **dermis** and shows through the epidermis. The cells of the dermis are remarkably stable, so the tattoo's ink will last, with minor fading and dispersion, for your entire life!

epidermis
the outmost layer of
skin

dermis
the layer of skin just
below the epidermis

The Tattoo Machine

5   The basic idea of the electrically powered tattoo machine is that a needle moves up and down like in a sewing machine, carrying ink into your skin in the process. Today, a tattoo machine is an electrically powered, vertically vibrating steel instrument that resembles a dentist's drill (and sounds a little like it, too). It is fitted with solid needles that puncture the skin at the rate of 50 to 3,000 times a minute. The sterilized needles

subcutaneous (diagram)
located, living, or made
under the skin

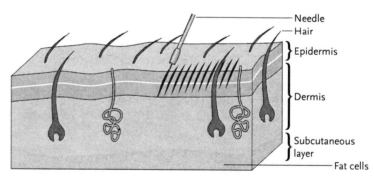

The tattoo needle inserts ink into the skin's dermal layer.

are installed in the machine and dipped in ink, which is sucked up through the machine's tube system. Then, powered by a foot switch much like that on a sewing machine, the tattoo machine uses an up-and-down motion to puncture the top layer of the skin and drive insoluble, micrometer-sized particles of ink into the second (dermal) layer of skin, about one-eighth inch deep.

Sterilization

6   Much of the tattoo application process focuses on safety, since any puncture wound—and that's what a tattoo machine is doing to your skin—holds the potential for infection and disease transfer. The only acceptable method of sterilization for killing every living microorganism is an autoclave, a heat/steam/pressure unit (used in hospitals) that achieves and maintains 250 degrees Fahrenheit (121 C) under 10 pounds of pressure for 30 minutes or up to 270 F (132 C) under 15 pounds of pressure for 15 minutes. (Most units run a 55-minute cycle from a cold start.)

7   Most tattoo materials—inks, ink cups, gloves, and needles—are used only once to eliminate the possibility of contamination of materials. All reusable materials, such as the needle bar and the tube, must be completely clean, put into special pouches, and sterilized in the autoclave. Indicator strips on the packages change color when processing has occurred. Other equipment includes razors (for shaving the skin, since hair clogs up the tubes and hinders application) and plastic barriers (bags) that are used on spray bottles, tattoo machines, and clip cords to prevent cross-contamination.

Prep Work

8   The tattoo artist, who has washed and inspected hands for cuts or abrasions and disinfected the work area with an EPA-approved viricidal, dons fresh gloves and generally follows this procedure:
- Places plastic bags on spray bottles
- Explains the sterilization process to client
- Opens up single-service, autoclave sterilized equipment in front of client
- Shaves and disinfects (with a mixture of water and antiseptic green soap) the area to be tattooed

8   With the outline (stencil) of the tattoo in place—or the outline of a custom tattoo drawn by hand onto the skin—the actual tattooing begins.

Making the Outline

9   Using one single-tipped needle, the artist starts at the bottom of the right-hand side and works up (lefties generally start on the left side), so the stencil won't be lost when the artist cleans a permanent line. For single- needle work, a thinner black ink than that used for shading is used, because thinner ink can be easily wiped away from the skin without smearing.

10   As this happens, the tattoo machine is buzzing and smooth clear lines should be emerging as the needle pierces the skin, applies the ink, and gradually lifts out of the skin in a steady motion. (Experts say this is where the professionals show their mettle: In order to create clear lines and proper depth, the tattoo artist must understand how deep the needles actually need to go to produce a permanent line. Not going deep enough will create scratchy lines after healing, and going too deep will cause excessive pain and bleeding.)

Shading

11   Once the outline is complete, the area is thoroughly cleaned with antiseptic soap and water. Then, the outline is thickened and shading is added. The tattoo artist will use a combination of needles. If this isn't done correctly, shadowed lines, excessive pain, and delayed healing will result. Again, everything must be autoclaved before use.

12   Using a thicker, blacker ink, the artist goes over the outline creating an even, solid line. Shading creates special effects. Each tattoo artist works differently, depending upon his or her training and preference.

Color

13   After the shading is done, the tattoo is cleaned again and is now ready for color. When applying color, the artist overlaps each line of color to ensure solid, even hues with no "holidays"—uneven areas where color has either lifted out during healing or where the tattoo artist simply missed a section of skin. The tattoo is again sprayed and cleaned

and pressure is applied using a disposable towel to remove any blood and plasma excreted during the tattooing process. According to medical experts, some bleeding always occurs in tattooing, but under normal conditions (no alcohol or illegal drugs in the system, no fatigue, no tattooing over scar tissue), most stops within a few minutes after the tattoo is completed. (Reputable tattoo artists won't tattoo those who are sick, drunk, high or pregnant, and they won't apply pornographic, racist, or gang tattoos.)

Identifying a Safe Tattoo Parlor

14   Other than the use of Universal Procedures and laws requiring that minors be tattooed only with parental permission, there are few regulations covering tattooing. Tattoo parlors must be licensed; this happens when artists qualify by completing a health department course on infectious disease transmission and passing an exam, but businesses aren't regularly inspected. (Legalization allows anyone to acquire a machine, get a license, and start tattooing whether they have any artistic ability or not—a situation that tattoo artists object to.) Here are some basic steps you can take to help ensure that you're choosing a safe tattoo parlor:

- Look around to see if the studio is clean and professional. That says a lot!
- Ask questions: Is there an autoclave? Are the needles and other materials single-use? Are EPA-approved disinfectants used? Are gloves being worn? (Professional tattoo artists won't mind the questions.)
- Play watchdog with the tattoo artist to be sure safety measures are being followed in the application of your tattoo.
- Make sure all needles are opened in front of you.
- Membership in professional organizations is not required, bur artists who participate are probably better informed about trends, innovations, and safety issues.

Other Considerations

15   After you've explored the tattoo process and learned about all the health/safety considerations, here are several more points to consider:

- Think long and hard about the fact that a tattoo is permanent. What's cool at 18 might not be very appealing on a 40-year-old you!
- *Tattoo removal* is considerably more painful and expensive than tattooing. The process usually takes several sessions and offers varying results. Doctors say tattoos can be lightened but not always completely removed.
- Consider your career interests and plans—will sporting a highly visible tattoo hinder your success or effectiveness later on?
- Consider the ramifications. For example, you won't be able to donate blood—the American Red Cross will not accept blood donations from someone who has been tattooed in the past year.

Getting Ready to Write
Reviewing the Reading

1. Early cultures used tattoos for different reasons. What were three of these reasons?
2. The writer compares the tattoo machine to which two other machines?
3. In order to prevent infections and the spread of disease, what must a tattoo artist do?
4. In tattooing, what is meant by a "holiday"? Is a holiday a good thing or a negative thing?
5. Why should anyone think long and hard before getting a tattoo?

Examining the Reading: Using Sequence Maps

To understand a narrative or process paragraph or essay, you must have a clear understanding of the sequence of events. A sequence map—a visual representation of key events or steps in the order in which they occur—can help you keep these straight.

Complete the sequence map below for "How Tattoos Work" by filling in the blank boxes.

Thinking Critically: Analyzing Tone

You can usually tell from a speaker's tone of voice how he or she feels. For example, you may be able to tell whether he or she is angry, serious, sincere, concerned, hostile, amused, or sympathetic. Although you cannot hear a writer's voice, you can sense how a writer feels about his or her subject. In other words, you can detect a *tone*. Tone is the writer's attitude toward the subject. Recognizing an author's tone is an important part of understanding, interpreting, and evaluating a piece of writing. Tone reveals feelings, attitudes, or viewpoints not directly expressed by the author. Can you sense the tone in each of the following statements?

- Anyone who throws litter out a car window should be severely punished. Not just a fine, but community service, jail time, *and* suspension of his or her driver's license.
- That poor woman's car broke down, right in the middle of the intersection. And it's so hot!
- After years of looking, I finally found the perfect job. It was a long search, but definitely worth the wait.

Idea Map

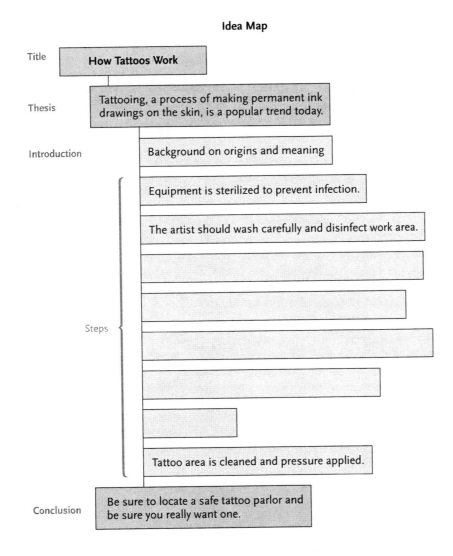

Do you sense the first author to be angry and judgmental, the second to be sympathetic and concerned, and the third to be relieved and happy? Tone is not always as obvious as in the above statements. But you often can detect tone by studying how the author approaches his or her topic. In particular, look at the language he or she uses to describe the subject.

Complete the following activity by selecting, from the list of terms below used to describe tone, two that describe the tone of "How Tattoos Work." For each term you selected, highlight several words, phrases, or sentences in the reading where this tone is obvious.

abstract	grim	persuasive	optimistic
instructive	righteous	sympathetic	distressed
bitter	cautionary	outraged	worried

Strengthening Your Vocabulary

Part A: Using the word's context, word parts, or a dictionary, write a brief definition of each of the following words as it is used in the reading.

1. insoluble (paragraph 5) _____

_____

2. viricidal (paragraph 8) _____

_____

3. mettle (paragraph 10) _____

_____

4. autoclaved (paragraph 11) _____

_____

5. legalization (paragraph 14) _____

_____

6. innovations (paragraph 14) _____

_____

7. ramifications (paragraph 15) _____

_____

Part B: Draw a word map for one of the words above.

Reacting to Ideas: Discussion and Journal Writing

1. Discuss the author's purpose for writing this article. Does the author indicate any attitude for or against tattooing?
2. Discuss why a tattoo that someone got when he or she was 16 could become something he or she is ashamed of or embarrassed about 30 years later.
3. Young people consider many things to be acceptable that adults know are potentially dangerous. Besides getting a tattoo, what might a teenager think is cool that his or her parents would find legitimately frightening?

Writing About the Reading
Paragraph Options

1. Write a paragraph about why you or someone you know might want to get a tattoo. Explain why a tattoo is desirable.
2. If you decided to get a tattoo, write a paragraph about what you would look for in a tattoo parlor. What would make you choose one parlor over another?
3. Think of a celebrity who is known for his or her tattoos. Write a paragraph about this person's style; what image he or she is trying to project, how you feel about it, and what kind of media attention it gets him or her. Do you think all of that would be different if their tattoos were removed—even if no other changes (haircut, clothes, makeup, etc.) were made?

Essay Options

4 Think of a rite of passage that you or someone you know has experienced. Write an essay explaining what the process involved. What age was the person when it occurred? Was it a ritual important to one particular culture or an event many people celebrate? Was it private or were there guests present?
5. Imagine you live in a society where tattoos are required for identification. Describe the tattoo you might create. In your essay, relate the design of your tattoo to your family background, culture, job or career, education, or any other feature of your life that is important in explaining who you are.
6. Currently, there are few regulations covering tattooing. Write an essay about your opinion on this issue. Is it good or bad that the rules are so loose? Would stricter laws make a difference to someone thinking of becoming a tattoo artist? What rules would you put in place if you were in charge of licensing tattoo parlors?

Revision Checklist

1. Is your paragraph or essay appropriate for your audience? Does it give them the background information they need? Will it interest them?
2. Will your paragraph or essay accomplish your purpose?
3. Is your main point clearly expressed in a topic sentence?
4. Is each detail relevant? In other words, does each detail directly explain or support the topic sentence?
5. Have you supported your topic sentence with sufficient detail to make it understandable and believable?
6. Do you use specific and vivid words to explain each detail?

For Process Writing

7. Does your topic sentence or thesis statement identify the process and explain its importance?
8. Are the steps arranged in the order in which they occurred? If not, will your reader be able to follow the sequence?
9. Have you used transitional words and phrases to help the reader follow the steps?
10. Have you used a consistent verb tense throughout your paragraph or essay?

9j CHAPTER REVIEW AND PRACTICE

Chapter Review

What is a process paragraph or essay?	A process paragraph or essay describes how something is done or how something works.
To write an effective process paragraph, what kind of topic should you choose?	You should choose a topic that is familiar.
What should the topic sentence of a process paragraph accomplish?	It should (1) identify the process or procedure you are writing about and (2) suggest its value or importance.
In a paragraph or essay about a process, how should details be arranged?	Details should be arranged in the order in which they occur.
What are the guidelines for writing process essays?	1. Give an overview of the process, if needed. 2. Organize steps into paragraphs. 3. Give examples or make comparisons, if needed. 4. Use a consistent verb tense.

ACTIVITIES: PROCESS ANALYSIS

Prewriting Activities

1. Imagine you're writing two essays: One *defines* the term "comparison shopping"; the other *contrasts* two different teaching styles. Jot down ways you might use process analysis in each essay.

2. Select *one* of the essay topics that follow and determine what your purpose, tone, and point of view would be for each audience indicated in parentheses. Then use brainstorming, questioning, mapping, or another prewriting technique to identify the points you'd cover for each audience. Finally, organize the raw material, noting the differences in emphasis and sequence for each group of readers.
   a. How to buy a car (*young people who have just gotten a driver's license; established professionals*)
   b. How children acquire their values (*first-time parents; elementary school teachers*)
   c. How to manage money (*grade-school children; college students*)
   d. How loans or scholarships are awarded to incoming students on your campus (*high school graduates applying for financial aid; high school guidance counselors*)
   e. How arguments can strengthen relationships (*preteen children; young adults*)
   f. How to relax (*college students; parents with young children*)

Revising Activities

3. Below is the brainstorming for a brief essay that describes the steps involved in making a telephone sales call. The paper has the following thesis: "Establishing rapport with customers is the most challenging and the most important part of phone sales." Revise the brainstormed material by deleting anything that undermines the paper's unity and organizing the steps in a logical sequence.
   - Keep customers on the phone as long as possible to learn what they need
   - The more you know about customers' needs the better
   - The tone of the opening comments is very important
   - Gently introduce the product
   - Use a friendly tone in opening comments
   - End on a friendly tone, too
   - Don't introduce the product right away
   - Growing rudeness in society. Some people hang up right away. Very upsetting.
   - Try in a friendly way to keep the person on the phone
   - Many people are so lonely they don't mind staying on the phone so they can talk to someone—anyone
   - How sad that there's so much loneliness in the world
   - Describe the product's advantages—price, convenience, installment plan
   - If person is not interested, try in a friendly way to find out why
   - Don't tell people that their reasons for not being interested are silly
   - Don't push people if they're not interested
   - Encourage credit card payment—the product will arrive earlier
   - Explain payment—check, money order, or credit card payment

4. Reprinted here is a paragraph from the first draft of a humorous essay advising shy college students how to get through a typical day. Written as a process analysis, the paragraph outlines techniques for surviving class. Revise the paragraph, deleting digressions that disrupt the paragraph's unity, eliminating unnecessary repetition, and sequencing the steps in the proper order. Also correct inappropriate shifts in person and add transitions where needed. Feel free to add any telling details.

Simply attending class can be stressful for shy people. Several strategies, though, can lessen the trauma. Shy students should time their arrival to coincide with that of most other class members—about two minutes before the class is scheduled to begin. If you arrive too early, you may be seen sitting alone, or, even worse, may actually be forced to talk with another early arrival. If you arrive late, all eyes will be upon you. Before heading to class, the shy student should dress in the least conspicuous manner possible—say, in the blue jeans, sweatshirt, and sneakers that 99.9 percent of your classmates wear. That way you won't stand out from everyone else. Take a seat near the back of the room. Don't, however, sit at the very back since professors often take sadistic pleasure in calling on students back there, assuming they chose those seats because they didn't want to be called on. A friend of mine who is far from shy uses just the opposite ploy. In an attempt to get in good with her professors, she sits in the front row and, incredibly enough, volunteers to participate. However, since shy people don't want to call attention to themselves, they should stifle any urge to sneeze or cough. You run the risk of having people look at you or offer you a tissue or cough drop. And of course, never, ever volunteer to answer. Such a display of intelligence is sure to focus all eyes on you. In other words, make yourself as inconspicuous as possible. How, you might wonder, can you be inconspicuous if you're blessed (or cursed) with great looks? Well, . . . have you ever considered earning your degree through the mail?

READING

Jessica Mitford

Dubbed "Queen of the Muckrakers" by *Time,* English-born Jessica Mitford (1917–96) came to the United States in 1939 at the age of twenty-one. Mitford worked as a bartender and salesperson before becoming an investigator for the Office of Price Administration in Washington. She didn't begin her writing career until the age of thirty-eight. Her books include two autobiographies, *Daughters and Rebels* (1960) and *A Fine Old Conflict* (1976); an examination of the American penal system, *Kind and Usual Punishment* (1974); a collection of essays, *Poison Penmanship* (1979); a critique of the birthing business, *The American Way of Birth* (1993); and a novel about celebrities and the media, *Grace Had an English Heart* (1989). The following selection is from the book *The American Way of Death* (1963), which earned Mitford a national reputation as an investigative writer. A scathing attack on the U.S. funeral industry, this book shocked readers and enraged morticians.

Pre-Reading Journal Entry

If you've ever attended a funeral, you know that efforts are made to avoid the appearance or even the mention of death. Many significant life experiences are also accompanied by elaborate rituals that obscure the real meaning of the events. List several such life events in your journal. For each, describe briefly the rituals that typically mark the event.

The American Way of Death

1   Embalming is indeed a most extraordinary procedure, and one must wonder at the docility of Americans who each year pay hundreds of millions of dollars for its perpetuation, blissfully ignorant of what it is all about, what is done, how it is done. Not one in ten thousand has any idea of what actually takes place. Books on the subject are extremely hard to come by. They are not to be found in most libraries or bookshops.

2   In an era when huge television audiences watch surgical operations in the comfort of their living rooms, when, thanks to the animated cartoon, the geography of the digestive system has become familiar territory even to the nursery school set, in a land where the satisfaction of curiosity about almost all matters is a national pastime, the secrecy surrounding embalming can, surely, hardly be attributed to the inherent gruesomeness of the subject. Custom in this regard has within this century suffered a complete reversal. In the early days of American embalming, when it was performed in the home of the deceased, it was almost mandatory for some relative to stay by the embalmer's side and witness the procedure. Today, family members who might wish to be in attendance would certainly be dissuaded by the funeral director. All others, except apprentices, are excluded by law from the preparation room.

3   A close look at what does actually take place may explain in large measure the undertaker's intractable reticence concerning a procedure that has become his major *raison d'étre*. Is it possible he fears that public information about embalming might lead patrons to wonder if they really want this service? If the funeral men are loath to discuss the subject outside the trade, the reader may, understandably, be equally loath to go on reading at this point. For those who have the stomach for it, let us part the formaldehyde curtain. . . .

4   The body is first laid out in the undertaker's morgue—or rather, Mr. Jones is reposing in the preparation room—to be readied to bid the world farewell.

5   The preparation room in any of the better funeral establishments has the tiled and sterile look of a surgery, and indeed the embalmer-restorative artist who does his chores there is beginning to adopt the term "dermasurgeon" (appropriately corrupted by some mortician-writers as "demisurgeon") to describe his calling. His equipment, consisting of scalpels, scissors, augers, forceps, clamps, needles, pumps, tubes, bowls and basins, is crudely imitative of the surgeon's, as is his technique, acquired in a nine- or twelve-month post-high-school course in an embalming school. He is supplied by an advanced chemical industry with a bewildering array of fluids, sprays, pastes, oils, powders, creams, to fix or soften tissue, shrink or distend it as needed, dry it here, restore the moisture there. There are cosmetics, waxes and paints to fill and cover features, even plaster of Paris to replace entire limbs. There are ingenious aids to prop and stabilize the cadaver: a Vari-Pose Head Rest, the Edwards Arm and Hand Positioner, the Repose Block (to support the shoulders during the embalming), and the Throop Foot Positioner, which resembles an old-fashioned stocks.

6   Mr. John H. Eckles, president of the Eckles College of Mortuary Science, thus describes the first part of the embalming procedure: "In the hands of a skilled practitioner, this work may be done in a comparatively short time and without mutilating the body other than by slight incision—so slight that it scarcely would cause serious inconvenience if made upon a living person. It is necessary to remove the blood, and doing this

not only helps in the disinfecting, but removes the principal cause of disfigurements due to discoloration."

7   Another textbook discusses the all-important time element: "The earlier this is done, the better, for every hour that elapses between death and embalming will add to the problems and complications encountered. . . ." Just how soon should one get going on the embalming? The author tells us, "On the basis of such scanty information made available to this profession through its rudimentary and haphazard system of technical research, we must conclude that the best results are to be obtained if the subject is embalmed before life is completely extinct—that is, before cellular death has occurred. In the average case, this would mean within an hour after somatic death." For those who feel that there is something a little rudimentary, not to say haphazard, about this advice, a comforting thought is offered by another writer. Speaking of fears entertained in early days of premature burial, he points out, "One of the effects of embalming by chemical injection, however, has been to dispel fears of live burial." How true; once the blood is removed, chances of live burial are indeed remote.

8   To return to Mr. Jones, the blood is drained out through the veins and replaced by embalming fluid pumped in through the arteries. As noted in *The Principles and Practices of Embalming*, "every operator has a favorite injection and drainage point—a fact which becomes a handicap only if he fails or refuses to forsake his favorites when conditions demand it." Typical favorites are the carotid artery, femoral artery, jugular vein, subclavian vein. There are various choices of embalming fluid. If Flextone is used, it will produce a "mild, flexible rigidity. The skin retains a velvety softness, the tissues are rubbery and pliable. Ideal for women and children." It may be blended with B. and G. Products Company's Lyf-Lyk tint, which is guaranteed to reproduce "nature's own skin texture . . . the velvety appearance of living tissue." Suntone comes in three separate tints: Suntan; Special Cosmetic Tint, a pink shade "especially indicated for young female subjects"; and Regular Cosmetic Tint, moderately pink.

9   About three to six gallons of a dyed and perfumed solution of formaldehyde, glycerin, borax, phenol, alcohol, and water is soon circulating through Mr. Jones, whose mouth has been sewn together with a "needle directed upward between the upper lip and gum and brought out through the left nostril," with the corners raised slightly "for a more pleasant expression." If he should be bucktoothed, his teeth are cleaned with Bon Ami and coated with colorless nail polish. His eyes, meanwhile, are closed with flesh-tinted eye caps and eye cement.

10   The next step is to have at Mr. Jones with a thing called a trocar. This is a long, hollow needle attached to a tube. It is jabbed into the abdomen, poked around the entrails and chest cavity, the contents of which are pumped out and replaced with "cavity fluid." This done, and the hole in the abdomen sewn up, Mr. Jones's face is heavily creamed (to protect the skin from burns which may be caused by leakage of the chemicals), and he is covered with a sheet and left unmolested for a while. But not for long—there is more, much more, in store for him. He has been embalmed, but not yet restored, and the best time to start the restorative work is eight to ten hours after embalming, when the tissues have become firm and dry.

11   The object of all this attention to the corpse, it must be remembered, is to make it presentable for viewing in an attitude of healthy repose. "Our customs require the presentation of our dead in the semblance of normality . . . unmarred by the ravages of ill-

ness, disease or mutilation," says Mr. J. Sheridan Mayer in his *Restorative Art*. This is rather a large order since few people die in the full bloom of health, unravaged by illness and unmarked by some disfigurement. The funeral industry is equal to the challenge: "In some cases the gruesome appearance of a mutilated or disease-ridden subject may be quite discouraging. The task of restoration may seem impossible and shake the confidence of the embalmer. This is the time for intestinal fortitude and determination. Once the formative work is begun and affected tissues are cleaned or removed, all doubts of success vanish. It is surprising and gratifying to discover the results which may be obtained."

12   The embalmer, having allowed an appropriate interval to elapse, returns to the attack, but now he brings into play the skill and equipment of sculptor and cosmetician. Is a hand missing? Casting one in plaster of Paris is a simple matter. "For replacement purposes, only a cast of the back of the hand is necessary; this is within the ability of the average operator and is quite adequate." If a lip or two, a nose or an ear should be missing, the embalmer has at hand a variety of restorative waxes with which to model replacements. Pores and skin texture are simulated by stippling with a little brush, and over this cosmetics are laid on. Head off? Decapitation cases are rather routinely handled. Ragged edges are trimmed, and head joined to torso with a series of splints, wires and sutures. It is a good idea to have a little something at the neck—a scarf or high collar—when time for viewing comes. Swollen mouth? Cut out tissue as needed from inside the lips. If too much is removed, the surface contour can easily be restored by padding with cotton. Swollen necks and cheeks are reduced by removing tissue through vertical incisions made down each side of the neck. "When the deceased is casketed, the pillow will hide the suture incisions . . . as an extra precaution against leakage, the suture may be painted with liquid sealer."

13   The opposite condition is more likely to present itself—that of emaciation. His hypodermic syringe now loaded with massage cream, the embalmer seeks out and fills the hollowed and sunken areas by injection. In this procedure the backs of the hands and fingers and the under-chin area should not be neglected.

14   Positioning the lips is a problem that recurrently challenges the ingenuity of the embalmer. Closed too tightly they tend to give a stern, even disapproving expression. Ideally, embalmers feel, the lips should give the impression of being ever so slightly parted, the upper lip protruding slightly for a more youthful appearance. This takes some engineering, however, as the lips tend to drift apart. Lip drift can sometimes be remedied by pushing one or two straight pins through the inner margin of the lower lip and then inserting them between the two front upper teeth. If Mr. Jones happens to have no teeth, the pins can just as easily be anchored in his Armstrong Face Former and Denture Replacer. Another method to maintain lip closure is to dislocate the lower jaw, which is then held in its new position by a wire run through holes which have been drilled through the upper and lower jaws at the midline. As the French are fond of saying, *il faut souffrir pour être belle.*[1]

15   If Mr. Jones has died of jaundice, the embalming fluid will very likely turn him green. Does this deter the embalmer? Not if he has intestinal fortitude. Masking pastes and cosmetics are heavily laid on, burial garments and casket interiors are color-corre-

---

[1]One has to suffer to be beautiful (editors' note).

lated with particular care, and Jones is displayed beneath rose-colored lights. Friends will say, "How *well* he looks." Death by carbon monoxide, on the other hand, can be rather a good thing from the embalmer's viewpoint: "One advantage is the fact that this type of discoloration is an exaggerated form of a natural pink coloration." This is nice because the healthy glow is already present and needs but little attention.

16   The patching and filling completed, Mr. Jones is now shaved, washed and dressed. Cream-based cosmetic, available in pink, flesh, suntan, brunette, and blond, is applied to his hands and face, his hair is shampooed and combed (and, in the case of Mrs. Jones, set), his hands manicured. For the horny-handed son of toil special care must be taken; cream should be applied to remove ingrained grime, and the nails cleaned. "If he were not in the habit of having them manicured in life, trimming and shaping is advised for better appearance—never questioned by kin."

17   Jones is now ready for casketing (this is the present participle of the verb "to casket"). In this operation his right shoulder should be depressed slightly "to turn the body a bit to the right and soften the appearance of lying flat on the back." Positioning the hands is a matter of importance, and special rubber positioning blocks may be used. The hands should be cupped slightly for a more lifelike, relaxed appearance. Proper placement of the body requires a delicate sense of balance. It should lie as high as possible in the casket, yet not so high that the lid, when lowered, will hit the nose. On the other hand, we are cautioned, placing the body too low "creates the impression that the body is in a box."

18   Jones is next wheeled into the appointed slumber room where a few last touches may be added—his favorite pipe placed in his hand or, if he was a great reader, a book propped into position. (In the case of little Master Jones a Teddy bear may be clutched.) Here he will hold open house for a few days, visiting hours 10 A.M. to 9 P.M.

Questions for Close Reading

1. What is the selection's thesis? Locate the sentence(s) in which Mitford states her main idea. If she doesn't state the thesis explicitly, express it in your own words.
2. Why, according to Mitford, do Americans know so little about the embalming process?
3. Mitford quotes from a textbook on embalming practices (paragraph 11). What does the passage reveal about the goals of mortuary science?
4. In what ways is the body made to look even better than it did when alive?
5. Refer to your dictionary as needed to define the following words used in the selection: *docility* (paragraph 1), *intractable* (3), *raison d'être* (3), *augers* (5), *distend* (5), *stippling* (12), and *jaundice* (15).

Questions About the Writer's Craft

1. **The pattern.** What are the main stages of the mortician's craft? What happens in each step? What words and phrases does Mitford use to indicate that she's moving from one step to the next?
2. Why does Mitford refer to the body being embalmed as Mr. Jones? What effect does this naming have on the reader?
3. Mitford interweaves her description of the embalming and restoring process with many quotations from mortuary science texts. Why do you suppose she does this? What do you notice about the writing style of the authors of these texts?
4. What is Mitford's tone in this essay? Do you feel she is being objective in her description of the funeral industry? Explain.

Writing Assignments Using Process Analysis as a Pattern of Development

1. Many important events in our lives are marked by celebrations or rituals. Often, the basic outlines of these rituals are established by tradition, but we can always personalize these traditions in one way or another. Select an important event that you will celebrate in the future and explain how you would like to experience the event. Your choice could include any of the following: your marriage, the birth of a child, your graduation, your parent's retirement, or some other notable occurrence.

2. Write a paper telling your survivors how you wish to be treated after death. Explain how they should conduct your funeral, whether they should embalm you, where they should put your remains, and, most important, what you would like said in your eulogy. Be as specific as possible as you outline the steps to be taken.

Writing Assignments Combining Patterns of Development

3. Write an essay *describing* a funeral or viewing that you attended. Focus on what seems to you the most important scene. Your thesis should express a dominant feeling about the scene and its *effect* on you: depression, grief, discomfort, fear, relief, or some other emotion. Alternatively, write an essay describing any other ceremony or ritual you have experienced (for example, a wedding, a bar or bat mitzvah, or a graduation). Your dominant feeling may be positive or negative.

4. Write an essay *arguing* that Americans often pretend that death doesn't exist or isn't really happening. Give *examples* drawn from your own life, your family's life, or public events. You might consider the following: the expressions we use with children ("Grandpa's gone away"; "Kitty is sleeping"); the euphemistic language we have for death ("passed away"; "no longer with us"); our obsession with looking young and keeping fit; our beliefs about "eternal life"; people's resistance to making a will.

Writing Assignment Using a Journal Entry as a Starting Point

5. Review your pre-reading journal entry, and select *one* major life event whose genuine significance is somehow masked by its accompanying rituals. Then write an essay describing this event and its rituals. If you need to supplement the material in your journal, interview others about their experiences and observations. Your essay may have a serious or a lighthearted tone.

READING

Clifford Stoll

An astronomer at the University of California at Berkeley, Clifford Stoll (1950–) is also a lecturer, commentator on MSNBC, and occasional visiting teacher of astronomy in elementary, middle, and high schools. He is the best-selling author of *The Cuckoo's Egg: Tracking a Spy Through the Maze of Computer Espionage* (1990) and *Silicon Snake Oil: Second Thoughts on the Information Superhighway* (1995), both of which address the complications of the computer age. As he reveals in the preface of *High-Tech Heretic: Reflections of a Computer Contrarian* (1999), despite having programmed and used computers since the mid-sixties, Stoll seeks to inject "a few notes of skepticism into the utopian dreams of a digital wonderland." According to his website, he is a "stay-at-home daddy" who lives with his family in the San Francisco Bay Area. The following essay appears as a chapter in *High-Tech Heretic*.

Pre-Reading Journal Entry

Over the past several years, the Internet has become increasingly popular as an educational resource. What do you think are the merits and the drawbacks of including the Internet as part of school assignments? Is your response affected by the age of the students in question? Record in your journal the pros and cons of requiring students—at the elementary, high school, and college levels, respectively—to access the Net as part of their studies.

Cyberschool

1   Welcome to the classroom of the future! Complete with electronic links to the world, it'll revolutionize education. Students will interact with information infrastructures and knowledge processors to learn group work and telework, whatever that means. You'll be enriched, empowered, and enabled by the digital classroom; immersed in an optimal learning environment. Yee-ha!

2   Worried that things rarely turn out as promised? Well, let me present a pessimal[1] view of the schoolroom of the future.

3   Suppose you're a harried school board member. Voters complain about high taxes. Teachers' unions strike for higher wages and smaller classes. Parents worry about plummeting scores on standardized tests. Newspapers criticize backward teaching methods, outdated textbooks, and security problems. Unruly students cut classes and rarely pay attention. Instructors teach topics which aren't in the curriculum or, worse, inject their own opinions into subject matter.

4   Sound like a tough call? Naw—it's easy to solve all these problems, placate the taxpayers, and get re-elected. High technology!

5   First, the school district buys a computer for every student. Sure, this'll set back the budget—maybe a few hundred dollars per student. Quantity discounts and corporate support should keep the price down, and classroom savings will more than offset the cost of the equipment.

6   Next buy a pile of CD-ROMs for the students, each preprogrammed with fun edutainment[2] programs. The educational games will exactly cover the curriculum . . . for every paragraph in the syllabus, the game will have an interactive aspect. As students climb to more advanced levels, the game naturally becomes more challenging and rewarding. But always fun.

7   Every student will work at her own pace. The youngest will watch happy cartoon characters and exciting animations. The kid that likes horses will listen to messages from a chatty pony; the child that dreams of fire engines will hear from Fred the Firefighter. High schoolers get multimedia images of film stars and rock and roll celebrities. With access to interactive video sessions, chat rooms, and e-mail, students can collaborate with each other. It's the ultimate in individualized, child-centered instruction.

8   Naturally, the edu-games will be programmed so that students become adept at standardized tests. No reason to teach anything that's not on the ACT, PSAT, or SAT exams. And the students will have fun because all this information will be built into

---

[1]The opposite of optimal?

[2]A term, coined by Stoll, combining the words *education* and *entertainment* (editors' note).

games like Myst, Dungeon, or Doom. They'll master the games, and automatically learn the material.

9   Meanwhile, the computers will keep score, like pinball machines. They'll send e-mail to parents and administrators . . . scores that will become part of each kid's permanent record. No more subjectivity in grading: The principal will know instantly how each child's doing. And if a student gets confused or falls behind, automated help will be just a mouse click away.

10   We'll update crowded classrooms, too. Replace desks with individual cubicles, comfortable chairs, and multimedia monitors. With no outside interruptions, kids' attention will be directed into the approved creative learning experiences, built into the software. Well compartmentalized, students will hardly ever see other . . . neatly ending classroom discipline problems.

11   Naturally, teachers are an unnecessary appendix at this cyberschool. No need for 'em when there's a fun, multimedia system at each student's fingertips. Should students have a question, they can turn to the latest on-line encyclopedia, enter an electronic chat room, or send e-mail to a professional educator. Those laid-off teachers can be retrained as data entry clerks.

12   As librarians and teachers become irrelevant, they'll be replaced by a cadre of instructional specialists, consultants, and professional hall monitors. Any discipline problems could be handled by trained security guards, who'd monitor the cubicles via remote video links.

13   Effect? With no more wasted time on student-teacher interactions or off-topic discussions, education will become more efficient. Since the computers' content would be directed at maximizing test performance, standardized test scores will zoom.

14   Eliminating teachers and luxuries such as art lessons and field trips will save enough to recoup the cost of those fancy computers. With little effort, this electronic education could even become a profit center. Merely sell advertising space in the edutainment programs. Corporate sponsors, eager to market their messages to impressionable minds, would pay school systems to plug their products within the coursework.

15   Concerned that such a system might be dehumanizing? Not to worry. Interactive chat sessions will encourage a sense of community and enhance kids' social skills. Should a student have questions, the Internet will put her in instant touch with a trained support mentor. When necessary, real-time instructors will appear on the distance learning displays, available to interact via two-way video.

16   The Cyberschool will showcase technology and train students for the upcoming electronic workplace. As local employment prospects change, the school board will issue updates to the curriculum over its interactive website. And the school board will monitor what each student learns—without idiosyncratic teachers to raise unpopular topics or challenge accepted beliefs.

17   Advanced students can sign up for on-line extracurricular activities—perhaps joining the Virtual Compassion Corps. There, students will be paired up across racial, gender, and class lines. Our children would offer foreigners advice and even arrange interviews with prospective employers. In this way, students will perform community service and mentor others, while displaying their cultural awareness over the network. All

without ever having to shake hands with a real person, travel to a distant country, or (gasp!) face the real problems of another culture.[3] Simple, safe, and sterile.

18   Should parents worry about Johnny's progress, they need only log in over the Internet to see their son's latest test scores. In addition, they'll receive e-mailed reports summarizing their child's work. And at any time, they can click on an icon to see live images of their young scholar, automatically uploaded by a school video camera.

19   Yep, just sign up for the future: the parent-pleasin', tax-savin', teacher-firin', interactive-educatin', child-centerin' Cyberschool. No stuffy classrooms. No more teacher strikes. No outdated textbooks. No expensive clarinet lessons. No boring homework. No learning. Coming soon to a school district near you.[4]

---

[3]An actual proposal from the director of MIT's Laboratory for Computer Science, Michael Dertouzos.

[4]Idea for a computer game: Cyberschool Superintendent. Players score by saving money. They could eliminate teachers, close libraries, or blow up music studios. Competitors advance by wiring schools, adding computers, and plugging in multimedia systems. Evil monstors might appear in the form of teachers, scholars, and librarians who insist that you read a book. Bonus points, labeled Pilot Project Grants, would be awarded for writing vapid press releases.

Questions for Close Reading

1. What is the selection's thesis? Locate the sentence(s) in which Stoll states his main idea. If he doesn't state the thesis explicitly, express it in your own words.
2. What process does Stoll describe in the essay? What are the basic steps of this process? What is Stoll's underlying attitude toward these measures?
3. What specific group of people does Stoll imagine as being especially in favor of the "cyberschool"? According to Stoll, how do these individuals justify using computers to teach children?
4. What role does Stoll indicate teachers will play in the "cyberschool"? What attitude does he convey about this role? Explain.
5. Refer to your dictionary as needed to define the following words used in the selection: *infrastructures* (paragraph 1), *optimal* (1), *harried* (3), *placate* (4), *adept* (8), *standardized* (8), *cubicles* (10), *compartmentalized* (10), *cadre* (12), *recoup* (14), and *idiosyncratic* (16).

Questions About the Writer's Craft

1. **The pattern.** Is Stoll's process analysis primarily directional or primarily informational? Explain. To what extent does Stoll try to persuade readers that the process he describes should be followed?
2. Focusing on his word choices, how would you characterize Stoll's tone in his essay? In your opinion, does his tone enhance or detract from the point he's trying to make? Explain.
3. **Other patterns.** Underlying Stoll's process analysis is an *argument* against a particular form of education. To write an effective argument, writers need to establish their own credibility. Based on what you learned about Stoll in his biography (page 185), what makes him appear qualified to write about his subject?
4. **Other patterns.** In his persona of pro-cyberschool spokesman, Stoll addresses opposition to idea of the cyberschool in paragraph 15. How does Stoll represent and rebut the *arguments* against the cyberschool? Are his arguments effective, in your opinion?

Writing Assignments Using Process-Analysis as a Pattern of Development

1. In his essay, Stoll offers a cynical recipe for creating an "optimal learning environment." Write an essay in which you present a process analysis of concrete ways the school you currently attend or one you have attended in the past could realistically be improved. You might, for in-

stance, discuss physical improvements such as updating the equipment in the computer lab, or less tangible measures such as cultivating a more interactive classroom environment. Brainstorm on your own or with others to generate specific ideas to include in your process.

2. In his essay, Stoll ironically suggests a course of action that he implies should not be taken in order to improve children's education. Taking a similarly ironic stance, write an essay *mis*guiding readers on how to "improve" some other significant institution or serious condition. For instance, you might discuss ways to increase the efficiency of a particular government agency, how to even out inequities between classes or races of people, how to protect the environment, and so on—all the while presenting steps that would work to the contrary. Like Stoll, you should ultimately reveal your true position in the concluding paragraph, preferably in a subtle way.

Writing Assignments Combining Patterns of Development

3. According to Stoll, computers serve as a distraction to students rather than a legitimate learning tool. What are other kinds of distractions students face? Write an essay in which you *classify* the different types of distractions that can make learning difficult. You may adopt a serious tone and address categories such as, for example, problems at home and pressure from peers. Or you might adopt a humorous tone and discuss distractions that include interest in the opposite sex and the temptation of computer games. Provide vivid *examples* to illustrate each of the categories you create. For additional viewpoints about the pressures to which students are subject, read Mary Sherry's "In Praise of the 'F' Word".

4. With the increasing popularity of the Internet, the future of traditional printed materials—such as books, magazines, and newspapers—has come into question. Write an essay in which you *compare* and *contrast* using printed materials with using the Internet in order to perform research. Be sure to provide at least one extended example or a few briefer examples to *illustrate* the differences and/or similarities you're pointing out. Your best source of information might be a "hands-on" approach: to research a topic using both methods in order to see for yourself what the differences are. By the end of your essay, make clear to your reader which of the two methods you find preferable, and why.

Writing Assignment Using a Journal Entry as a Starting Point

5. In an indirect way, Stoll argues against the wholesale computerization of the classroom. Write an essay in which you argue that the Internet in specific should *or* should not play a significant role in the education of *one* particular age group of students (elementary, high school, or college). In formulating your argument, refer to the material you generated in your pre-reading journal entry. For additional perspectives on this issue, you might consider doing some research on this topic in the library and/or on the Internet. In writing your essay, you should acknowledge and rebut opposing points of view.

READING

Paul Roberts

Paul Roberts (1917–67) was a scholar of linguistics and a respected teacher whose textbooks helped scores of high school and college students become better writers. Roberts's works include *English Syntax* (1954) and *Patterns of English* (1956). The following selection is from his best-known book, *Understanding English* (1958).

Pre-Reading Journal Entry

Many educators argue that first-year college students write bland essays because their high school English classes didn't teach them how to think clearly and creatively. Do you agree? Take some time to reflect in your journal about your best and worst high school English classes. For each class, focus on teaching style, classroom atmosphere, assignments, activities, and so on.

How to Say Nothing in 500 Words

Nothing About Something

1   It's Friday afternoon, and you have almost survived another week of classes. You are just looking forward dreamily to the weekend when the English instructor says: "For Monday you will turn in a five-hundred-word composition on college football."

2   Well, that puts a good big hole in the weekend. You don't have any strong views on college football one way or the other. You get rather excited during the season and go to all the home games and find it rather more fun than not. On the other hand, the class has been reading Robert Hutchins in the anthology and perhaps Shaw's "Eighty-Yard Run," and from the class discussion you have got the idea that the instructor thinks college football is for the birds. You are no fool, you. You can figure out what side to take.

3   After dinner you get out the portable typewriter that you got for high school graduation. You might as well get it over with and enjoy Saturday and Sunday. Five hundred words is about two double-spaced pages with normal margins. You put in a sheet of paper, think up a title, and you're off:

Why College Football Should Be Abolished

4   College football should be abolished because it's bad for the school and also bad for the players. The players are so busy practicing that they don't have any time for their studies.

5   This, you feel, is a mighty good start. The only trouble is that it's only thirty-two words. You still have four hundred and sixty-eight to go, and you've pretty well exhausted the subject. It comes to you that you do your best thinking in the morning, so you put away the typewriter and go to the movies. But the next morning you have to do your washing and some math problems, and in the afternoon you go to the game. The English instructor turns up too, and you wonder if you've taken the right side after all. Saturday night you have a date, and Sunday morning you have to go to church. (You shouldn't let English assignments interfere with your religion.) What with one thing and another, it's ten o'clock Sunday night before you get out the typewriter again. You make a pot of coffee and start to fill out your views on college football. Put a little meat on the bones.

Why College Football Should Be Abolished

6   In my opinion, it seems to me that college football should be abolished. The reason why I think this to be true is because I feel that football is bad for the colleges in nearly every respect. As Robert Hutchins says in his article in our anthology in which he discusses college football, it would be better if the colleges had race horses and had races with one another, because then the horses would not have to attend classes. I

firmly agree with Mr. Hutchins on this point, and I am sure that many other students would agree too.

7   One reason why it seems to me that college football is bad is that it has become too commercial. In the olden times when people played football just for the fun of it, maybe college football was all right, but they do not play football just for the fun of it now as they used to in the old days. Nowadays college football is what you might call a big business. Maybe this is not true at all schools, and I don't think it is especially true here at State, but certainly this is the case at most colleges and universities in America nowadays, as Mr. Hutchins points out in his very interesting article. Actually the coaches and alumni go around to the high schools and offer the high school stars large salaries to come to their colleges and play football for them. There was one case where a high school star was offered a convertible if he would play football for a certain college.

8   Another reason for abolishing college football is that it is bad for the players. They do not have time to get a college education, because they are so busy playing football. A football player has to practice every afternoon from three to six, and then he is so tired that he can't concentrate on his studies. He just feels like dropping off to sleep after dinner, and then the next day he goes to his classes without having studied and maybe he fails the test.

(Good ripe stuff so far, but you're still a hundred and fifty-one words from home. One more push.)

9   Also I think college football is bad for the colleges and the universities because not very many students get to participate in it. Out of a college of ten thousand students only seventy-five or a hundred play football, if that many. Football is what you might call a spectator sport. That means that most people go to watch it but do not play it themselves.

(Four hundred and fifteen. Well, you still have the conclusion, and when you retype it, you can make the margins a little wider.)

10   These are the reasons why I agree with Mr. Hutchins that college football should be abolished in American colleges and universities.

11   On Monday you turn it in, moderately hopeful, and on Friday it comes back marked "weak in content" and sporting a big "D."

12   This essay is exaggerated a little, not much. The English instructor will recognize it as reasonably typical of what an assignment on college football will bring in. He knows that nearly half of the class will contrive in five hundred words to say that college football is too commercial and bad for the players. Most of the other half will inform him that college football builds character and prepares one for life and brings prestige to the school. As he reads paper after paper all saying the same thing in almost the same words, all bloodless, five hundred words dripping out of nothing, he wonders how he allowed himself to get trapped into teaching English when he might have had a happy and interesting life as an electrician or a confidence man.

13   Well, you may ask, what can you do about it? The subject is one on which you have few convictions and little information. Can you be expected to make a dull subject interesting? As a matter of fact, this is precisely what you are expected to do. This is the writer's essential task. All subjects, except sex, are dull until somebody makes them interesting. The writer's job is to find the argument, the approach, the angle, the wording that will take the reader with him. This is seldom easy, and it is particularly hard in subjects that have been much discussed: College Football, Fraternities, Popular Music, Is Chivalry Dead?, and the like. You will feel that there is nothing you can do with such subjects except repeat the old bromides. But there are some things you can do which will make your papers, if not throbbingly alive, at least less insufferably tedious than they might otherwise be.

Avoid the Obvious Content

14   Say the assignment is college football. Say that you've decided to be against it. Begin by putting down the arguments that come to your mind: it is too commercial, it takes the students' minds off their studies, it is hard on the players, it makes the university a kind of circus instead of an intellectual center, for most schools it is financially ruinous. Can you think of any more arguments just off hand? All right. Now when you write your paper, *make sure that you don't use any of the material on this list.* If these are the points that leap to your mind, they will leap to everyone else's too, and whether you get a "C" or a "D" may depend on whether the instructor reads your paper early when he is fresh and tolerant or late, when the sentence "In my opinion, college football has become too commercial," inexorably repeated, has brought him to the brink of lunacy.

15   Be against college football for some reason or reasons of your own. If they are keen and perceptive ones, that's splendid. But even if they are trivial or foolish or indefensible, you are still ahead so long as they are not everybody else's reasons too. Be against it because the colleges don't spend enough money on it to make it worth while, because it is bad for the characters of the spectators, because the players are forced to attend classes, because the football stars hog all the beautiful women, because it competes with baseball and is therefore un-American and possibly Communist inspired. There are lots of more or less unused reasons for being against college football.

16   Sometimes it is a good idea to sum up and dispose of the trite and conventional points before going on to your own. This has the advantage of indicating to the reader that you are going to be neither trite nor conventional. Something like this:

17   We are often told that college football should be abolished because it has become too commercial or because it is bad for the players. These arguments are no doubt very cogent, but they don't really go to the heart of the matter.

Then you go to the heart of the matter.

Take the Less Usual Side

18   One rather simple way of getting interest into your paper is to take the side of the argument that most of the citizens will want to avoid. If the assignment is an essay on dogs, you can, if you choose, explain that dogs are faithful and lovable companions, intelligent, useful as guardians of the house and protectors of children, indispensable in

police work—in short, when all is said and done, man's best friends. Or you can suggest that those big brown eyes conceal, more often than not, a vacuity of mind and an inconstancy .of purpose; that the dogs you have known most intimately have been mangy, ill-tempered brutes, incapable of instruction; and that only your nobility of mind and fear of arrest prevent you from kicking the flea-ridden animals when you pass them on the street.

19   Naturally, personal convictions will sometimes dictate your approach. If the assigned subject is "Is Methodism Rewarding to the Individual?" and you are a pious Methodist, you have really no choice. But few assigned subjects, if any, will fall in this category. Most of them will lie in broad areas of discussion with much to be said on both sides. They are intellectual exercises and it is legitimate to argue now one way and now another, as debaters do in similar circumstances. Always take the side that looks to you hardest, least defensible. It will almost always turn out to be easier to write interestingly on that side.

20   This general advice applies where you have a choice of subjects. If you are to choose among "The Value of Fraternities" and "My Favorite High School Teacher" and "What I Think About Beetles," by all means plump for the beetles. By the time the instructor gets to your paper, he will be up to his ears in tedious tales about the French teacher at Bloombury High and assertions about how fraternities build character and prepare one for life. Your views on beetles, whatever they are, are bound to be a refreshing change.

21   Don't worry too much about figuring out what the instructor thinks about the subject so that you can cuddle up with him. Chances are his views are no stronger than yours. If he does have convictions and you oppose them, his problem is to keep from grading you higher than you deserve in order to show he is not biased. This doesn't mean that you should always cantankerously dissent from what the instructor says; that gets tiresome too. And if the subject assigned is "My Pet Peeve," do not begin, "My pet peeve is the English instructor who assigns papers on 'my pet peeve.'" This was still funny during the War of 1812, but it has sort of lost its edge since then. It is in general good manners to avoid personalities.

Slip Out of Abstraction

22   If you will study the essay on college football . . . you will perceive that one reason for its appalling dullness is that it never gets down to particulars. It is just a series of not very glittering generalities: "football is bad for the colleges," "it has become too commercial," "football is a big business," "it is bad for the players," and so on. Such round phrases thudding against the reader's brain are unlikely to convince him, though they may well render him unconscious.

23   If you want the reader to believe that college football is bad for the players, you have to do more than say so. You have to display the evil. Take your roommate, Alfred Simkins, the second-string center. Picture poor old Alfy coming home from football practice every evening, bruised and aching, agonizingly tired, scarcely able to shovel the mashed potatoes into his mouth. Let us see him staggering up to the room, getting out his econ textbook, peering desperately at it with his good eye, falling asleep and failing the test in the morning. Let us share his unbearable tension as Saturday draws near. Will he fail, be demoted, lose his monthly allowance, be forced to return to the coal

mines? And if he succeeds, what will be his reward? Perhaps a slight ripple of applause when the third-string center replaces him, a moment of elation in the locker room if the team wins, of despair if it loses. What will he look back on when he graduates from college? Toil and torn ligaments. And what will be his future? He is not good enough for pro football, and he is too obscure and weak in econ to succeed in stocks and bonds. College football is tearing the heart from Alfy Simkins and, when it finishes with him, will callously toss aside the shattered hulk.

24   This is no doubt a weak enough argument for the abolition of college football, but it is a sight better than saying, in three or four variations, that college football (in your opinion) is bad for the players.

25   Look at the work of any professional writer and notice how constantly he is moving from the generality, the abstract statement, to the concrete example, the facts and figures, the illustration. If he is writing on juvenile delinquency, he does not just tell you that juveniles are (it seems to him) delinquent and that (in his opinion) something should be done about it. He shows you juveniles being delinquent, tearing up movie theatres in Buffalo, stabbing high school principals in Dallas, smoking marijuana in Palo Alto. And more than likely he is moving toward some specific remedy, not just a general wringing of the hands.

26   It is no doubt possible to be *too* concrete, too illustrative or anecdotal, but few inexperienced writers err this way. For most the soundest advice is to be seeking always for the picture, to be always turning general remarks into seeable examples. Don't say, "Sororities teach girls the social graces." Say "Sorority life teaches a girl how to carry on a conversation while pouring tea, without sloshing the tea into the saucer." Don't say, "I like certain kinds of popular music very much." Say, "Whenever I hear Gerber Spinklittle play 'Mississippi Man' on the trombone, my socks creep up my ankles."

Get Rid of Obvious Padding

27   The student toiling away at his weekly English theme is too often tormented by a figure: five hundred words. How, he asks himself, is he to achieve this staggering total? Obviously by never using one word when he can somehow work in ten.

28   He is therefore seldom content with a plain statement like "Fast driving is dangerous." This has only four words in it. He takes thought, and the sentence becomes:

In my opinion, fast driving is dangerous.

Better, but he can do better still:

In my opinion, fast driving would seem to be rather dangerous.

If he is really adept, it may come out:

In my humble opinion, though I do not claim to be an expert on this complicated subject, fast driving, in most circumstances, would seem to be rather dangerous in many respects, or at least so it would seem to me.

Thus four words have been turned into forty, and not an iota of content has been added.

29   Now this is a way to go about reaching five hundred words, and if you are content with a "D" grade, it is as good a way as any. But if you aim higher, you must work differently. Instead of stuffing your sentences with straw, you must try steadily to get rid of

the padding, to make your sentences lean and tough. If you are really working at it, your first draft will greatly exceed the required total, and then you will work it down, thus:

> It is thought in some quarters that fraternities do not contribute as much as might be expected to campus life.
>
> Some people think that fraternities contribute little to campus life.

> The average doctor who practices in small towns or in the country must toil night and day to heal the sick.
>
> Most country doctors work long hours.

> When I was a little girl, I suffered from shyness and embarrassment in the presence of others.
>
> I was a shy little girl.

> It is absolutely necessary for the person employed as a marine fireman to give the matter of steam pressure his undivided attention at all times.
>
> The fireman has to keep his eye on the steam gauge.

30   You may ask how you can arrive at five hundred words at this rate. Simply. You dig up more real content. Instead of taking a couple of obvious points off the surface of the topic and then circling warily around them for six paragraphs, you work in and explore, figure out the details. You illustrate. You say that fast driving is dangerous, and then you prove it. How long does it take to stop a car at forty and at eighty? How far can you see at night? What happens when a tire blows? What happens in a head-on collision at fifty miles an hour? Pretty soon your paper will be full of broken glass and blood and headless torsos, and reaching five hundred words will not really be a problem.

Call a Fool a Fool

31   Some of the padding in freshman themes is to be blamed not on anxiety about the word minimum but on excessive timidity. The student writes, "In my opinion, the principal of my high school acted in ways that I believe every unbiased person would have to call foolish." This isn't exactly what he means. What he means is, "My high school principal was a fool." If he was a fool, call him a fool. Hedging the thing about with "in-my-opinion's" and "it-seems-to-me's" and "as-I-see-it's" and "at-least-from-my-point-of-view's" gains you nothing. Delete these phrases whenever they creep into your paper.

32   The student's tendency to hedge stems from a modesty that in other circumstances would be commendable. He is, he realizes, young and inexperienced, and he half suspects that he is dopey and fuzzy-minded beyond the average. Probably only too true. But it doesn't help to announce your incompetence six times in every paragraph. Decide what you want to say and say it as vigorously as possible, without apology and in plain words.

33   Linguistic diffidence can take various forms. One is what we call *euphemism*. This is the tendency to call a spade "a certain garden implement" or women's underwear "unmentionables." It is stronger in some eras than others and in some people than others but it always operates more or less in subjects that are touchy or taboo: death, sex, madness, and so on. Thus we shrink from saying "He died last night" but say

instead "passed away," "left us," "joined his Maker," "went to his reward." Or we try to take off the tension with a lighter cliché: "kicked the bucket," "cashed in his chips," "handed in his dinner pail." We have found all sorts of ways to avoid saying *mad:* "mentally ill," "touched," "not quite right upstairs," "feeble-minded," "innocent," "simple," "off his trolley," "not in his right mind." Even such a now plain word as *insane* began as a euphemism with the meaning "not healthy."

34   Modern science, particularly psychology, contributes many polysyllables in which we can wrap our thoughts and blunt their force. To many writers there is no such thing as a bad schoolboy. Schoolboys are maladjusted or unoriented or misunderstood or in need of guidance or lacking in continued success toward satisfactory integration of the personality as a social unit, but they are never bad. Psychology no doubt makes us better men or women, more sympathetic and tolerant, but it doesn't make writing any easier. Had Shakespeare been confronted with psychology, "To be or not to be" might have come out, "To continue as a social unit or not to do so. That is the personality problem. Whether 'tis a better sign of integration at the conscious level to display a psychic tolerance toward the maladjustments and repressions induced by one's lack of orientation in one's environment or—" But Hamlet would never have finished the soliloquy.

35   Writing in the modern world, you cannot altogether avoid modern jargon. Nor, in an effort to get away from euphemism, should you salt your paper with four-letter words. But you can do much if you will mount guard against those roundabout phrases, those echoing polysyllables that tend to slip into your writing to rob it of its crispness and force.

Beware of the Pat Expression

36   Other things being equal, avoid phrases like "other things being equal." Those sentences that come to you whole, or in two or three doughy lumps, are sure to be bad sentences. They are no creation of yours but pieces of common thought floating in the community soup.

37   Pat expressions are hard, often impossible, to avoid, because they come too easily to be noticed and seem too necessary to be dispensed with. No writer avoids them altogether, but good writers avoid them more often than poor writers.

38   By "pat expressions" we mean such tags as "to all practical intents and purposes," "the pure and simple truth," "from where I sit," "the time of his life," "to the ends of the earth," "in the twinkling of an eye," "as sure as you're born," "over my dead body," "under cover of darkness," "took the easy way out," "when all is said and done," "told him time and time again," "parted the best of friends," "stand up and be counted," "gave him the best years of her life," "worked her fingers to the bone." Like other clichés, these expressions were once forceful. Now we should use them only when we can't possibly think of anything else.

39   Some pat expressions stand like a wall between the writer and thought. Such a one is "the American way of life." Many student writers feel that when they have said that something accords with the American way of life or does not they have exhausted the subject. Actually, they have stopped at the highest level of abstraction. The American way of life is the complicated set of bonds between a hundred and eighty million ways. All of us know this when we think about it, but the tag phrase too often keeps us from thinking about it.

40   So with many another phrase dear to the politician: "this great land of ours," "the man in the street," "our national heritage." These may prove our patriotism or give a clue to our political beliefs, but otherwise they add nothing to the paper except words.

Colorful Words

41   The writer builds with words, and no builder uses a raw material more slippery and elusive and treacherous. A writer's work is a constant struggle to get the right word in the right place, to find that particular word that will convey his meaning exactly, that will persuade the reader or soothe him or startle or amuse him. He never succeeds altogether—sometimes he feels that he scarcely succeeds at all—but such successes as he has are what make the thing worth doing.

42   There is no book of rules for this game. One progresses through everlasting experiment on the basis of ever-widening experience. There are few useful generalizations that one can make about words as words, but there are perhaps a few.

43   Some words are what we call "colorful." By this we mean that they are calculated to produce a picture or induce an emotion. They are dressy instead of plain, specific instead of general, loud instead of soft. Thus, in place of "Her heart beat," we may write "Her heart *pounded, throbbed, fluttered, danced.*" Instead of "He sat in his chair," we may say, "He *lounged, sprawled, coiled.*" Instead of "It was hot," we may say, "It was *blistering, sultry, muggy, suffocating, steamy, wilting.*"

44   However, it should not be supposed that the fancy word is always better. Often it is as well to write "Her heart beat" or "It was hot" if that is all it did or all it was. Ages differ in how they like their prose. The nineteenth century liked it rich and smoky. The twentieth has usually preferred it lean and cool. The twentieth-century writer, like all writers, is forever seeking the exact word, but he is wary of sounding feverish. He tends to pitch it low, to understate it, to throw it away. He knows that if he gets too colorful, the audience is likely to giggle.

45   See how this strikes you: "As the rich, golden glow of the sunset died away along the eternal western hills, Angela's limpid blue eyes looked softly and trustingly into Montague's flashing brown ones, and her heart pounded like a drum in time with the joyous song surging in her soul." Some people like that sort of thing, but most modern readers would say, "Good grief," and turn on the television.

Colored Words

46   Some words we would call not so much colorful as colored—that is, loaded with associations, good or bad. All words—except perhaps structure words—have associations of some sort. We have said that the meaning of a word is the sum of the contexts in which it occurs. When we hear a word, we hear with it an echo of all the situations in which we have heard it before.

47   In some words, these echoes are obvious and discussable. The word *mother,* for example, has, for most people, agreeable associations. When you hear *mother* you probably think of home, safety, love, food, and various other pleasant things. If one writes, "She was like a mother to me," he gets an effect which he would not get in "She was like an aunt to me." The advertiser makes use of the associations of *mother* by working it in when he talks about his product. The politician works it in when he talks about himself.

48   So also with such words as *home, liberty, fireside, contentment, patriot, tenderness, sacrifice, childlike, manly, bluff, limpid.* All of these words are loaded with favorable associations that would be rather hard to indicate in a straightforward definition. There is more than a literal difference between "They sat around the fireside" and "They sat around the stove." They might have been equally warm and happy around the stove, but *fireside* suggests leisure, grace, quiet tradition, congenial company, and *stove* does not.

49   Conversely, some words have bad associations. *Mother* suggests pleasant things, but *mother-in-law* does not. Many mothers-in-law are heroically lovable and some mothers drink gin all day and beat their children insensible, but these facts of life are beside the point. The thing is that *mother* sounds good and *mother-in-law* does not.

50   Or consider the word *intellectual.* This would seem to be a complimentary term, but in point of fact it is not, for it has picked up associations of impracticality and ineffectuality and general dopiness. So also with such words as *liberal, reactionary, Communist, socialist, capitalist, radical, schoolteacher, truck driver, undertaker, operator, salesman, huckster, speculator.* These convey meanings on the literal level, but beyond that—sometimes, in some places—they convey contempt on the part of the speaker.

51   The question of whether to use loaded words or not depends on what is being written. The scientist, the scholar, try to avoid them; for the poet, the advertising writer, the public speaker, they are standard equipment. But every writer should take care that they do not substitute for thought. If you write, "Anyone who thinks that is nothing but a Socialist (or Communist or capitalist)," you have said nothing except that you don't like people who think that, and such remarks are effective only with the most naïve readers. It is always a bad mistake to think your readers more naïve than they really are.

Colorless Words

52   But probably most student writers come to grief not with words that are colorful or those that are colored but with those that have no color at all. A pet example is *nice,* a word we would find it hard to dispense with in casual conversation but which is no longer capable of adding much to a description. Colorless words are those of such general meaning that in a particular sentence they mean nothing. Slang adjectives, like *cool* ("That's real cool") tend to explode all over the language. They are applied to everything, lose their original force, and quickly die.

53   Beware also of nouns of very general meaning, like *circumstances, cases, instances, aspects, factors, relationships, attitudes, eventualities,* etc. In most circumstances you will find that those cases of writing which contain too many instances of words like these will in this and other aspects have factors leading to unsatisfactory relationships with the reader resulting in unfavorable attitudes on his part and perhaps other eventualities, like a grade of "D." Notice also what "etc." means. It means "I'd like to make this list longer, but I can't think of any more examples."

Questions for Close Reading

1. What is the selection's thesis? Locate the sentence(s) in which Roberts states his main idea. If he doesn't state the thesis explicitly, express it in your own words.
2. According to Roberts, what do students assume they have to do to get a good grade on an English composition?

3. How do "colorful words," "colored words," and "colorless words" differ? Which should be used in essay writing? Why?

4. What are Roberts's most important pieces of advice for the student writer?

5. Refer to the dictionary as needed to define the following words used in the selection: *bromides* (paragraph 13), *insufferably* (13), *inexorably* (14), *dissent* (21), *abolition* (24), *adept* (28), *euphemism* (33), and *insensible* (49).

Questions About the Writer's Craft

1. **The pattern.** What two processes does Roberts analyze in this essay? Is each process informational, directional, or a combination of the two?

2. Why do you think Roberts uses the second person "you" throughout the essay? How does this choice of point of view affect your response to the essay?

3. What is Roberts's tone in the essay? Find some typical examples of his tone. How does Roberts achieve this tone? Considering the author's intended audience, is this tone a good choice? Explain.

4. Does Roberts "practice what he preaches" about writing? Review the section headings of the essay and find examples of each piece of advice in the essay.

Writing Assignments Using Process Analysis as a Pattern of Development

1. Write a humorous essay showing how to avoid doing schoolwork, household chores, or anything else most people tend to put off. You may use the second person as Roberts does. Or you may use the first person and describe your typical method of avoidance. Before writing, read Bill Bryson's "Your New Computer" and Clifford Stoll's "Cyberschool", two humorous models for a how-*not*-to guide.

2. Borrowing some of Roberts's lively techniques, make a routine, predictable process interesting to read about. You might choose an activity such as how to register to vote, apply for a driver's license, sign up for college courses, take care of laundry, play a simple game, study for an exam, or some other familiar process. Caroline Rego's "The Fine Art of Complaining" may give you some ideas on how to explain a process in a helpful yet entertaining way.

Writing Assignments Combining Patterns of Development

3. Should a composition course be required of all first-year college students? Write an essay *arguing* the value—or lack of value—of such a course. Follow Roberts's advice for writing a lively composition: avoid obvious padding, choose unusual points and *examples*, avoid abstractions, go to the heart of the matter, use colorful words.

4. Write a paper detailing your experiences as a student in English classes—from elementary school up to now. Using several *examples, describe* how successfully or unsuccessfully English has been taught, and recommend any specific reforms or changes you feel are needed.

Writing Assignment Using a Journal Entry as a Starting Point

5. Write an essay describing an ideal high school English class. What kind of teacher would be at the helm? What kind of learning atmosphere would prevail? What sorts of skills would be covered? How? To formulate your position, review your pre-reading journal entry, drawing upon your experiences as a guide. End the essay by briefly discussing the factors that might prevent English classes from being like the ideal one you've described. To broaden your perspective on the issues involved, consider discussing the topic with friends and classmates.

READING

Caroline Rego

Caroline Rego was born in 1950 in Edmond, Oklahoma. A graduate of the University of Oklahoma, she began her journalistic career as a police reporter for a daily newspaper in Montana. Later, while filling in for a vacationing colleague in the features section of another newspaper, she found her true calling: writing consumer-affairs articles that teach readers how to protect themselves against shoddy service, dangerous products, and inefficiency. A sought-after public speaker, Rego talks frequently to students and community groups on strategies for becoming an informed consumer. The following selection is part of a work in progress on consumer empowerment.

Pre-Reading Journal Entry

When you're disappointed with someone or something, how do you typically react—passively, assertively, or in some other way? In your journal, list a few disappointments you've experienced. How did you respond on each occasion? In retrospect, are you happy with your responses? Why or why not?

The Fine Art of Complaining

1   *You waited forty-five minutes for your dinner, and when it came it was cold—and not what you ordered in the first place. You washed your supposedly machine-washable, preshrunk T-shirt (the one the catalogue claimed was "indestructible"), and now it's the size of a napkin. Your new car broke down a month after you bought it, and the dealer says the warranty doesn't apply.*

2   Life's annoyances descend on all of us—some pattering down like gentle rain-drops, others striking with the bruising force of hailstones. We dodge the ones we can, but inevitably, plenty of them make contact. And when they do, we react fairly predictably. Many of us—most of us, probably—grumble to ourselves and take it. We scowl at our unappetizing food but choke it down. We stash the shrunken T-shirt in a drawer, vowing never again to order from a catalogue. We glare fiercely at our checkbooks as we pay for repairs that should have been free.

3   A few of us go to the other extreme. Taking our cue from the crazed newscaster in the 1976 movie *Network,* we go through life mad as hell and unwilling to take it anymore. In offices, we shout at hapless receptionists when we're kept waiting for appointments. In restaurants, we make scenes that have fellow patrons craning their necks to get a look at us. In stores, we argue with salespeople for not waiting on us. We may notice after a while that our friends seem reluctant to venture into public with us, but hey—we're just standing up for our rights. Being a patsy doesn't get you anywhere in life.

4   It's true—milquetoasts live unsatisfying lives. However, people who go through the day in an eye-popping, vein-throbbing state of apoplectic rage don't win any prizes either. What persons at both ends of the scale need—what could empower the silent sufferer and civilize the Neanderthal—is a course in the gentle art of *effective* complaining.

5   Effective complaining is not apologetic and half-hearted. It's not making one awk-ward attempt at protest—"Uh, excuse me, I don't think I ordered the squid and

onions"—and then slinking away in defeat. But neither is it roaring away indiscriminately, attempting to get satisfaction through the sheer volume of our complaint.

6   Effective complainers are people who act businesslike and important. Acting important doesn't mean puffing up your chest and saying, "Do you know who I am?"—an approach that would tempt anyone to take you down a peg or two. It doesn't mean shouting and threatening—techniques that will only antagonize the person whose help you need. It *does* mean making it clear that you know your request is reasonable and that you are confident it will be taken care of. People are generally treated the way they expect to be treated. If you act like someone making a fair request, chances are that request will be granted. Don't beg, don't explain. Just state your name, the problem, and what you expect to have done. Remain polite. But be firm. "My car has been in your garage for three days, and a mechanic hasn't even looked at it yet," you might say. "I want to know when it is going to be worked on." Period. Now it is up to them to give you a satisfactory response. Don't say, "Sorry to bother you about this, but . . ." or "I, uh, was sort of expecting. . . ." You're only asking people to remedy a problem, after all; that is not grounds for apology.

7   If your problem requires an immediate response, try to make your complaint in person; a real, live, in-the-flesh individual has to be dealt with in some way. Complaining over the telephone, by contrast, is much less effective. When you speak to a disembodied voice, when the person at the other end of the line doesn't have to face you, you're more likely to get a runaround.

8   Most importantly, complain to the right person. One of the greatest frustrations in complaining is talking to a clerk or receptionist who cannot solve your problem and whose only purpose seems to be to drive you crazy. Getting mad doesn't help; the person you're mad at probably had nothing to do with your actual problem. And you'll have to repeat everything you've said to the clerk once you're passed along to the appropriate person. So make sure from the start that you're talking to someone who can help—a manager or supervisor.

9   If your problem doesn't require an immediate response, complaining by letter is probably the most effective way to get what you want. A letter of complaint should be brief, businesslike, and to the point. If you have a new vacuum cleaner that doesn't work, don't spend a paragraph describing how your Uncle Joe tried to fix the problem and couldn't. As when complaining in person, be sure you address someone in a position of real authority. Here's an example of an effective letter of complaint.

10   Ms. Anne Lublin
Manager
Mitchell Appliances
80 Front Street
Newton, MA 02159

11   Dear Ms. Lublin:

12   *First section: Explain the problem. Include facts to back up your story.*

13   On August 6, I purchased a new Perma-Kool freezer from your store (a copy of my sales receipt is enclosed). In the two weeks I have owned the freezer, I have had to call your repair department three times in an at-

tempt to get it running properly. The freezer ran normally when it was installed, but since then it has repeatedly turned off, causing the food inside to spoil. My calls to your repair department have not been responded to promptly. After I called the first time, on August 10, I waited two days for the repair person to show up. It took three days to get a repair person here after my second call, on August 15. The freezer stopped yet again on August 20. I called to discuss this recent problem, but no one has responded to my call.

14   *Second section: Tell how you trust the company and are confident that your reader will fix the problem. This is to "soften up" the reader a bit.*

15   I am surprised to receive such unprofessional service and poor quality from Mitchell Appliances since I have been one of your satisfied customers for fifteen years. In the past, I have purchased a television, air conditioner, and washing machine from your company. I know that you value good relations with your customers, and I'm sure you want to see me pleased with my most recent purchase.

16   *Third section: Explain exactly what you want to be done—repair, replacement, refund, etc.*

17   Although your repair department initially thought that the freezer needed only some minor adjustments, the fact that no one has been able to permanently fix the problem convinces me that the freezer has some serious defect. I am understandably unwilling to spend any more time having repairs made. Therefore, I expect you to exchange the freezer for an identical model by the end of this week (August 30). Please call me to arrange for the removal of the defective freezer and the delivery of the new one.

18   Sincerely,

Janice Becker

19   *P.S. (Readers always notice a P.S.) State again when you expect the problem to be taken care of, and what you will do if it isn't.*

20   P.S. I am confident that we can resolve this problem by August 30. If the defective freezer is not replaced by then, however, I will report this incident to the Better Business Bureau.

21   Notice that the P.S. says what you'll do if your problem isn't solved. In other words, you make a threat—a polite threat. Your threat must be reasonable and believable. A threat to burn down the store if your purchase price isn't refunded is neither reasonable nor believable—or if it *were* believed, you could end up in jail. A threat to report the store to a consumer-protection agency, such as the Better Business Bureau, however, is credible.

22   Don't be too quick to make one of the most common—and commonly empty—threats: "I'll sue!" A full-blown lawsuit is more trouble, and more expensive, than most problems are worth. On the other hand, most areas have a small-claims court where suits involving modest amounts of money are heard. These courts don't use complex legal language or procedures, and you don't need a lawyer to use them. A store or

company will often settle with you—if your claim is fair—rather than go to small-claims court.

23   Whether you complain over the phone, in person, or by letter, be persistent. One complaint may not get results. In that case, keep on complaining, and make sure you keep complaining to the same person. Chances are he or she will get worn out and take care of the situation, if only to be rid of you.

24   Someday, perhaps, the world will be free of the petty annoyances that plague us all from time to time. Until then, however, toasters will break down, stores will refuse to honor rainchecks, and bills will include items that were never purchased. You can depend upon it—there will be grounds for complaint. You might as well learn to be good at it.

Questions for Close Reading

1. What is the selection's thesis? Locate the sentence(s) in which Rego states her main idea. If she doesn't state the thesis explicitly, express it in your own words.
2. In Rego's opinion, what types of actions and statements are *not* helpful when making a complaint?
3. What should be included in a letter of complaint? What should be omitted?
4. What does Rego suggest doing if a complaint is ignored?
5. Refer to your dictionary as needed to define the following words used in the selection: *hapless* (paragraph 3), *venture* (3), *patsy* (3), *milquetoasts* (4), *apoplectic* (4), *Neanderthal* (4), *indiscriminately* (5), *disembodied* (7), and *credible* (21).

Questions About the Writer's Craft

1. **The pattern.** Is Rego's process analysis primarily directional or primarily informational? Explain. To what extent does Rego try to persuade readers to follow her process?
2. **Other patterns.** Where does Rego include *narrative elements in her essay*? What do these brief narratives add to the piece?
3. **Other patterns.** Numerous oppositions occur throughout the essay. How do these *contrasts* enliven the essay and help Rego persuade readers to adopt her suggestions?
4. Reread the essay, noting where Rego shifts point of view. Where does she use the second-person (*you*), the first-person-plural (*we*), and the third-person-plural (*they*) points of view? How does her use of multiple points of view add to the essay's effectiveness?

Writing Assignments Using Process Analysis as a Pattern of Development

1. Write an essay explaining to college students how to register—with someone in a position of authority—an effective complaint about a campus problem. You could show, for example, how to complain to a professor about a course's grading policy, to the bookstore manager about the markup on textbooks, to security about the poorly maintained college parking lots. Feel free to adapt some of Rego's recommendations, but be sure to invent several strategies of your own. In either case, provide—as Rego does—lively examples to illustrate the step-by-step procedure for registering an effective complaint with a specific authority figure on campus.
2. Rego argues that "people who go through the day in an eye-popping, vein-throbbing state of apoplectic rage don't win any prizes." But sometimes, getting mad can be appropriate—even productive. Write an essay explaining the best process for expressing anger effectively. Explain how to vent emotion safely, communicate the complaint in a nonthreatening way, encourage more honest interaction, and prompt change for the better. Illustrate the process by drawing upon your own experiences and observations.

Writing Assignments Combining Patterns of Development

3. Think about a service or product that failed to live up to your expectations. Perhaps you were disgruntled about your mechanic's car repair, a store's return policy, or a hotel's accommodations. Using Rego's suggestions, write a letter of complaint in which you *describe* the problem, convey confidence in the reader's ability to resolve the problem, and state your request for specific action. Remember that a firm but cordial tone will *persuade* your reader that you have legitimate grounds for seeking the resolution you propose.

4. Rego shows that events often don't turn out as we had hoped. In an essay, *contrast* how you thought a specific situation would be with the way it actually turned out. Was the unexpected outcome better or worse than what you had expected? Did you have trouble adjusting, or did you adapt with surprising ease? Provide vivid *specifics* about the unforeseen turn of events and your *reaction* to it.

Writing Assignment Using a Journal Entry as a Starting Point

5. Write an essay contrasting the way you reacted to a specific disappointment with the way you wish you had reacted. Reread your pre-reading journal entry, and select *one* incident that illustrates this discrepancy most dramatically. Use vigorous narrative details to make the contrast vivid and real. In your conclusion, indicate what you've learned in hindsight.

ADDITIONAL WRITING TOPICS

Process Analysis

General Assignments

Develop one of the following topics through process analysis. Explain the process one step at a time, organizing the steps chronologically. If there's no agreed-on sequence, design your own series of steps. Use transitions to ease the audience through the steps in the process. You may use any tone you wish, from serious to light.

Directional: How to Do Something

1. How to improve a course you have taken
2. How to drive defensively
3. How to get away with _____
4. How to succeed at a job interview
5. How to relax
6. How to show appreciation to others
7. How to get through school despite personal problems
8. How to be a responsible pet owner
9. How to conduct a garage or yard sale
10. How to look fashionable on a limited budget
11. How to protect a home from burglars
12. How to meet more people
13. How to improve the place where you work
14. How to gain or lose weight
15. How to get over a disappointment

Informational: How Something Happens

1. How a student becomes burned out
2. How a library's card catalog or computerized catalog organizes books
3. How a dead thing decays (or how some other natural process works)
4. How the college registration process works
5. How *Homo sapiens* chooses a mate
6. How a VCR (or some other machine) works

7. How a bad habit develops
8. How people fall into debt
9. How someone becomes an Internet addict/junkie
10. How a child develops a love of reading

Assignments With a Specific Purpose, Audience, and Point of View

On Campus

1. As an experienced campus tour guide for prospective students, you've been asked by your school's Admissions Office to write a pamphlet explaining to new tour guides how to conduct a tour of your school's campus. When explaining the process, keep in mind that tour guides need to portray the school in its best light.

2. You write an "advice to the lovelorn" column for the campus newspaper. A correspondent writes saying that he or she wants to break up with a steady girlfriend/boyfriend but doesn't know how to do this without hurting the person. Give the writer guidance on how to end a meaningful relationship with a minimal amount of pain.

At Home or in the Community

3. To help a sixteen-year-old friend learn how to drive, explain a specific driving maneuver one step at a time. You might, for example, describe how to make a three-point turn, parallel park, or handle a skid. Remember, your friend lacks self-confidence and experience.

4. Your best friend plans to move into his or her own apartment but doesn't know the first thing about how to choose one. Explain the process of selecting an apartment—where to look, what to investigate, what questions to ask before signing a lease.

On the Job

5. As a staff writer for a consumer magazine, you've been asked to write an article on how to shop for a certain product. Give specific steps explaining how to save money, buy a quality product, and the like.

6. An author of books for elementary school children, you want to show children how to do something—take care of a pet, get along with siblings, keep a room clean. Explain the process in terms a child would understand yet not find condescending.

READING

Garry Trudeau

Garry Trudeau, born in New York City in 1948, is most famous for his internationally acclaimed comic strip Doonesbury. *He attended Yale University and in 1970 was awarded a Master of Fine Arts degree from Yale's School of Art and Architecture.* Doonesbury *appears in newspapers nationwide and has been collected in numerous books. In 1975, Trudeau won the Pulitzer Prize for editorial cartooning. In 1977 he was nominated for an Academy Award for the animated film,* A Doonesbury Special.

Anatomy of a Joke

This short essay was first published August 1, 1993, in the opinion section of *The New York Times*. In it, Trudeau traces in detail a single *Tonight Show* joke, from its inception to Jay Leno's delivery.

As you read Trudeau's description, you might be surprised at the time, detail, and calculation that go into a seemingly impromptu and fleeting television joke. Consider why such meticulous and expensive attention would be given to something so inconsequential.

1   In the wake of last week's press "availabilities" of funnymen Dave Letterman, Jay Leno, Chevy Chase et al., there was much rim-shot critiquing, all of it missing the point.

2   The real jokes, the ones that count, occur not at press events but during those extraordinary little pieces called monologues. Despite the popular conception of the monologue as edgy and unpredictable, it is actually as formal and structured as anything found in traditional kabuki. The stakes are too high for it to be otherwise. Even the ad-libs, rejoinders, and recoveries are carefully scripted. While it may suit Leno's image to portray the "Tonight" show monologue as something that's banged out over late-night pizza with a few cronies, in fact each joke requires the concerted effort of a crack team of six highly disciplined comedy professionals. To illustrate how it works, let's follow an actual topical joke, told the night of Monday, July 26, as it makes its way through the pipeline.

3   The inspiration for a topical joke is literally torn from the headlines by a professional comedy news "clipper." Comedy news reading is sometimes contracted out to consultants, but the big-budget "Tonight" show has 12 of its own in-house clippers who peruse some 300 newspapers every day. Clippers know that the idea for the joke must be contained in the headline or, at worst, the subhead. If the idea is in the body text, then the general public has probably missed it and won't grasp the reference the joke is built around. In this case, the clipper has spied an item about flood relief.

A20   Friday, July 23, 1993

House Delays Final Flood Aid Vote
$3 Billion Package Stalls in Dispute Over Budget Limits

The Washington Post

---

4   The news clip is then passed on to a comedy "engineer," whose job is to decide what shape the joke should take. After analyzing the headline, the engineer decides how many parts the joke should have, the velocity of its build, whether it contains any red herrings (rare on the "Tonight" show), and the dynamics of the payoff and underlaughing. With Monday's joke, the engineer chose a simple interrogatory setup, which telegraphs to the often sleepy audience that the next line contains a payoff. The finished sequencing is then sent on to the "stylist."

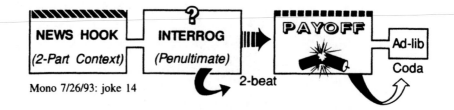

NEWS HOOK (2-Part Context) — INTERROG (Penultimate) — 2-beat — PAYOFF — Ad-lib / Coda

Mono 7/26/93: joke 14

5   The comedy stylist is the writer who actually fashions the raw joke. The stylist is the prima donna of the team, the best paid, the worst dressed—and never in the office. The stylist, who is typically a per diem session player, is faxed the original headline, the structural scheme, and a gross time count, and from those elements creates the rough draft for the joke. It's up to him to find the joke's "spring," that tiny component of universal truth that acts as the joke's fulcrum. In this case, the joke hinges on the public's resentment of Congress, a hoary but proven truism. The stylist then faxes his finished rough to the "polish man."

1./It looks like the House of Representatives is having trouble voting flood relief because they're worried about where to appropriate the money from.
2./Here's my question.
3./How come when the House votes itself a pay raise, they never worry about that appropriation?

---

6   The polish man, usually a woman, is the joke's editor, charged with burnishing the joke until it gleams. Obscure references, awkward phrasing, and puns are all removed, and any potentially offensive material is run by an outside anti-defamation consultant. Unlike the stylist, who usually works at his beach house, the polish man is always on the premises, available in the event of emergency rewrites. For Monday's joke, the polish man adds a "fall from the sky" coda that will allow Leno some physical business. The decision to use it, however, ultimately rests with the "timing coach."

7   The timing coach is responsible for timing out the phrasing and pauses, and bringing the 21-joke routine in under its seven-minute limit. Running over is a major no-no. During the Carson era, a timing coach, who asked not to be identified, signed off on a monologue that ran 13.5 seconds long, a deficit that came out of Barbra Streisand's guest segment. The coach was summarily sacked. Such errors are rare today, however, as the monologues are now digitalized on disk. A timer can modulate the phrasing pattern to within 0.01 of a second, well beyond the performance sensitivity of any comic but Robin Williams.

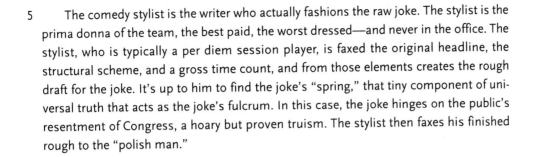

(6.3 sec. to pause) IT LOOKS LIKE . . . FLOOD RELIEF . . . WORRIED . . . MONEY
IS GOING TO COME FROM. (.95 sec. beat) NOW, HERE'S MY QUESTION; (.6 second
beat; 3.45 sec. to ad-lib) HOW COME . . . BIG PAY RAISE . . . WHERE <u>THAT</u>
MONEY'S COMING FROM? (ad-lib under laugh; see menu).

---

8   The final joke is then e-mailed to the "talent," in this case Jay Leno. Leno dry-runs
the joke in his office, adding spin and body movement, and locks in his ad-libs, including recovery lines in case the joke bombs. (Carson had such good recovery material that
he used to commission intentionally bad jokes, but Leno has not yet reached that pinnacle of impeccability.) Once Leno approves the joke, it is transferred to a hard disk and
laser-printed on cue cards with a special font to make it look hand-lettered. Finally, at
exactly 5:30 P.M., California taping time, Leno walks on stage and reads it to 15 million
people.

Meaning and Purpose

1. Now that you have read the essay, what significance does the title have for you?
2. Why are news headlines used as the bases for jokes in the *Tonight Show* monologue?
3. In paragraph 7, Trudeau says, "The timing coach is responsible for timing out the phrasing and
   pauses, and bringing in the 21-joke routine in under its seven-minute limit." Why are the subject, structure, and timing of a TV joke given such meticulous care?
4. What is the thesis of the essay? Where has Trudeau placed it?

Strategy

1. What is each stage of the joke process Trudeau describes?
2. Trudeau often disrupts the strict chronology of his process to give descriptions and explanations. Find two examples of this strategy. Why does he include these interruptions?
3. Trudeau is careful to use clear transitions. What transitions does he use to move the reader
   through each stage of the process? What other transitions does he use to clarify his ideas?
4. Why does Trudeau include visual illustrations? Do they help to clarify his ideas or not?

Style

1. Trudeau employs many colloquialisms in his essay. After finding several, determine why he uses
   them.
2. What specialized vocabulary does he use? Why?
3. Look up the following words in a dictionary: *anatomy* (title); *wake* (paragraph 1); *kabuki,
   cronies, pipeline* (2); *peruse* (3); *velocity, red herrings, dynamics, interrogatory* (4); *prima donna,
   per diem, gross, fulcrum, hoary* (5); *burnishing, anti-defamation, coda* (6); *summarily, digitalized,
   modulate* (7); *pinnacle, impeccability* (8).

WRITING TASKS

1. Choose something in your own life that lends itself to an informative process analysis. Then
   write a paper in which you clearly explain how, precisely, that thing in your life happens or how
   it works. Take care to carry the reader along with transitional expressions. Like Trudeau, include clarifying descriptions, explanations, and examples.
2. Trudeau traces the meticulous detail and care that goes into a single, fleeting TV joke. Consider
   why such care would be taken for such a seemingly trivial pursuit. What would the payoff be
   for such time, expense, and attention? Consider other pursuits that entail similar attention to

detail: many medical procedures, many aspects of the space program, the creative process (art and writing, in particular), many legal matters, much neurotic and psychotic behavior. Write a paper in which you describe one or more processes that demand a meticulous attention to detail and result in a compensating payoff for that attention.

READING

Donald M. Murray

Donald M. Murray was born in 1924 in Boston. He has had a long and distinguished career as a writer and teacher. Murray has published fiction, nonfiction, and poetry, served as an editor of Time *magazine, and won the Pulitzer Prize for editorial writing in 1959. His teaching career at the University of New Hampshire, Durham, and the textbooks he has published on how to write—* A Writer Teaches Writing, Write to Learn, *and* Read to Write—*have established him as one of America's most influential teachers of writing. He sees the writing teacher as a coach and is convinced that a student must want to learn and be willing to exert much effort in order to write well.*

The Maker's Eye
Revising Your Own Manuscripts

Originally published in *The Writer*, this essay demonstrates the process professional writers go through to revise their manuscripts. Murray distinguishes the differences in attitudes that student writers and professional writers take to the revising process and cites other professional writers to argue for the essential importance of meticulous revision.

As you read, note any differences between the methods you use to revise a paper and the methods the professional writer uses. Jot down advice you might find helpful in improving your own writing.

1   When students complete a first draft, they consider the job of writing done—and their teachers too often agree. When professional writers complete a first draft, they usually feel that they are at the start of the writing process. When a draft is completed, the job of writing can begin.

2   That difference in attitude is the difference between amateur and professional, inexperience and experience, journeyman and craftsman. Peter F. Drucker, the prolific business writer, calls his first draft "the zero draft"—after that he can start counting. Most writers share the feeling that the first draft, and all of those which follow, are opportunities to discover what they have to say and how best they can say it.

3   To produce a progression of drafts, each of which says more and says it more clearly, the writer has to develop a special kind of reading skill. In school we are taught to decode what appears on the page as finished writing. Writers, however, face a different category of possibility and responsibility when they read their own drafts. To them the words on the page are never finished. Each can be changed and rearranged, can set off a chain reaction of confusion or clarified meaning. This is a different kind of reading, which is possibly more difficult and certainly more exciting.

4   Writers must learn to be their own best enemy. They must accept the criticism of others and be suspicious of it; they must accept the praise of others and be even more suspicious of it. Writers cannot depend on others. They must detach themselves from

their own pages so that they can apply both their caring and their craft to their own work.

5   Such detachment is not easy. Science fiction writer Ray Bradbury supposedly puts each manuscript away for a year to the day and then rereads it as a stranger. Not many writers have the discipline or the time to do this. We must read when our judgment may be at its worst, when we are close to the euphoric moment of creation.

6   Then the writer, counsels novelist Nancy Hale, "should be critical of everything that seems to him most delightful in his style. He should excise what he most admires, because he wouldn't thus admire it if he weren't . . . in a sense protecting it from criticism." John Ciardi, the poet, adds, "The last act of the writing must be to become one's own reader. It is, I suppose, a schizophrenic process, to begin passionately and to end critically, to begin hot and to end cold; and, more important, to be passion-hot and critic-cold at the same time."

7   Most people think that the principal problem is that writers are too proud of what they have written. Actually, a greater problem for most professional writers is one shared by the majority of students. They are overly critical, think everything is dreadful, tear up page after page, never complete a draft, see the task as hopeless.

8   The writer must learn to read critically but constructively, to cut what is bad, to reveal what is good. Eleanor Estes, the children's book author, explains: "The writer must survey his work critically, coolly, as though he were a stranger to it. He must be willing to prune, expertly and hard-heartedly. At the end of each revision, a manuscript may look . . . worked over, torn apart, pinned together, added to, deleted from, words changed and words changed back. Yet the book must maintain its original freshness and spontaneity."

9   Most readers underestimate the amount of rewriting it usually takes to produce spontaneous reading. This is a great disadvantage to the student writer, who sees only a finished product and never watches the craftsman who takes the necessary step back, studies the work carefully, returns to the task, steps back, returns, steps back, again and again. Anthony Burgess, one of the most prolific writers in the English-speaking world, admits, "I might revise a page twenty times." Roald Dahl, the popular children's writer, states, "By the time I'm nearing the end of a story, the first part will have been reread and altered and corrected at least 150 times. . . . Good writing is essentially rewriting. I am positive of this."

10   Rewriting isn't virtuous. It isn't something that ought to be done. It is simply something that most writers find they have to do to discover what they have to say and how to say it. It is a condition of the writer's life.

11   There are, however, a few writers who do little formal rewriting, primarily because they have the capacity and experience to create and review a large number of invisible drafts in their minds before they approach the page. And some writers slowly produce finished pages, performing all the tasks of revision simultaneously, page by page, rather than draft by draft. But it is still possible to see the sequence followed by most writers most of the time in rereading their own work.

12   Most writers scan their drafts first, reading as quickly as possible to catch the larger problems of subject and form, then move in closer and closer as they read and write, reread and rewrite.

13   The first thing writers look for in their drafts is *information*. They know that a good piece of writing is built from specific, accurate, and interesting information. The writer must have an abundance of information from which to construct a readable piece of writing.

14   Next writers look for *meaning* in the information. The specifics must build a pattern of significance. Each piece of specific information must carry the reader toward meaning.

15   Writers reading their own drafts are aware of *audience*. They put themselves in the reader's situation and make sure that they deliver information which a reader wants to know or needs to know in a manner which is easily digested. Writers try to be sure that they anticipate and answer the questions a critical reader will ask when reading the piece of writing.

16   Writers make sure that the *form* is appropriate to the subject and the audience. Form, or genre, is the vehicle which carries meaning to the reader, but form cannot be selected until the writer has adequate information to discover its significance and an audience which needs or wants that meaning.

17   Once writers are sure the form is appropriate, they must then look at the *structure*, the order of what they have written. Good writing is built on a solid framework of logic, argument, narrative, or motivation which runs through the entire piece of writing and holds it together. This is the time when many writers find it most effective to outline as a way of visualizing the hidden spine by which the piece of writing is supported.

18   The element on which writers may spend a majority of their time is *development*. Each section of a piece of writing must be adequately developed. It must give readers enough information so that they are satisfied. How much information is enough? That's as difficult as asking how much garlic belongs in a salad. It must be done to taste, but most beginning writers underdevelop, underestimating the reader's hunger for information.

19   As writers solve development problems, they often have to consider questions of *dimension*. There must be a pleasing and effective proportion among all the parts of the piece of writing. There is a continual process of subtracting and adding to keep the piece of writing in balance.

20   Finally, writers have to listen to their own voices. *Voice* is the force which drives a piece of writing forward. It is an expression of the writer's authority and concern. It is what is between the words on the page, what glues the piece of writing together. A good piece of writing is always marked by a consistent, individual voice.

21   As writers read and reread, write and rewrite, they move closer and closer to the page until they are doing line-by-line editing. Writers read their own pages with infinite care. Each sentence, each line, each clause, each phrase, each word, each mark of punctuation, each section of white space between the type has to contribute to the clarification of meaning.

22   Slowly the writer moves from word to word, looking through language to see the subject. As a word is changed, cut, or added, as a construction is rearranged, all the words used before that moment and all those that follow that moment must be considered and reconsidered.

23   Writers often read aloud at this stage of the editing process, muttering or whispering to themselves, calling on the ear's experience with language. Does this sound right—or that? Writers edit, shifting back and forth from eye to page to ear to page.

I find I must do this careful editing in short runs, no more than fifteen or twenty minutes at a stretch, or I become too kind with myself. I begin to see what I hope is on the page, not what actually is on the page.

24 This sounds tedious if you haven't done it, but actually it is fun. Making something right is immensely satisfying, for writers begin to learn what they are writing about by writing. Language leads them to meaning, and there is the joy of discovery, of understanding, of making meaning clear as the writer employs the technical skills of language.

25 Words have double meanings, even triple and quadruple meanings. Each word has its own potential for connotation and denotation. And when writers rub one word against the other, they are often rewarded with a sudden insight, an unexpected clarification.

26 The maker's eye moves back and forth from word to phrase to sentence to paragraph to sentence to phrase to word. The maker's eye sees the need for variety and balance, for a firmer structure, for a more appropriate form. It peers into the interior of the paragraph, looking for coherence, unity, and emphasis, which make meaning clear.

27 I learned something about this process when my first bifocals were prescribed. I had ordered a larger section of the reading portion of the glass because of my work, but even so, I could not contain my eyes within this new limit of vision. And I still find myself taking off my glasses and bending my nose towards the page, for my eyes unconsciously flick back and forth across the page, back to another page, forward to still another, as I try to see each evolving line in relation to every other line.

28 When does this process end? Most writers agree with the great Russian writer Tolstoy, who said, "I scarcely ever reread my published writings, if by chance I come across a page, it always strikes me: all this must be rewritten; this is how I should have written it."

29 The maker's eye is never satisfied, for each word has the potential to ignite new meaning. This article has been twice written all the way through the writing process, and it was published four years ago. Now it is to be republished in a book. The editors make a few small suggestions, and then I read it with my maker's eye. Now it has been re-edited, re-revised, re-read, re-re-edited, for each piece of writing to the writer is full of potential and alternatives.

30 A piece of writing is never finished. It is delivered to a deadline, torn out of the typewriter on demand, sent off with a sense of accomplishment and shame and pride and frustration. If only there were a couple more days, time for just another run at it, perhaps then . . .

Meaning and Purpose

1. According to Murray, what are the differences in the ways in which professional writers and student writers view their first drafts? Do his observations ring true? Do both types of writers share any common problems?
2. What two kinds of reading skills does the author distinguish? How does the writer's reading skill differ from that of the normal readers?
3. What does Murray mean when he says, "Writers must learn to be their own best enemy" (paragraph 4)? Explain.
4. In paragraphs 12–30, Murray takes the reader chronologically through each of the elements that a writer must consider to revise a manuscript. Describe the ways in which a writer must consider each of these elements.
5. Murray distinguishes between "information" and "meaning." Explain the difference between the two.
6. Explain Murray's contention that "A piece of writing is never finished" (paragraph 30).

Strategy

1. What is the essay's thesis? Where is it stated?
2. Is the essay an example of directive or informative process analysis? Explain.
3. Murray cites other writers in his description of the revision process. Why?
4. Explain the author's seemingly odd statement that "most writers share the feeling that the first draft, and all of those which follow, are opportunities to discover what they have to say" (paragraph 2).
5. Murray doesn't actually begin a description of the professional writer's revision process until paragraph 12. What is the purpose of such a long introduction?

Style

1. Murray changes from the third person ("writer," "writers," "the maker") to the first person ("I") in paragraphs 23, 27, and 29. What effect does he create by this change of person?
2. Why does Murray end the essay in midsentence?
3. Use a dictionary to determine the meanings of these words: *journeyman, prolific* (paragraph 2); *euphoric* (5); *schizophrenic* (6); *connotation, denotation* (25).

WRITING TASKS

1. Write an essay in which you detail the way in which you revise an essay. In the process, explain why this method might work better for you than the method explained by Murray.
2. If you use a computer to write, explain the advantages of revising on a computer.
3. Write an essay in which you explain to the reader a process that you do regularly and well. Without being moralistic, demonstrate how this might actually benefit the reader.

CHAPTER 10

Argument

CHAPTER OBJECTIVES

In this chapter you will learn to:

- Write argument paragraphs and essays.

- Identify an issue.

- Present a position on the issue.

- Develop convincing support for the position.

- Write effective topic sentences.

10a   WRITE ABOUT IT!

Study the above photograph. What issues does the photograph address? Choose one issue. Write a paragraph that answers the following questions: What position (pro or con) does the bumper sticker take on the issue? What are the possible reasons for agreeing with this position?

    The paragraph you have just written is a brief argument. An **argument** presents logical reasons and evidence to support a point of view on an issue. Many everyday, academic, and workplace situations require you to use argument. A few examples are shown below. In this chapter you will learn how to plan an argument, select convincing reasons and evidence to support it, and present them effectively.

Everyday Scenarios

- An effort to convince your manager that you need Saturday nights off
- A plan for an evening out with friends that urges them to see a particular movie

Academic Scenarios

- A sociology paper defending or rejecting a new theory
- A position paper for environmental science on pollution controls for industry
- An essay on your college goals for a scholarship application

Workplace Scenarios

- A memo defending a budget request
- A letter to support an employee's promotion
- A proposal to secure a contract with a prospective client

10b UNDERSTANDING ARGUMENT

What Is Argumentative Writing?

An **argument** is line of reasoning intended to persuade the reader or listener to agree with a particular viewpoint or take a particular action. If you turn on the television or radio, or open a magazine or newspaper, you are sure to encounter the most common form of argument—advertising. Commercials and ads are attempts to persuade you to buy a particular product or service. Here are a few examples:

1. "You've tried just about everything for your hay fever.... Now try your doctor. Your doctor has an advanced prescription medicine called Seldane that can relieve your allergy symptoms without causing drowsiness."
2. "We fit a square meal into a round bowl. (So we didn't have room for the fat.)—Healthy Choice."

10c EXERCISE 10-1

Directions: Working alone or with another student, brainstorm a list of situations in which you have recently used argument.

The Parts of an Argument

An argument presents reasons for accepting a belief or position or for taking a specific action. It has three essential parts:

- **An issue** This is the problem or controversy that the argument addresses. It is also the topic of an argument paragraph.
- **A position** A position is the particular point of view a writer has on an issue. There are always at least two points of view on an issue—pro and con. For example, you may be for or against gun control. You may favor or oppose lowering the legal drinking age.
- **Support** Support consists of the details that demonstrate your position is correct and should be accepted. There are three types of support: reasons, evidence, and emotional appeals.

Here are a few examples:

Issue	Position	Support
Welfare	The welfare system is unjust and needs reform.	People cheat, deserving system people cannot get benefits, and it costs taxpayers too much money.
Plus-minus	The plus-minus grading system is confusing and unnecessary.	It costs instructors extra grading time, employers do not system understand it, and it complicates the computation of GPA.

You can visualize an argument paragraph as follows:

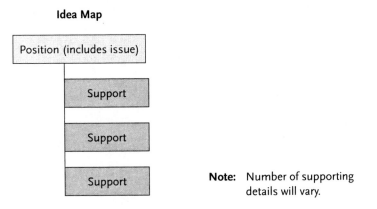

Idea Map

Note: Number of supporting details will vary.

Here is a sample argument paragraph:

Year-round school is advantageous to both parents and children, and more school districts should adopt a full-year calendar. Most parents work year round and find child care and supervision troublesome and expensive during the summer months when their children are not in school. Further, continuous year-round application of skills will prevent forgetting and strengthen students' academic preparation. Finally, children themselves admit they are bored in the summer and end up hanging out in malls, staying up late, and sleeping in the mornings to kill time. A well-rounded school year will produce well-rounded children and happy parents.

You can visualize this paragraph as follows:

Idea Map

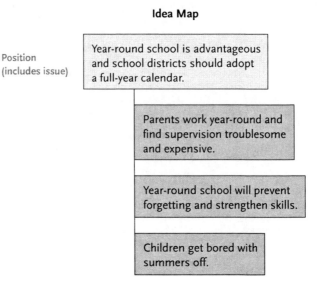

Position
(includes issue)

Year-round school is advantageous and school districts should adopt a full-year calendar.

Parents work year-round and find supervision troublesome and expensive.

Year-round school will prevent forgetting and strengthen skills.

Children get bored with summers off.

10d EXERCISE 10-2

Directions: For each of the following issues, write a sentence that takes a position on the issue.

1. Community service
2. Health insurance
3. Sports fan behavior
4. Air travel safety
5. Minimum wage

Writing Your Topic Sentence

Your topic sentence should do the following:

- identify the issue
- state your position on the issue

In a lengthy argument, it may also suggest the major reasons you will offer to support your position. The following topic sentence makes it clear that the writer will argue against the use of animals for medical research:

> The use of animals in medical research should be outlawed because it is cruel, unnecessary, and disrespectful of animals' place in the chain of life.

Notice that this thesis identifies the issue and makes it clear that the writer opposes animal research. It also suggests the three major reasons she will present: (1) it is cruel, (2) it is unnecessary, and (3) it is disrespectful. You do not always have to include the major points of your argument in your topic sentence, but including them does help the reader to know what to expect. This topic sentence also makes clear what action the author thinks is appropriate: using animals in medical research should be outlawed.

Here are a few more topic sentences. Notice that they use the verbs *should, would,* and *must.*

If we expect industries to dispose of their wastes properly, then we <u>should</u> provide tax breaks to cover the extra expense.

It <u>would</u> be a mistake to assume racial discrimination has been eliminated or even reduced significantly over the past twenty years.

The proportion of tenured women and minority faculty on our campus <u>must</u> be increased.

10e EXERCISE 10-3

Writing in Progress

Directions: For three of the following issues, take a position and write a topic sentence.

1. Employee health care benefits
2. The right of insurance companies to deny medical coverage to certain individuals
3. Banning smoking in public places
4. Outlawing sport hunting of wild animals
5. Mandatory counseling for drunken drivers
6. Buying American-made products
7. Volunteer work
8. Athletes and the use of steroids

Supporting Your Position

There are two primary types of support that can be used to explain why your position should be accepted:

- **Reasons** Reasons are general statements that back up a position. Here are a few reasons to support an argument in favor of parental Internet controls:

  The Internet contains sites that are not appropriate for children.

  The Internet is a place for sexual predators to find victims.

  No one else polices the Internet, so parents must do so.

- **Evidence** The most common types of evidence are facts and statistics, quotations from authorities, examples, and personal experience. Each is discussed in more detail below.

Facts and Statistics

Facts are statements that can be verified as correct. As in writing any other type of paragraph or essay, you must choose facts that directly support the position you express in your topic sentence. Here is an excerpt from an argument that uses facts as evidence to argue that African Americans have made significant gains in the nation's political system:

Changes in political representation show mixed results. On the positive side, the mayors of many large U.S. cities are African American, and of 435 representatives, 39 are African American. But of 100 senators, none is African American, when we would expect about 12 based on population. Of the 495,000 elected officials in the United States, only about 9,000 are African American (*Statistical Abstract* 2001: Table 399). African Americans, who number 34.6 million, make up about 12 percent of the population, but they hold only about 2 percent of the elected offices. Yet, compared with the past, this small amount represents substantial gains in the U.S. political system.

James M. Henslin, *Social Problems*

Facts expressed as numbers are called *statistics*. It is usually more effective to present more than one statistic. Suppose you are writing to persuade taxpayers that state lotteries have become profitable businesses. You might state that more than 60 percent of the adult population now buy lottery tickets regularly. This statistic would have little meaning by itself. However, if you were to state that 60 percent of adults now purchase lottery tickets, whereas five years ago only 30 percent purchased them, the first statistic would become more meaningful.

In selecting statistics to support your position, be sure to:

1. **Obtain statistics from reliable print or online sources.** These include almanacs, encyclopedias, articles in reputable journals and magazines, or other trustworthy reference material from your library. Online sources include databases, online journals, and scholarly Web sites.
2. **Use up-to-date information, preferably from the past year or two.** Dated statistics may be incorrect or misleading.
3. **Make sure you define terms and units of measurement.** For example, if you say that 60 percent of adults regularly play the lottery, you should define what "regularly" means. Does it mean daily, weekly, or monthly?
4. **Verify that the statistics you obtain from more than one source are comparable.** For example, if you compare the crime rates in New York City and Los Angeles, be sure that each crime rate was computed the same way, that each represents the same types of crimes, and that report sources were similar.

Quotations from Authorities

You can also support your position by using expert or authoritative statements of opinion or conclusions. Experts or authorities are those who have studied your subject extensively, conducted research on it, or written widely about it. For example, if you are writing an essay calling for stricter preschool-monitoring requirements to prevent child abuse, the opinion of a psychiatrist who works extensively with abused children would provide convincing support.

Examples

Examples are specific situations that illustrate a point. In a persuasive essay, your examples must represent your position and should illustrate as many aspects of your position as possible. Suppose your position is that a particular movie should have been X-rated because it contains excessive violence. The evidence you choose to support this position should be clear, vivid examples of violent scenes.

The examples you choose should also, if possible, relate to your audience's experience. Familiar examples are more appealing, convincing, and understandable. Suppose you are writing to present a position on abortion. Your audience consists of career women between 30 and 40 years old. It would be most effective to use as examples women of the same age and occupational status.

Personal Experience

If you are knowledgeable about a subject, your personal experiences can be convincing evidence. For example, if you were writing an essay supporting the position that physical separation from parents encourages a teenager or young adult to mature, you could discuss your own experiences with leaving home and assuming new responsibilities.

10f EXERCISE 10-4

Writing in Progress

Directions: Generate reasons and evidence to support one of the topic sentences you wrote for Exercise 10-3.

Researching Your Topic

An argument essay must provide specific and convincing evidence that supports the topic sentence. Often it is necessary to go beyond your own knowledge and experience. You may need to research your topic. For example, if you were writing to urge the creation of an environmentally protected wetland area, you would need to find out what types of wildlife live there, which are endangered, and how successful other wetlands have been in protecting wildlife.

At other times, you may need to interview people who are experts on your topic or directly involved with it. Suppose you are writing a memo urging other employees in your department to participate in a walk-a-thon. It is being held to benefit a local shelter for homeless men and women. The director of the shelter or one of her employees could offer useful statistics, share personal experiences, and provide specific details about the clientele the shelter serves that would help you make a convincing case.

10g EXERCISE 10-5

Writing in Progress

Directions: Evaluate the evidence you collected in Exercise 10-4, and research your topic further if needed. Write the first draft of the paragraph.

Applying Your Skills to Essay Writing: Argument

The skills you learned for writing an argument paragraph apply to essay writing as well. Use the guidelines described below to write an effective argument essay.

Guidelines for Writing Argument Essays

1. Thesis Statement Your thesis statement should identify the issue and state your position on the issue. It may also suggest the primary reasons for accepting the position. Place your thesis statement where it will be most effective. There are three common placements:

a. Thesis statement in the beginning

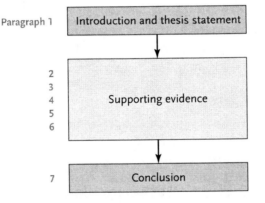

b. Thesis statement after responding to objections

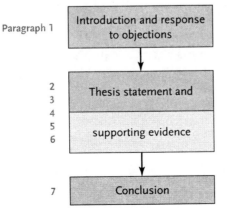

c. Thesis statement at the end

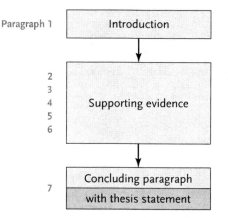

In general, placing the thesis in the beginning is best when addressing an audience in agreement with your position or one that is neutral about the topic under discussion. For an audience that does not agree with your argument, a later placement gives you the opportunity to respond to the audience's objections before you present your thesis.

2. Develop Convincing Support   The support you provide determines the effectiveness of your argument. Be sure to offer convincing reasons and sufficient evidence to explain each reason. Here is a sample argument written by one student. Note how she presents reasons and evidence for taking a specific action.

Buckle Up

As a paramedic, I am the first to arrive at the scene of many grim and tragic accidents. One horrid accident last month involved four women in one car. The front-seat passenger died instantly, another died during a mercy flight to the nearest hospital, one lost both legs, and one walked away from the accident without serious injury. Only one woman was wearing a seat belt. Guess which one? Though many people protest and offer excuses, seat belts do save lives.

Many people avoid wearing seat belts and say they'd rather be thrown free from an accident. Yet they seldom realize that the rate at which they will be thrown is the same rate at which the car is moving. Others fear being trapped inside by their seat belt in case of a fire. However, if not ejected, those without a belt are likely to be stunned or knocked unconscious on impact and will not be alert enough to escape uninjured.

Seat belts save lives by protecting passengers from impact. During a crash, a body slams against the windshield or steering wheel with tremendous force if unbelted. The seat belt secures the passenger in place and protects vital organs from injury.

Recent statistics demonstrate that a passenger is five times more likely to survive a crash if a seat belt is worn. Life is a gamble, but those are good odds. Buckle up!

This writer introduces the topic with a startling example from her personal experience. The thesis statement occurs at the end of the first paragraph. The second and third paragraphs offer evidence that supports the writer's thesis. The last paragraph concludes the essay by offering a convincing statistic and reminding the reader of the thesis "Buckle up." You can visualize this short argument as follows:

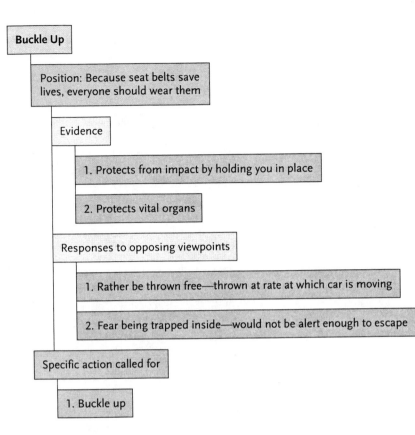

3. The Introduction and Conclusion The introduction of an argument essay should interest the reader in the issue and suggest why the issue is important. The introduction may include your thesis statement, a definition of a key term, or other explanatory information.

If you delay stating your thesis until the end of your essay, make sure your conclusion contains a clear, direct thesis statement. If you state your thesis earlier, then your conclusion should summarize key points and make a final call for action. You may request that your reader take specific action, such as writing a letter to a congressional leader or joining a local environmental protection group.

4. Opposing Viewpoints An opposing viewpoint is the position that is the opposite of the one you took. It is effective to recognize opposing viewpoints because it builds your credibility and shows that you are open minded. For example, suppose you are arguing that gays should be allowed in the military. You could also recognize or admit that opponents believe that the presence of gays in a military unit may compromise its cohesiveness. You may also decide to refute or argue against opposing viewpoints. You could refute the notion that gays in the military compromises cohesiveness by stating that soldiers are unified against the enemy, not each other. Think of refutation as a process of finding weaknesses in the opponent's argument.

NEED TO KNOW

Analyzing Your Audience

Analyzing your audience is a crucial step in planning a convincing argument. There are three types of audiences:

- **Audiences who agree with your position** These are the easiest to write for because they already accept most of what you will say. Audiences in agreement with you are likely to have positive feelings toward you because you think the way they do about the issue. For this audience, state your position and explain why you think it is correct.

- **Neutral audiences** These readers have not made up their minds or have not given much thought to the issue. They may have questions, they may misunderstand the issue, or they may have heard arguments supporting the opposing viewpoint. An essay written for a neutral audience should be direct and straightforward, like those written for an audience in agreement with your point of view. However, a fuller explanation of the issue is necessary to answer questions, clear up misunderstandings, and respond to opposing arguments.

- **Audiences who disagree with your position** These are the most difficult to address. Some members will have thought about the issue and taken a position that opposes yours. Others who disagree may not have examined the issue at all and are making superficial judgments or are relying on misinformation. Both types think their position is correct, so they will not be eager to change their minds. They may also distrust you, because you think differently from them. For such an audience, your biggest challenge is to build trust and confidence. Before writing, carefully analyze this audience and try to answer these questions:

  - Why does your audience disagree with your position?
  - Is their position based on real facts and sound evidence, or on personal opinion? If it is based on evidence, what type?
  - What type of arguments or reasons are most likely to appeal to your audience? For example, will they be persuaded by facts and statistics, or by statements made by authorities? Would personal anecdotes and examples work well?

  Once you understand how your audience thinks, you can plan your essay more effectively.

AN ACADEMIC SCENARIO

A Student Essay

The Academic Writer and the Writing Task

Ebtisam Abusamak is a student at Central Piedmont Community College. For a journalism class, she was asked to choose an issue and write a paper taking a position on the issue. For her paper, Abusamak chose smoking in public places. As you read, study the annotations to help you evaluate her argument.

Interest-catching title

Cigarettes, Anyone?
Ebtisam Abusamak

Background

As a non-smoking student at Central Piedmont College, I believe my freedom is being restricted by the secondhand smoke of others. This is a violation of my constitutional rights to life—which I can only achieve if my body is healthy—liberty, and the pursuit of happiness, none of which is possible when I am surrounded by smokers.

Thesis statement

A smoking ban for all public places would protect my constitutional rights and help smokers, as well.

Personal experience as evidence

Reason 1

When someone near me smokes, I am forced to inhale their smoke and come home smelling like an ashtray, or get up and move, even if it is completely inconvenient for me to do so. This is not just indoors. There have been countless times that I have gone outside to get fresh air and have instead been blasted with a super-sized combo of chemicals and deadly toxins with a side of rat poison. To protect my health, I must compromise my freedom of movement, which is not only completely unfair but unconstitutional as well.

Secondhand smoke is known to cause thousands of deaths in the United States each year. It has been linked to an endless list of serious health problems ranging from bronchitis and asthma to lung cancer and heart disease—even Sudden Infant Death Syndrome. Many nonsmokers who are exposed to secondhand tobacco smoke suffer immediate symptoms including breathing difficulty, eye irritation, and headache, nausea, and asthma attacks.

Reason 2
Examples as evidence

Smoking related diseases are a preventable waste of money. If smoking was abolished, cancer levels would drop and hospitals would have much-needed extra beds. There have been many cases of non-smokers working in restaurants and bars who are diagnosed with serious illnesses due to exposure to cigarette smoke. It's ironic that, while these people are working to live, they are increasing their chances of dying due to the bad choices of the people they serve. Many smokers argue that a smoking section might help the problem. However, having a smoking section in a bar or restaurant is like having a peeing-allowed section in a public swimming pool—the stuff spreads! Would you swim there?

Reason 3
Facts as evidence
Comparison

A ban on smoking in public places would not only improve the lives of non-smokers but would encourage smokers to quit or reduce their smoking. States such as California, where smoking in public places has been banned entirely have proven that a smoke-free environment reduces both the number of smokers in the population and the number of cigarettes they smoke.

Reason 4

Smokers believe that they have a right to make the choice because it's a personal decision. However, their choices not only affect them but everyone around them. People who want to smoke in public areas like to point out the examples of people living past 100 years old who have smoked their entire adult lives or the many cases of lung cancer that were not caused by smoking. There is concern for the restaurant owners whose businesses will suffer because of smoking bans. There is also a concern for tobacco farmers and the entire cigarette industry. But, when all things are considered, the inevitable loss of thousands of lives seems to greatly outweigh the challenges posed to farmers, restaurant owners, and big businesses. Would it be wrong to sacrifice the satisfaction of one customer for the life of another?

Recognition of opposing viewpoint
Refutation of opposing viewpoint

We all have the freedom to make choices regarding our own bodies, but no one has the right to willingly and knowingly put others at risk when making these choices. California and several other states have set the precedent by outlawing smoking in the work place. Other states are sure to follow, but the debate is likely to continue. Unfortunately, you will probably be affected by the effects of smoking at least once in your life, either personally or through the illness or death of a loved one. This is a life-altering issue that needs to be dealt with immediately through smoking bans in all public places. For once, I would like to take a breath of fresh air.

Conclusion
Review of primary reasons
Call for action

Examining Academic Writing

1. For what type of audience is Abusamak writing—neutral, in agreement, or not in agreement?
2. Did you find her argument convincing? Why or why not?
3. What other reasons could she have included?
4. Abusamak did not use research to write her paper. Would facts and statistics have strengthened her essay? If so, what should she have included?

Academic Writing Assignments

1. You are taking an ecology class. You have been asked to select a type of environmental pollution and develop an argument urging steps be taken to control it in your community.
2. You are taking a political science class and you are studying voter registration and participation. Your instructor has asked you to write an editorial for your local newspaper urging that either more citizens become registered voters or more voters use their voting privilege.
3. You are taking a zoology class and are studying the function of zoos. You are considering such questions as: Do zoos protect animals or put them on display? Do they preserve endangered species or do they sacrifice animal needs for those of humans? Write an essay that takes a position on zoos. Develop an argument that supports your position.

A WORKPLACE SCENARIO

A Petition

The Workplace Writer and the Writing Task

Juanita Garcia is a nurse at Valley Visiting Nurses Association. She is also president of the nurses bargaining unit. Because Juanita has two small children, she is interested in reducing her work hours and sharing her job responsibilities with another nurse. She has written the following petition to present to the association's board of directors:

To all nurses at VVNA: PLEASE add your signature at the bottom if you agree it's time we were allowed to job share!

PETITION

We, the undersigned employees at Valley Visiting Nurses Association, are submitting this petition in the belief that everyone at VVNA—nurses and administration alike—would benefit from instituting a job-sharing policy.

There has been a dramatic shift in the workplace over the past century. According to the Bureau of Labor Statistics, the percentage of American women in the labor force rose from 33 percent in 1950 to 60 percent by 2000, and that in 61 percent of American homes, both husband and wife work outside the home. Yet of these working couples, only 1 percent of full-time child care is provided by men.

As a small company administrator, news of a pregnancy from one of your employees may not be cause for congratulations. Who will do that person's job when it comes time for parental leave? And what if that employee decides not to return when the leave is up? For many parents, it can be a wrenching decision to leave a young child and return to work. For them and for you the solution lies in a flexible job-sharing policy.

Job sharing is just what it sounds like: two employees sharing one position. In a company like ours, it would be extremely easy to implement, as we all do essentially the same job, taking care of patients. You hired each of us because we have the appropriate education, training, and compassion. There is not one among us who could not do the job of any of the others. Job sharing would in no way have a negative effect on the company. In fact, employees who job share would have more energy and be less distracted in a four-hour day than they might in an eight-hour one, especially after a long night with a child.

Other benefits to you, the employer, would include:
- increased flexibility, with more workers trained and ready to meet an increase in demand.
- greater continuity when one worker is sick or on vacation.
- a reduction in employee absenteeism, sickness, and stress.
- an increase in employee commitment and loyalty.

As for the last point, employee loyalty is cost-effective. Lower turnover saves the company money in the long run. Think about the time and money you spend hiring and training new employees. By offering your workers the flexibility of job sharing, they will be more likely to return to work after parental leave, even if their hearts lie in being hands-on parents. You will not have to advertise for a new worker, or take time out to interview or train someone new.

Good nurses are in short supply. We believe that by having a job-sharing policy, VVNA will be able to attract and retain the best workers. After all, we are not selling pencils or shoes; we are selling care and compassion. In order to maintain the high level of service we provide, it is necessary that we feel supported by our company. For this reason, as well as the others stated above, we urge you to begin allowing job sharing.

Examining Workplace Writing

1. What is the issue and what position does Garcia take on the issue?
2. What types of evidence does Garcia offer?
3. For what type of audience does Garcia seem to be writing?
4. Is the argument convincing? Why or why not?
5. Why does Garcia focus on benefits to the employer rather than on benefits to the nurses?

Workplace Writing Assignments

1. You are a nurse at a residential care center for developmentally disabled children. You are organizing a holiday party for the children, but you need the staff to contribute money for gifts and food. Write a letter to the center's staff urging them to participate.
2. You are a high school science teacher, and your students do not have Internet access in the school building. Write a memo or letter to your principal explaining why Internet access is important and urging him or her to support your budget request for an Internet provider service.
3. You are a member of a health and wellness committee where you work. The committee has received numerous complaints from employees about the lack of appetizing and nutritional food in the company cafeteria. On behalf of the committee, write a letter to the cafeteria manager urging her to revise the menu. Make specific suggestions about the types of foods that should be served.

10h WRITING ABOUT A READING

Paired Readings

Both "The Captive Panther" and "Predators on the Prowl" deal with wild animals and their relationship to humans. "The Captive Panther" takes a single position on keeping animals in zoos. "Predators on the Prowl" examines two viewpoints about wild animals that hunt and kill other animals and occasionally humans. Read each to examine the arguments they present.

Thinking Before Reading
Reading 1: The Captive Panther

"The Captive Panther" first appeared in the book *Inhumane Society: The American Way of Exploiting Animals* by Michael W. Fox. The author presents arguments against keeping wild animals in captivity. As you read, notice how Fox builds his persuasive argument.

1. Preview the reading.
2. Connect the reading to your own experience by answering the following questions:
   a. How do you feel when you visit a zoo or aquarium?
   b. What purposes do zoos or aquariums serve?

READING

The Captive Panther
Michael W. Fox

psyche

the mind

1   Some experiences can be so painfully intense that they are soon forgotten. Amnesia protects the **psyche**. Then again, in anticipation of vicarious suffering, we may simply tune out certain experiences altogether. Other times, perhaps for good reason, the psyche is not so protected. It is as if the soul—the observing, feeling self—is actually burned by certain experiences. The imprint is branded so indelibly that we can go back and review every detail so completely that the experience is actually relived. I had just such an experience with a panther in a zoo many years ago.

2   The first time that I ever really *saw* an animal in a cage was in a small zoo at the Jardin des Plantes, a natural history museum in Paris. I entered a large, ornate Victorian rotunda that housed a few animals in small wrought-iron cages. I now recall seeing only one animal there. At first it appeared not to see me even though I stood beside its cage for a long time.

3   Time did end that day as a part of me separated and was incorporated as part of the creature in the cage.

4   In retrospect, I was probably mesmerized by what at first appeared to be a shiny black serpent in constant motion. Its liquid form brushed across the front of the cage. After insinuating itself around some artificial rocks and a body-polished tree stump toward the back of the enclosure, it ricocheted off a ceramic-tiled wall to again caress the front of the cage. Form and motion were so unified and the pattern of movement within the confines of the cage so repetitive that at first encounter the creature was barely recognizable as a panther, or black leopard. Her movements were executed with such precision—even to the point of always touching the tree trunk with her left hip and the same ceramic tile with her right front paw—that she was more like a perpetual motion machine than a **sentient** being.

sentient

conscious,
experiencing feeling

5   And then I saw the blood—a streak of blood down her left thigh, draining from an open sore that would never heal until the cat was freed from the hypnotic lines she traced and was so inexorably bound to execute. Each scraping turn around the tree trunk kept the sore open, like a broken heart bleeding for the loss of all that was wild and free.

6   I wondered if she felt any pain. Her yellow-green eyes were like cold glass, with neither fire nor luster. Perhaps this was a slow ritual form of suicide, gradually grinding and rubbing and shredding the body to pieces to free the wild spirit within. I saw the glint of white bone—or was it tendon—through the cat's thigh muscles winking as she turned and paced before me. And there was no pad left on the right front paw that struck the tile wall polished ocher with the patina of dried blood and serum. Yet still the crippled creature continued her measured **minuet**.

minuet

a certain type of dance

7   The panther body, denied freedom of expression and fulfillment of purpose, had become a prison for the creature spirit within. Following and anticipating every movement she made, I began to breathe in rhythm with the cat. I felt part of myself entering her cage while the rotunda started to revolve faster and faster around that part of my

consciousness that remained in my body outside of the cage. Then when I entered the prison of her body the other visitors strolling around the rotunda became **ephemeral** shadow-beings, as if they were part of a dream and the only thing that was real was the measured universe of the tortured panther.

ephemeral
short-lived

8   Confined in such limited space, how else could this boundless spirit of the jungle respond? Her rhythmic, trancelike actions were more than thwarted attempts to escape. Was her compulsive animation designed simply to help her cope with the emptiness of existing in body without any purpose for the spirit, a kind of living death?

9   The cage may be the last refuge for many endangered species, but such "protective custody" is a sad reflection indeed of how far we have desecrated nature's creation. Zoos have been as slow to address the psychological needs of the animals they keep as they have to question their own purpose. But times are changing; more and more people have begun to feel and see the world through the eyes of the animals. The cage bars are disappearing as we begin to empathize and come to realize that the fate of the animal kingdom is inextricably linked with the fate of humanity. The black panther in the cage is a mirror reflecting our own condition. And we are not helpless to do something about both.

10   But when we reach into the cage with our hearts, we may feel very differently about keeping animals in zoos or ever visiting a zoo again.

11   Do zoos educate the public adequately to political action and compassionate concern for the plight of wildlife and nature? Are they not too tame, sanitized, and beautiful? They are becoming facsimiles of how animals once were in the wild. Some zoo safari parks are run for profit and secondarily for entertainment. And zoos are also an illusion, a false assurance to the public that lions and cheetahs and tigers and elephants are plentiful and lead free and easy lives. Some amusement parks even have safari zoos purely for public entertainment. This is surely an unethical exploitation of wildlife.

12   Even the best of zoos cannot justify their existence if they do not sufficiently inform and even shock the public into compassionate concern and political action. I know of no zoo that exhibits crippled but otherwise healthy animals that have been maimed by trappers and hunters.

13   Regarding the claim that the best zoos are helping save species from extinction by breeding them in captivity, it may be best to let them become extinct if there is no place for them in the wild. Life in captivity can never fulfill any species or individual, because the animal *is* its natural environment, and no species lives in isolation from others. Certainly the better zoos have seminatural environments—miniswamps, artificial rivers, climatrons, and mixed-species exhibits. But to what end? For exhibition. They are not conserving nature by creating high-tech facsimiles thereof. And even if such artificial environments enhance the overall welfare and reproductivity of endangered species, where are their offspring to go? To other zoo collections.

14   I believe that even the best zoos and aquaria in the world are not doing an adequate job of nature conservation. They have taken more species from the wild than they have ever put back, and until this situation is dramatically reversed, zoos cannot make any claim to effective nature conservation. Breeding endangered species in captivity is animal preservation, not conservation, and animals preserved forever in a cage or synthetic habitat are at best unreal.

15   As for zoos' often high-blown research into exotic animal diseases, nutrition, and reproduction, all of this would be unnecessary if we had just left wildlife alone and respected their rights and protected their habitats.

16   Are zoos a necessary evil? Wildlife's last refuge? Sometimes I think so. Sometimes I think not. I respect the many people who are dedicated to good zoo management, research, species preservation, and veterinary medicine. But all this dedication may be seriously misplaced if we lose sight of the fact that the problems of zoo animals and the crisis of wildlife's threatened **annihilation** are primarily man-made.

17   Building better zoos at the expense of efforts to conserve nature is wrong. We should need no zoos and we are misguided if we do not work toward this end, however far into the future it might be. Zoos are not so much a necessary evil as they are a tragic mirror of an evil for which we may yet atone.

18   As it is estimated that at the current rate of habitat destruction, some 500,000 to 2 million plant and animal (including insect) species will soon be extinct, obviously captive breeding in zoos is not the answer. Habitat protection is the only solution, and all nations and peoples must be prepared to make the necessary adjustments and sacrifices if the health and vitality of the Earth is to be preserved.

annihilation

destruction

19   One of the best exhibits in any zoo that I have ever visited was a large mirror behind bars. The caption read: **Homo sapiens**, a dangerous, predatorial tool- and weapon-
making primate. Status: endangered by its own doing.

20   There can be no communion with our animal kin when they are held captive, no
matter what the justifications may be for their "protective custody." The zoo is a trick
mirror that can delude us into believing that we love and respect animals and are helping to preserve them. And like the animal circus, the zoo can have a pernicious influence on children's attitudes toward wild creatures. We cannot recognize or celebrate
the sanctity and dignity of nonhuman life under such conditions. There can be no communion: only amusement, curiosity, amazement, and perhaps sympathy. The depriva-
tion of these creatures and the loss of wildness and wilderness are ours also. When we
fail collectively to feel these things, and in the process come to accept and patronize the
zoo as some cultural norm, we lose something of our own humanity—that intuitive wisdom and a sense of reverence for all life that are the hallmarks of a truly civilized society.

Fox, *Inhumane Society: The American Way of Exploiting Animals*

Homo sapiens

species of modern
human beings

Getting Ready to Write

Reviewing the Reading

1. Describe the panther that Fox encountered. How did seeing this animal affect him?
2. For what purposes do zoos exist?
3. Name some fundamental faults with zoos. What needs have zoos failed to meet for their animals? How might this problem be fixed?
4. How does the author refute the argument that zoos save animals from extinction?
5. What does the author believe to be the real reason for the existence of zoos?

Examining the Reading: Using Idea Maps to Examine Persuasive Essays

One of the best ways to understand persuasive writing is to reduce the ideas in an essay to a simple map
or outline. Examining the major pieces of evidence in the essay will allow you to analyze the relationship among the ideas objectively. Use the following format to map the major steps of an argument. Fill
in the missing parts of the following idea map that organizes "The Captive Panther."

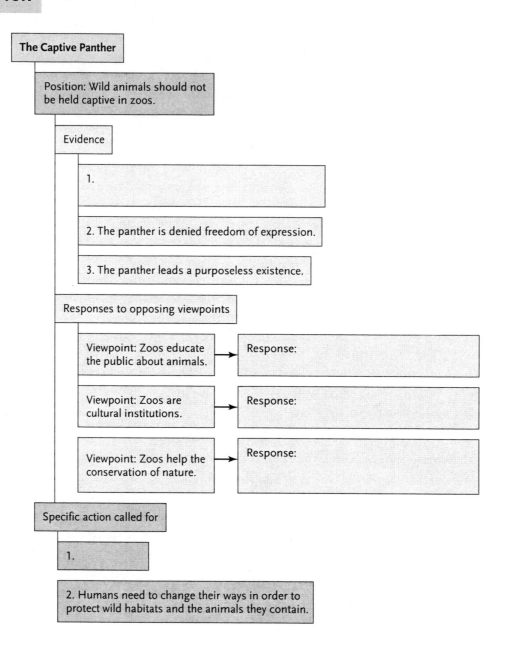

Thinking Critically: Evaluating Persuasive Writing

Persuasive writing is meant to be convincing. As you read a convincing piece, it is easy to be swept along by the writer's line of reasoning. Fox begins his essay with a graphic description that tugs at the reader's emotions. Not all writers do this, but when they do, it is difficult not to accept their arguments.

The best way to read persuasive writing is with a critical, questioning attitude. As you read, ask yourself questions such as these: Why should I believe this? How do I know this is correct? Mark and annotate as you read. Place question marks next to ideas you want to question or consider further. Use the questions listed in Table 10-1 to evaluate the evidence a writer provides.

Using the questions in Table 10-1, evaluate the strength of the arguments that Fox presents. Write a paragraph on each argument explaining why you accept or reject it.

Table 10-1 Critical Questions

Facts and Statistics

Are they relevant?
Are they up-to-date?
Do they logically connect with the issue in question?

Quotations from Authorities

Are the persons quoted experts?
Would other experts agree?
What do the quotations contribute to the writer's ideas?

Examples

Is each example relevant to the issue?
Does each example illustrate something that is typical or exceptional?
Can you think of other examples that would confirm or disprove the writer's position?

Personal Experience

Is the writer's personal experience relevant to the issue?
Is the writer's personal experience typical of most people's?
Can you think of other personal experiences that would confirm or disprove the writer's position?

Strengthening Your Vocabulary

Part A: Using the word's context, word parts, or a dictionary, write a brief definition of each of the following words or phrases as it is used in the reading.

1. vicarious (paragraph 1) _____

   _____

2. indelibly (paragraph 1) _____

   _____

3. insinuating (paragraph 4) _____

   _____

4. inexorably (paragraph 5) _____

   _____

5. desecrated (paragraph 9) _____

   _____

6. pernicious (paragraph 20) _____

   _____

7. reverence (paragraph 20) _____

   _____

Part B: Choose one of the above words and draw a word map.

Reacting to Ideas: Discussion and Journal Writing

1. Analyze the audience for whom the essay is written. Does Fox perceive his audience as agreeing, disagreeing, or neutral?

2. What is the most and least convincing evidence Fox offers?
3. Why did Fox begin the essay with the description of the panther?
4. What is the difference between animal preservation and animal conservation?
5. Do you agree that the zoo is "a trick mirror," which deludes us into believing that we love and respect animals?

Writing About the Reading
Paragraph Options

1. Write a paragraph describing an animal you have observed. Reveal your attitude toward the animal through your description.
2. Write a paragraph about an effort in your community to conserve nature or preserve the habitat of wildlife. How have people in your area reacted to this effort?
3. Fox mentions a sign he saw which stated that the human species is "Endangered by its own doing." Write a paragraph that explains this statement and reflects your opinion toward this statement.

Essay Options

4. Write a persuasive essay to your state or local officials (a) urging the closing of a nearby zoo, (b) the building of a more humane zoo, or (c) the expansion of the existing zoo.
5. Write a persuasive essay arguing for or against using animals in a circus or in other animal performances such as at Sea World.
6. Write an essay for or against people wearing coats made of animal fur.

Thinking Before Reading
Reading 2: Predators on the Prowl

Marc Peyser wrote this article, "Predators on the Prowl" for the January 8, 1996 edition of *Newsweek*. He describes arguments for and against the hunting of mountain lions. As you read, notice the types of evidence he uses to show the various sides of this issue.

1. Preview the reading.
2. Connect the reading to your own experience by answering the following questions:
   a. Have you ever encountered a wild animal? What did you do?
   b. How do you feel about hunting for sport?

READING

Predators on the Prowl
Marc Peyser

1   For Iris Kenna, Cuyamaca Rancho State Park near San Diego was like a second home. By day, she strolled its fields in search of exotic birds. At night, the 56-year-old high-school counselor sometimes slept under the stars. But one morning almost exactly a year ago, Kenna encountered something unfamiliar, and it saw her first. Without warning, a 140-pound male mountain lion pounced on her from behind. The struggle was brief. The animal dragged the dying, 5-foot-4 Kenna into dense brush to hide her from competing **predators**. Rangers found her only after two hikers spotted a pair of

predators

animals that hunt, kill, and eat other animals

glasses, a backpack and a human tooth by the path she had been on. The rangers followed a trail of her clothes for 30 yards until they came to Kenna's body. The back of her scalp was ripped off; the rest of her was riddled with bites. No one had heard a scream, or even a roar.

2   Kenna is the most vivid symbol of an angry, shifting debate over how people and predators can coexist. In the high-growth Western states, many residents love living near the wild, and they are inclined to preserve it no matter what the risks. But violent deaths like Kenna's—and a string of other mountain-lion attacks—are making a powerful case for fighting back. Californians will vote in March [1996] on opening the way to mountain-lion hunting, which has been prohibited there for more than 20 years.* But Oregon, Arizona and Colorado recently changed their hunting laws to ensure that predatory animals—including bears, wolves and coyotes—would be protected. "It's overwhelmingly popular to have these animals in our **ecosystems**," says Tom Dougherty of the National Wildlife Federation. "But if they're in your backyard, some people aren't loving it."

ecosystems

groups of organisms that depend on each other for survival

3   The most acute mountain-lion problem is in California. That's partly because the state's human population has doubled every 25 years this century. As more people built more houses, they usurped territory once largely inhabited by wild animals. But the mountain lion (alternately called cougar, puma and panther) has also been questionably served by environmentalists. In 1972, preservation-minded Californians banned hunting the majestic animals (except when they pose an imminent danger to people or livestock). The cougar population ballooned, from an estimated 2,400 lions to 6,000 today. Without hunters to thin the ranks, increased competition for food has sent hungry

mountain lions to suburban backyards, shopping centers and elementary schools in search of nourishment—a deer or, lacking that, a collie. Even children have been mauled. "People are afraid to go on a picnic without taking a firearm," says state Sen. Tim Leslie, a prominent anti-cougar advocate. In the wake of Kenna's death, Gov. Pete Wilson authorized the March [1996] ballot initiative—one that could lead to controlling the cougar population.

4   But in other places, sentiment favors animals at least as much as people. A survey of Coloradans living near the Rockies found that 80 percent believe that development in mountain-lion territory should be restricted. What's more, when wildlife authorities killed the cougar that killed a woman named Barbara Schoener in California in 1994, donors raised $21,000 to care for the cougar's cub—but only $9,000 for Schoener's two children. Arizona recently outlawed trapping cougars (though hunting is legal), while Colorado and Oregon don't allow mountain-lion hunters to use bait or dogs. "There's a value shift about how people view wildlife, a high willingness to accept mountain lions on the **urban fringe**—even if they kill people," says Michael Manfredo, who conducted the survey at Colorado State University. That open-mindedness will certainly be tested as Westerners reintroduce predators—grizzly bears in Idaho, wolves in New Mexico and in Yellowstone National Park. It's a jungle out there—and it's getting more jungle-like every day.

urban fringe

edges of a city

*The measure did not pass and the ban on mountain-lion hunting remains in California. However, during the 2005–2006 session, a state assemblyman once again proposed legislation to lift the ban. The bill was in committee as of this book's publication.

Getting Ready to Write
Reviewing the Reading

1. What happened to Iris Kenna? Why is her story significant?
2. Where is the hunting of predators illegal, according to the reading?
3. Summarize the mountain lion problem in California.
4. What are some other names for the mountain lion?
5. What are some future challenges in the debate over introducing predators to the wild?

Examining the Reading: Using Idea Maps to Examine Argument Essays

One of the best ways to understand a piece of persuasive writing is to reduce the ideas in it to a simple map or outline. Examining the major pieces of evidence in an essay will allow you to analyze the relationship among the ideas objectively. Use the following format to map the major steps of an argument. Fill in the missing parts of this idea map that organizes "Predators on the Prowl."

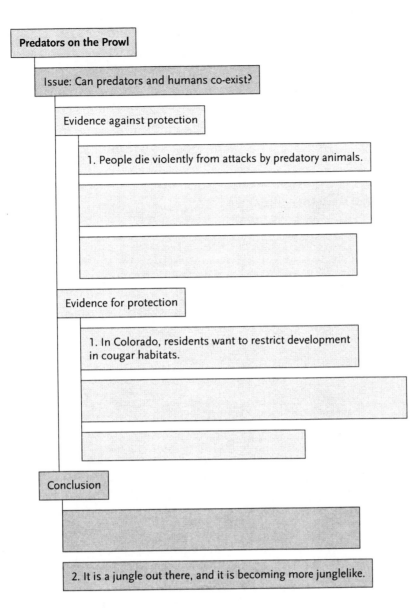

Thinking Critically: Evaluating Alternative Viewpoints

Using the questions listed in Table 10-1, evaluate the evidence and arguments presented by Peyser. What types of evidence are offered? Which evidence is most relevant? Which arguments are most convincing? How would you find out more about this issue?

Strengthening Your Vocabulary

Part A: Using the word's context, word parts, or a dictionary, write a brief definition of each of the following words or phrases as it is used in the reading.

1. riddled (paragraph 1) _____

_____

2. symbol (paragraph 2) _____

_____

3. acute (paragraph 3) _____

_____

4. usurped (paragraph 3) _____

_____

5. imminent (paragraph 3) _____

_____

6. sentiment (paragraph 4) _____

_____

Part B: Choose one of the above words and draw a word map.

Reacting to Ideas: Discussion and Journal Writing

1. Why do you think the public contributed more money to caring for the cougar's cub than to caring for Barbara Schoener's children? To which fund would you prefer to contribute?
2. What do you think those in favor of protecting predators would say to Iris Kenna's family if the state of California urged tighter restrictions on predators? What arguments might those in favor of protection raise?
3. Who do you think should have first rights to an area of land—the people who own it or the animals who live there?

Writing About the Reading
Paragraph Options

1. Write a paragraph about the use of public elections (votes) to decide matters such as mountain lion hunting. Should these kinds of issues be left to legislators to decide? Should the general public vote on them?
2. Write a paragraph about development in your area. Do you think builders are encroaching on too many wild areas? How does your community react to development?
3. Michael Manfredo is quoted in the article as saying, "It's a jungle out there—and it's getting more junglelike everyday." Write a paragraph that explains this quote. Describe how this notion affects your life.

Essay Options

4. Write an essay discussing whether the author is for or against restricting wildlife predators. Refer to sections of the reading to support your points.
5. What is your position on the issue of restricting wildlife predators? If you are in favor of it, write an essay describing what laws should be enacted, restrictions imposed, or guarantees offered. If you oppose restriction, what actions should be taken to protect wildlife predators?
6. Write an essay describing what you think Iris Kenna's family would say to those who want to protect predators. Summarize the arguments they might use.

Writing About the Readings
"The Captive Panther"
"Predators on the Prowl"

Both "The Captive Panther" and "Predators on the Prowl" deal with wild animals and their relationship to humans. Using these two readings as sources, write an essay discussing the problem of wild animals interacting with humans. What issues are involved? What problems arise?

Revision Checklist

1. Is your essay appropriate for your audience? Does it give them the background information they need? Will it interest them?
2. Will your essay accomplish your purpose?

3. Have you narrowed your topic so that you can cover your subject thoroughly in your essay?
4. Is your main point clearly expressed in a thesis statement in the introductory paragraph? Does your introductory paragraph capture the reader's interest and lead into the body of the essay?.
5. Does each paragraph of your essay have a topic sentence that supports your essay's main point?
6. Is each paragraph's topic sentence supported by relevant and sufficient detail?
7. Are your paragraphs arranged in a logical sequence and connected by transitional words and phrases?
8. Is the tone of your essay appropriate for your purpose and audience?
9. Does your conclusion reemphasize your thesis statement and draw the essay to a close?
10. Does your title identify the topic and interest the reader?

For Argument Essays

11. Have you analyzed the position your audience takes on the issue about which you are writing?
12. Have you researched your topic to obtain adequate and convincing evidence?
13. Does your thesis statement identify the issue and state your position on it?
14. Does your thesis statement foreshadow your supporting points?
15. Have you provided convincing evidence?
16. Have you proofread?

10i CHAPTER REVIEW AND PRACTICE

Chapter Review

What is an argument?	An argument is a line of reasoning intended to persuade the reader to accept a viewpoint or take an action.
Define the three parts of an argument.	1. **Issue**—The problem or controversy that the argument addresses 2. **Position**—The point of view on the issue 3. **Support**—The reasons or evidence that indicates the position should be accepted
What should your topic sentence contain?	It should identify the issue and state your position on the issue.
What are the two primary types of support?	The two types of primary support are reasons and evidence.
What are the common types of evidence?	Common evidence includes facts and statistics, quotations from authorities, examples, and personal experience.
Why is research sometimes necessary?	Research is sometimes necessary to locate sufficient evidence to support your position.
What are the guidelines for writing argument essays?	1. Choose an appropriate placement of your thesis statement. 2. Develop convincing support. 3. The introduction should interest the reader; the conclusion should present a final call to action or a review of key points.
Why should you analyze your audience?	How you write your essay and the types of evidence you offer depends on your audience.

STUDENT ESSAY

The following student essay was written by Mark Simmons in response to this assignment:

Mary Sherry's "In Praise of the 'F' Word" invites controversy by attacking the popular notion that failing students is a harmful practice. Select another controversial issue, one that you feel strongly about. Conduct library research to gather evidence in support of your position, and brainstorm with others to identify some points that might be raised by those who oppose your view. Then, using logic and formal, documented evidence, convince readers that your viewpoint is valid.

Your instructor may not ask you to include research in your essay. But, if you're asked—as Mark was—to research your paper and to provide *formal documentation*, you'll want to pay special attention to the way Mark credits his sources. (In *your* paper, the Works Cited list should be double-spaced— along with the rest of the paper—and placed at the end on a separate page.)

Whether or not you include research in your paper, the annotations on Mark's essay and the comments following it will help you determine how well it applies the principles of argumentation-persuasion.

Compulsory National Service
by Mark Simmons

Beginning of two-paragraph introduction

1   Our high school history class spent several weeks studying the events of the 1960s. The most interesting thing about that decade was the spirit of service and social commitment among young people. In the '60s, young people thought about issues beyond themselves; they joined the Peace Corps, worked in poverty-stricken Appalachian communities, and participated in freedom marches against segregation. Most young people today, despite their concern with careers and getting ahead, would also like an opportunity to make a worthwhile contribution to society.

Common knowledge: No need to document

2   Convinced that many young adults are indeed eager for such an opportunity, President Bill Clinton's administration implemented in 1994 a pilot program of voluntary national service. The following year, the program was formalized, placed under the management of the Corporation for National Service (CNS), and given the name AmeriCorps. In the years 1994–2003, approximately 250,000 AmeriCorps volunteers provided varied assistance in communities across the country ("AmeriCorps: Who We Are"). Such voluntary national service was also endorsed by President George W. Bush. Following the devastating terrorist attacks on September 11, 2001, President Bush urged Americans to volunteer as a way of assisting in the nation's recovery and of demonstrating a spirit of national unity. He issued an executive order in early 2002 establishing USA Freedom Corps, an organization seeking to persuade Americans to perform 4,000 hours of volunteer service over a lifetime (Hutcheson A2). In general, programs such as USA Freedom Corps and the more established AmeriCorps hold out so much promise that it seems only natural to go one step further and make young people's participation in these programs or some kind of national service mandatory. By instituting a program of compulsory national service, the country could tap youth's idealistic desire to make a difference. Such a system would yield significant benefits.

Parenthetic citation of unpaged anonymous material obtained through the Internet

Start of two-sentence thesis

Definition paragraph

3   What exactly is meant by compulsory national service? Traditionally, it has tended to mean that everyone between the ages of seventeen and twenty-five would serve the country for two years. These young people could choose between two major options: military service or a public-service corps. They could serve their time at any point within an eight-year span. The unemployed or the uncertain could join immediately after high

school; college-bound students could complete their education before joining the national service. Years ago, Senator Sam Nunn and Representative Dave McCurdy gave a new twist to the definition of compulsory national service. They proposed a plan that would require all high school graduates applying for federal aid for college tuition to serve either in the military or in a Citizens Corps. Anyone in the Citizens Corps would be required to work full-time at public-service duties for one or two years. During that time, participants would receive a weekly stipend, and, at the end, be given a voucher worth $10,000 for each year of civilian service. The voucher could then be applied toward college credit, employment training, or a down payment on a house (Sudo 9).

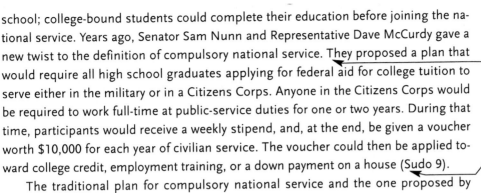

Beginning of summary of a source's ideas

Parenthetic citation—page number and author are given since the author is not cited earlier in the sentence

4   The traditional plan for compulsory national service and the one proposed by Nunn and McCurdy are just two of many variations that have been discussed over the years. While this country debates the concept, some nations such as France have gone ahead and accepted it enthusiastically. The idea could be workable in this country too. Unfortunately, opponents are doing all they can to prevent the idea from taking hold. They contend, first of all, that the program would cost too much. A great deal of money, they argue, would be spent administering the program, paying young people's wages, and providing housing for participants. Another argument against compulsory national service is that it would demoralize young people; supposedly, the plan would prevent the young from moving ahead with their careers and would make them feel as though they were engaged in work that offered no personal satisfaction. A third argument is that compulsory service would lay the groundwork for a dictatorship. The picture is painted of an army of young people, controlled by the government, much like the Hitler Youth of World War II.

Topic sentence

Beginning of summary of three points made by the opposing viewpoint

5   Despite opponents' claims that compulsory national service would involve exorbitant costs, the program would not have to be that expensive to run. AmeriCorps has already provided an excellent model for achieving substantial benefits at reasonable cost. For example, a study conducted by universities in Iowa and Michigan showed that each dollar spent on AmeriCorps programs yielded $2.60 in reduced welfare costs, increased earnings, and other benefits (Garland 120). Also, the sums required for wages and housing could be reduced considerably through payments made by the towns, cities, and states using the corps' services. And the economic benefits of the program could be significant. AmeriCorps's official website gives an idea of the current scope of the program's activities. Volunteers provide crucial services including building affordable homes for families, reducing crime in neighborhoods, responding to natural disasters, and tutoring children ("AmeriCorps"). A compulsory national corps could also clean up litter, provide day care services, staff libraries, immunize children, and care for the country's growing elderly population (Clinton; Eng). All these projects would help solve many of the problems that plague our nation, and they would probably cost less than if they were handled by often inefficient government bureaucracies.

Topic sentence: Refutation of first point

Information comes from two sources. Sources, separated by a semicolon, are given in the order they appear in the Works Cited list. First source is unpaged electronic text. No page given for second source because it runs only one page.

6   Also, rather than undermining the spirit of young people, as opponents contend, the program would probably boost their morale. Many young people feel enormous pressure and uncertainty; they are not sure whether they want to find a job or further their education. Compulsory national service could give these young people much-needed breathing space. As Edward Lewis, president of St. Mary's College, says,

Topic sentence: Refutation of second point

Attribution giving author's full name and area of expertise

Full-sentence quotation is preceded by a comma and begins with a capital letter

Where secondary source was quoted

Quotation is blended into the sentence (no comma and the quotation begins with a lowercased word)

Quotation with ellipsis

Just the page number is provided because the author's name is cited in the preceding attribution

Parenthetic citation for electronic source having two authors. No page given since electronic text is unpaged.

Topic sentence: Refutation of third point

"Many students are not ready for college at seventeen or eighteen. This kind of program responds to that need" (qtd. in Fowler 3). Robert Coles, psychiatrist and social activist, argues that a public service stint enriches participants' lives in yet another way. Coles points out that young people often have little sense of the job market. When they get involved in community service, though, they frequently "discover an area of interest . . . that launches them on a career" (93). Equally important, compulsory national service can provide an emotional boost for the young; all of them would experience the pride that comes from working hard, reaching goals, acquiring skills, and handling responsibilities (Waldman and Wofford). A positive mind-set would also result from the sense of community that would be created by serving in the national service. All young people—rich or poor, educated or not, regardless of sex and social class—would come together and perceive not their differences but their common interests and similarities (Waldman and Wofford). As President Clinton proclaimed at the Year 2000 swearing-in of AmeriCorps's recruits in Philadelphia, AmeriCorps gives volunteers a chance "to tear down barriers of distrust and misunderstanding and old-fashioned ignorance, and build a genuine American community" (Clinton).

7   Finally, in contrast to what opponents claim, compulsory national service would not signal the start of a dictatorship. Although the service would be required, young people would have complete freedom to choose any two years between the ages of seventeen and twenty-five. They would also have complete freedom to choose the branch of the military or public service corps that suits them best. And the corps would not need to be outfitted in military uniforms or to live in barrack-like camps. It could be set up like a regular job, with young people living at home as much as possible, following a nine-to-five schedule, enjoying all the personal freedoms that would ordinarily be theirs. Also, a dictatorship would no more likely emerge from compulsory national service than it has from our present military system. We would still have a series of checks and balances to prohibit the taking of power by one group or individual. We should also keep in mind that our system is different from that of fascist regimes; our long tradition of personal liberty makes improbable the seizing of absolute power by one person or faction. A related but even more important point to remember is that freedom does not mean people are guaranteed the right to pursue only their individual needs. That is mistaking selfishness for freedom. And, as everyone knows, selfishness leads only to misery. The national service would not take away freedom. On the contrary, serving in the corps would help young people grasp this larger concept of freedom, a concept that is badly needed to counteract the deadly "look out for number one" attitude that is spreading like a poison across the nation.

Beginning of two-paragraph conclusion

8   Perhaps there will never be a time like the 1960s when so many young people were concerned with remaking the world. Still, a good many of today's young people want meaningful work. They want to feel that what they do makes a difference. A program of compulsory national service would harness this idealism and help young people realize the best in themselves. Such a program would also help resolve some of the country's most critical social problems.

Attribution leading to a long quotation. Attribution is followed by a colon since the lead-in is a full sentence. If the lead-in isn't a full sentence, use a comma after the attribution.

9   Almost two decades ago, political commentator Donald Eberly expressed his belief in the power of national service. Urging the inauguration of such a program, Eberly wrote the following:

The promise of national service can be manifested in many ways: in cleaner air and fewer forest fires; in well-cared-for infants and old folks; in a better-educated citizenry and better-satisfied work force; perhaps in a more peaceful world. National service has a lot of promise. It's a promise well worth keeping. (651)

Several years later, President Clinton took office, gave his support to the concept, and AmeriCorps was born. This advocacy of public service was then championed, at least in word, by President Bush. During his administration, however, AmeriCorps was threatened by deep budget cuts advocated by opponents of the program and its Clintonian legacy. Fortunately, despite these measures, Congress voted in 2003 with overwhelming bipartisan support to save AmeriCorps and salvage a portion of its budget ("Timely Help"). In the words of a Philadelphia Inquirer editorial, "The civic yield from that investment is incalculable" ("Ill Served"). An efficient and successful program of voluntary service, AmeriCorps has paved the way. Now seems to be the perfect time to expand the concept and make compulsory national service a reality.

Works Cited

"AmeriCorps: Who We Are." AmeriCorps. The Corporation for National Service. 11 July 2003: 5 pars. 26 Jan. 2004 <http://www.americorps.org/whoweare.html>.

Clinton, William. "Remarks by the President to AmeriCorps." AmeriCorps. The Corporation for National Service. 11 Oct. 2000: 28 pars. 7 Jan. 2004 <http://www.americorps.org/news/pr/ potus_remarks101100.html>.

Coles, Robert. The Call of Service. Boston: Houghton Mifflin, 1993.

Eberly, Donald. "What the President Should Do About National Service." Vital Speeches of the Day 15 Aug. 1989: 561–63.

Eng, Lily. "Congressional Pressure Puts AmeriCorps Under the Gun." Philadelphia Inquirer 18 Apr. 1996, late ed.: B1.

Fowler, Margaret. "New Interest in National Youth Corps." New York Times 16 May 1989, natl. ed.: A25.

Garland, Susan B. "A Social Program CEOs Want to Save." Business Week 19 June 1996: 120–21.

Hutcheson, Ron. "Bush Moves to Establish His New Volunteer Program." Philadelphia Inquirer 31 Jan. 2002: A2.

"Ill Served." Editorial. Philadelphia Inquirer Online 27 June 2003. 1 Mar. 2004 <http://www.philly.com/mld/inquirer/ news/editorial/6180250.htm>.

Sudo, Phil. "Mandatory National Service?" Scholastic Update 23 Feb. 1990: 9.

"Timely Help for AmeriCorps." Editorial. New York Times Online 17 July 2003: 4 pars. 28 Feb 2004 <http:// www.nytimes.com/2003/07/17/opinion/17THU4.html>.

Waldman, Steven, and Harris Wofford. "AmeriCorps the Beautiful? Habitat for Conservative Values." Policy Review Sept.–Oct. 1997: 49 pars. CD-ROM. EBSCOhost.

Long quotation is indented ten spaces. Don't leave any extra space within, above, or below the quotation.

For an indented quotation, the period is placed *before* the parenthetic citation.

In *your* paper, the Works Cited list would be double-spaced like the rest of the paper, with no extra space after the heading or between entries. Also, in *your* paper, the Works Cited would start on a *separate* page.

Anonymous material obtained on the Internet. Names of website and of sponsoring organization appear. Electronic text is 5 paragraphs long. Web address always required.

Published speech

Authored material on the Internet. Dates the material was published and accessed, respectively, are provided.

Book by one author

Newspaper article whose text is only one page

Article from weekly magazine

Internet article with unnumbered paragraphs or pages

Article (by two authors) from scholarly journal on CD-ROM

COMMENTARY

Blend of Argumentation and Persuasion.

In his essay, Mark tackles a controversial issue. He takes the position that compulsory national service would benefit both the country as a whole and its young people in particular. Mark's essay is a good example of the way argumentation and persuasion often mix: Although the paper presents Mark's position in a logical, well-reasoned manner (argumentation), it also appeals to readers' personal values and suggests a course of action (persuasion).

Audience Analysis

When planning the essay, Mark realized that his audience—his composition class—would consist largely of two kinds of readers. Some, not sure of their views, would be inclined to agree with him if he presented his case well. Others would probably be reluctant to accept his view. Because of this mixed audience, Mark knew he couldn't depend on *pathos* (an appeal to emotion) to convince readers. Rather, his argument had to rely mainly on *logos* (reason) and *ethos* (credibility). So Mark organized his essay around a series of logical arguments—many of them backed by expert opinion—and he evoked his own authority by drawing on his knowledge of history and his "inside" knowledge of young people.

Introduction and Thesis

Mark introduces his subject by discussing an earlier decade when large numbers of young people worked for social change. Mark's references to the Peace Corps, community work, and freedom marches reinforce his image as a knowledgeable source and establish a context for his position. These historical references, combined with the comments about AmeriCorps, the program of voluntary national service, lead into the two-sentence thesis at the end of the two-paragraph introduction: "By instituting a program of compulsory national service, the country could tap youth's idealistic desire to make a difference. Such a system would yield significant benefits."

The second paragraph in the introduction also illustrates Mark's first use of outside sources. Because the assignment called for research in support of an argument, Mark went to the library and online and identified sources that helped him defend his position. If Mark's instructor had required extensive investigation of an issue, Mark would have been obligated both to dig more deeply into his subject and to use more scholarly and specialized sources. But given the instructor's requirements, Mark proceeded just as he should have: He searched out expert opinion that supported his viewpoint; he presented that evidence clearly; he documented his sources carefully.

Background Paragraph and Use of Outside Sources

The third paragraph provides a working *definition* of compulsory national service by presenting two common interpretations of the concept. Such background information guarantees that Mark's readers will share his understanding of the essay's central concept.

Acknowledging the Opposing Viewpoint

Having explained the meaning of compulsory national service, Mark is now in a good position to launch his argument. Even though he wasn't required to research the opposing viewpoint, Mark wisely decided to get together with some friends to brainstorm some issues that might be raised by the dissenting view. He acknowledges this position in the *topic sentence* of the essay's fourth paragraph: "Unfortunately, opponents are doing all they can to prevent the idea from taking hold." Next he summarizes the main points the dissenting opinion might advance: compulsory national service would be expensive, demoralizing to young people, and dangerously authoritarian. Mark uses the rest of the essay to counter these criticisms.

Refutation

The next three paragraphs (5–7) *refute* the opposing stance and present Mark's evidence for his position. Mark structures the essay so that readers can follow his *counterargument* with ease. Each paragraph argues against one opposing point and begins with a *topic sentence* that serves as Mark's response to the dissenting view. Note the way the italicized portion of each topic sentence recalls a dissenting point cited earlier: "Despite opponents' claims that *compulsory national service would involve exorbitant costs,* the program would not have to be that expensive to run" (paragraph 5); "Also, rather than *undermining the spirit of young people,* as opponents contend, the program would probably boost their morale" (6); "Finally, in contrast to what opponents claim, *compulsory national service would not signal the start of a dictatorship*" (7). Mark also guides the reader through the various points in the refutation by using *transitions* within paragraphs: "*And* the economic benefits . . . could be significant" (5); "*Equally important,* compulsory national service could provide an emotional boost . . ." (6); "*Also,* a dictatorship would no more likely emerge . . ." (7).

Throughout the three-paragraph refutation, Mark uses outside sources to lend power to his argument. If the assignment had called for in-depth research, he would have cited facts, statistics, and case studies to develop this section of his essay. Given the nature of the assignment, though, Mark's reliance on expert opinion is perfectly acceptable.

Mark successfully incorporates material from these outside sources into his refutation. He doesn't, for example, string one quotation numbingly after another; instead he usually develops his refutation by *summarizing* expert opinion and saves *direct quotations* for points that deserve emphasis. Moreover, whenever Mark quotes or summarizes a source, he provides clear signals to indicate that the material is indeed borrowed.

Some Problems with the Refutation

Overall, Mark's three-paragraph refutation is strong, but it would have been even more effective if the paragraphs had been resequenced. As it now stands, the last paragraph in the refutation (7) seems anticlimactic. Unlike the preceding two paragraphs, which are developed through fairly extensive reference to outside sources, paragraph 7 depends entirely on Mark's personal feelings and interpretations for its support. Of course, Mark was under no obligation to provide research in all sections of the paper. Even so, the refutation would have been more persuasive if Mark had placed the final paragraph in the refutation in a less emphatic position. He could, for example, have put it first or second in the sequence, saving for last either of the other two more convincing paragraphs.

You may also have felt that there's another problem with the third paragraph in the refutation. Here, Mark seems to lose control of his counterargument. Beginning with "And, as everyone knows . . . ," Mark falls into the *logical fallacy* called *begging the question*. He shouldn't assume that everyone agrees that a selfish life inevitably brings misery. He also indulges in charged emotionalism when he refers—somewhat melodramatically—to the "deadly 'look out for number one' attitude that is spreading like a poison across the nation."

Inductive Reasoning

In part, Mark arrived at his position *inductively*, through a series of *inferences* or *inductive leaps*. He started with some personal *observations* about the nation and its young people. Then, to support those observations, he added his friends' insights as well as information gathered through research. Combined, all this material led him to the general *conclusion* that compulsory national service would be both workable and beneficial.

Combining Patterns of Development

To develop his argument, Mark draws on several patterns of development. The third paragraph relies on *definition* to clarify what is meant by compulsory national service. The first paragraph of both the introduction and conclusion *compares* and *contrasts* young people of the 1960s with those of today. And, to support his position, Mark uses a kind of *causal analysis;* he both speculates on the likely consequences of compulsory national service and cites expert opinion to illustrate the validity of some of those speculations.

Conclusion

Despite some problems in the final section of his refutation, Mark comes up with an effective two-paragraph conclusion for his essay. In the first closing paragraph, he echoes the point made in the introduction about the 1960s and restates his thesis. That done, he moves to the second paragraph of his conclusion. There, he quotes a dramatic statement from a knowledgeable source, cites efforts to undermine AmeriCorps, and ends by pointing out that AmeriCorps has earned the respect of some unlikely supporters. All that Mark does in this final paragraph lends credibility to the crisp assertion and suggested course of action at the very end of his essay.

Revising the First Draft

Given the complex nature of his argument, Mark found that he had to revise his essay several times. One way to illustrate some of the changes he made is to compare his final introduction with the original draft reprinted here:

Original Version of the Introduction

"There's no free lunch." "You can't get something for nothing." "You have to earn your way." In America, these sayings are not really true. In America, we gladly take but give back little. In America, we receive economic opportunity, legal protection, the right to vote, and, most of all, a personal freedom unequaled throughout the world. How do we repay our country for such gifts? In most cases, we don't. This unfair relationship must be changed. The best way to make a start is to institute a system of national compulsory service for young people. This system would be of real benefit to the country and its citizens.

When Mark met with a classmate for a peer review session, he found that his partner had a number of helpful suggestions for revising various sections of the essay. But Mark's partner focused most of her comments on the essay's introduction because she felt it needed special attention. Following his classmate's suggestion, Mark deleted the original introduction's references to Americans in general. He made this change because he wanted readers to know—from the very start of the essay—that the paper would focus not on all Americans but on American youth. To reinforce this emphasis, he also added the point about the social commitment characteristic of young people in the 1960s. This reference to an earlier period gave the discussion an important historical perspective and lent a note of authority to Mark's argument. The decision to mention the '60s also helped Mark realize that his introduction should point out more recent developments—specifically, the promise of AmeriCorps. Mark was pleased to see that adding this new material not only gave the introduction a sharper focus, but it also provided a smoother lead-in to his thesis.

These are just a few of the many changes Mark made while reworking his essay. Because he budgeted his time carefully, he was able to revise thoroughly. With the exception of some weak spots in the refutation, Mark's essay is well-reasoned and convincing.

ACTIVITIES: ARGUMENTATION-PERSUASION

Prewriting Activities

1. Imagine you're writing two essays: One *defines* hypocrisy; the other *contrasts* license and freedom. Identify an audience for each essay (college students, professors, teenagers, parents, employers, employees, or some other group). Then jot down how each essay might argue the merits of certain ways of behaving.

2. Following are several thesis statements for argumentation-persuasion essays. For each thesis, determine whether the three audiences indicated in parentheses are apt to be supportive, wavering, or hostile. Then select *one* thesis and use group brainstorming to identify, for each audience, specific points you would make to persuade each group.
   a. Students should not graduate from college until they have passed a comprehensive exam in their majors (*college students, their parents, college officials*).
   b. Abandoned homes owned by the city should be sold to low-income residents for a nominal fee (*city officials, low-income residents, general citizens*).
   c. The town should pass a law prohibiting residents who live near the reservoir from using pesticides on their lawns (*environmentalists, homeowners, members of the town council*).
   d. Faculty advisors to college newspapers should have the authority to prohibit the publication of articles that reflect negatively on the school (*alumni, college officials, student journalists*).

Revising Activities

3. Each set of statements that follows contains at least one of the logical fallacies described earlier in the. Identify the fallacy or fallacies in each set and explain why the statements are invalid.

a. Grades are irrelevant to learning. Students are in college to get an education, not good grades. The university should eliminate grading altogether.

b. The best policy is to put juvenile offenders in jail so that they can get a taste of reality. Otherwise, they will repeat their crimes again and again.

c. So-called sex education programs do nothing to decrease the rate of teenage pregnancy. Further expenditures on these programs should be curtailed.

d. If we allow abortion, people will think it's acceptable to kill the homeless or pull the plug on sick people—two groups that are also weak and frail.

e. The curfews that some towns impose on teenagers are as repressive as the curfews in totalitarian countries.

4. Following is the introduction from the first draft of an essay advocating the elimination of mandatory dress codes in public schools. Revise the paragraph, being sure to consider these questions: How effectively does the writer deal with the opposing viewpoint? Does the paragraph encourage those who might disagree with the writer to read on? Why or why not? Do you see any logical fallacies in the writer's thinking? Where? Does the writer introduce anything that veers away from the point being discussed? Where? Before revising, you may find it helpful to do some brainstorming—individually or in a group—to find ways to strengthen the paragraph.

After reworking the paragraph, take a few minutes to consider how the rest of the essay might unfold. What persuasive strategies could be used? How could Rogerian argument win over readers? What points could be made? What action could be urged in the effort to build a convincing argument?

In three nearby towns recently, high school administrators joined forces to take an outrageously strong stand against students' constitutional rights. Acting like fascists, they issued an edict in the form of a preposterous dress code that prohibits students from wearing expensive jewelry, designer jeans, leather jackets—anything that the administrators, in their supposed wisdom, consider ostentatious. Perhaps the next thing they'll want to do is forbid students to play rock music at school dances. What prompted the administrators' dictatorial prohibition against certain kinds of clothing? Somehow or other, they got it into their heads that having no restrictions on the way students dress creates an unhealthy environment, where students vie with each other for the flashiest attire. Students and parents alike should protest this and any other dress code. If such codes go into effect, we might as well throw out the Constitution.

READING

Mary Sherry

Following her graduation from Dominican University in 1962 with a degree in English, Mary Sherry (1940–) wrote freelance articles and advertising copy while raising her family. Over the years, a love of writing and an interest in education have been integral to all that Sherry does professionally. Founder and owner of a small research and publishing firm in Minnesota, she has taught creative and remedial writing to adults for more than twenty years. The following selection first appeared as a 1991 "My Turn" column in *Newsweek*.

Pre-Reading Journal Entry

Imagine you had a son or daughter who didn't take school seriously. How would you go about motivating the child to value academic success? Would your strategies differ depending on the age and gender of the child? If so, how and why? What other factors might influence your approach? Use your journal to respond to these questions.

In Praise of the "F" Word

1 Tens of thousands of 18-year-olds will graduate this year and be handed meaningless diplomas. These diplomas won't look any different from those awarded their luckier classmates. Their validity will be questioned only when their employers discover that these graduates are semiliterate.

2 Eventually a fortunate few will find their way into educational repair shops—adult-literacy programs, such as the one where I teach basic grammar and writing. There, high-school graduates and high-school dropouts pursuing graduate-equivalency certificates will learn the skills they should have learned in school. They will also discover they have been cheated by our educational system.

3 As I teach, I learn a lot about our schools. Early in each session I ask my students to write about an unpleasant experience they had in school. No writers' block here! "I wish someone would have had made me stop doing drugs and made me study." "I liked to party and no one seemed to care." "I was a good kid and didn't cause any trouble, so they just passed me along even though I didn't read well and couldn't write." And so on.

4 I am your basic do-gooder, and prior to teaching this class I blamed the poor academic skills our kids have today on drugs, divorce and other impediments to concentration necessary for doing well in school. But, as I rediscover each time I walk into the classroom, before a teacher can expect students to concentrate, he has to get their attention, no matter what distractions may be at hand. There are many ways to do this, and they have much to do with teaching style. However, if style alone won't do it, there is another way to show who holds the winning hand in the classroom. That is to reveal the trump card[1] of failure.

5 I will never forget a teacher who played that card to get the attention of one of my children. Our youngest, a world-class charmer, did little to develop his intellectual talents but always got by. Until Mrs. Stifter.

6 Our son was a high-school senior when he had her for English. "He sits in the back of the room talking to his friends," she told me. "Why don't you move him to the front row?" I urged, believing the embarrassment would get him to settle down. Mrs. Stifter looked at me steely-eyed over her glasses. "I don't move seniors," she said. "I flunk them." I was flustered. Our son's academic life flashed before my eyes. No teacher had ever threatened him with that before. I regained my composure and managed to say that I thought she was right. By the time I got home I was feeling pretty good about this. It was a radical approach for these times, but, well, why not? "She's going to flunk you," I told my son. I did not discuss it any further. Suddenly English became a priority in his life. He finished out the semester with an A.

---

[1] In cards, an advantage held in reserve until it's needed (editors' note).

7   I know one example doesn't make a case, but at night I see a parade of students who are angry and resentful for having been passed along until they could no longer even pretend to keep up. Of average intelligence or better, they eventually quit school, concluding they were too dumb to finish. "I should have been held back" is a comment I hear frequently. Even sadder are those students who are high-school graduates who say to me after a few weeks of class, "I don't know how I ever got a high-school diploma."

8   Passing students who have not mastered the work cheats them and the employers who expect graduates to have basic skills. We excuse this dishonest behavior by saying kids can't learn if they come from terrible environments. No one seems to stop to think that—no matter what environments they come from—most kids don't put school first on their list unless they perceive something is at stake. They'd rather be sailing.

9   Many students I see at night could give expert testimony on unemployment, chemical dependency, abusive relationships. In spite of these difficulties, they have decided to make education a priority. They are motivated by the desire for a better job or the need to hang on to the one they've got. They have a healthy fear of failure.

10   People of all ages can rise above their problems, but they need to have a reason to do so. Young people generally don't have the maturity to value education in the same way my adult students value it. But fear of failure, whether economic or academic, can motivate both.

11   Flunking as a regular policy has just as much merit today as it did two generations ago. We must review the threat of flunking and see it as it really is—a positive teaching tool. It is an expression of confidence by both teachers and parents that the students have the ability to learn the material presented to them. However, making it work again would take a dedicated, caring conspiracy between teachers and parents. It would mean facing the tough reality that passing kids who haven't learned the material— while it might save them grief for the short term—dooms them to long-term illiteracy. It would mean that teachers would have to follow through on their threats, and parents would have to stand behind them, knowing their children's best interests are indeed at stake. This means no more doing Scott's assignments for him because he might fail. No more passing Jodi because she's such a nice kid.

12   This is a policy that worked in the past and can work today. A wise teacher, with the support of his parents, gave our son the opportunity to succeed—or fail. It's time we return this choice to all students.

Questions for Close Reading

1. What is the selection's thesis? Locate the sentence(s) in which Sherry states her main idea. If she doesn't state the thesis explicitly, express it in your own words.
2. Sherry opens her essay with these words: "Tens of thousands of 18-year-olds will graduate this year and be handed meaningless diplomas." Why does Sherry consider these diplomas meaningless?
3. According to Sherry, what justification do many teachers give for "passing students who have not mastered the work" (paragraph 8)? Why does Sherry think that it is wrong to pass such students?
4. What does Sherry think teachers should do to motivate students to focus on school despite the many "distractions . . . at hand" (4)?

5. Refer to your dictionary as needed to define the following words used in the selection: *validity* (paragraph 1), *semiliterate* (1), *equivalency* (2), *impediments* (4), *composure* (6), *radical* (6), *priority* (6), *resentful* (7), *testimony* (9), *motivate* (10), *merit* (11), *conspiracy* (11), and *illiteracy* (11).

Questions About the Writer's Craft

1. **The pattern.** To write an effective argumentation-persuasion essay, writers need to establish their credibility. How does Sherry convince readers that she is qualified to write about her subject? What does this attempt to establish credibility say about Sherry's perception of her audience's point of view?

2. Sherry's title is deliberately misleading. What does her title lead you to believe the essay will be about? Why do you think Sherry chose this title?

3. Why do you suppose Sherry quotes her students rather than summarizing what they had to say? What effect do you think Sherry hopes the quotations will have on readers?

4. **Other patterns.** What *example* does Sherry provide to show that the threat of failure can work? How does this example reinforce her case?

Writing Assignments Using Argumentation-Persuasion as a Pattern of Development

1. Like Sherry, write an essay arguing your position on a controversial school-related issue. Possibilities include but need not be limited to the following: College students should *or* should not have to fulfill a physical education requirement; high school students should *or* should not have to demonstrate computer proficiency before graduating; elementary school students should *or* should not be grouped according to ability; a course in parenting should *or* should not be a required part of the high school curriculum. Once you select a topic, brainstorm with others to gather insight into varying points of view. When you write, restrict your argument to one level of education, and refute as many opposing arguments as you can. The following essays will help you identify educational issues worth writing about: Clifford Stoll's "Cyberschool", Paul Roberts's "How to Say Nothing in 500 Words", and Jacques D'Amboise's "Showing What Is Possible".

2. Sherry acknowledges that she used to blame students' poor academic skills on "drugs, divorce and other impediments." To what extent should teachers take these and similar "impediments" into account when grading students? Are there certain situations that call for leniency, or should out-of-school forces affecting students not be considered? To gain perspective on this issue, interview several friends, classmates, and instructors. Then write an essay in which you argue your position. Provide specific examples to support your argument, being sure to acknowledge and—when possible—to refute opposing viewpoints.

Writing Assignments Combining Patterns of Development

3. You probably feel, as Sherry does, that Mrs. Stifter is a strong, committed professional. Write an essay *illustrating* the qualities you think a teacher needs to have to be effective. Ask friends, classmates, family members, and instructors for their opinions; however, in your paper, focus on only those attributes you believe are most critical. To highlight the importance of these qualities, begin with a dramatic *contrasting* example of an ineffective teacher—someone who lacks the attributes you consider most important. To gain insight into some of the factors that make teachers effective or ineffective, read Jacques D'Amboise's "Showing What Is Possible".

4. Where else, besides in the classroom, do you see people acting irresponsibly, expending little effort, and taking the easy way out? You might consider the workplace, a school-related club or activity, family life, or interpersonal relationships. Select *one* area and write an essay *illustrating* the *effects* of this behavior on everyone concerned. For a broader perspective on the issue of personal responsibility, read John M. Darley and Bibb Latané's "Why People Don't Help in a Crisis".

Writing Assignment Using a Journal Entry as a Starting Point

5. Write the text for a brochure presenting parents with a step-by-step guide for dealing with academically unmotivated students. Focus your discussion on a specific level of schooling. From your pre-reading journal entry, select those strategies you consider most realistic and productive. When presenting your ideas, take into account children's likely resistance to the strategies described, and instruct parents how to deal with this resistance. Interviewing others (especially parents) and doing some research in the library and/or on the Internet will broaden your understanding of the issues involved.

READING

Yuh Ji-Yeon

At the age of five, Yuh Ji-Yeon (1965–) immigrated from Seoul, Korea, to the United States, settling in Chicago with her parents. After graduating from Stanford University, she worked as a reporter for the *Omaha World-Herald* and *New York Newsday*. She received a doctorate from the University of Pennsylvania following her dissertation examining the experiences of Korean women immigrating to the United States as wives of U.S. soldiers, which she expanded into her book *Beyond the Shadow of Camptown* (2002). Nearly all of Yuh's writing reflects the concerns of people struggling for liberation in the face of oppression. She currently teaches history at Northwestern University. The following selection first appeared in the *Philadelphia Inquirer* in 1991.

Pre-Reading Journal Entry

Which events in American history do you consider shameful? List these events in your journal. For each, jot down what your teachers taught you about the event when you were a child. Does what you were taught as a child differ from what you know now? In what way? If you did later on learn harsher truths about these events, how did you feel? Do you believe that you should have been told the truth from the beginning? Why or why not?

Let's Tell the Story of All America's Cultures

1   I grew up hearing, seeing and almost believing that America was white—albeit with a little black tinge here and there—and that white was best.

2   The white people were everywhere in my 1970s Chicago childhood: Founding Fathers, Lewis and Clark, Lincoln, Daniel Boone, Carnegie, presidents, explorers and industrialists galore. The only black people were slaves. The only Indians were scalpers.

3   I never heard one word about how Benjamin Franklin was so impressed by the Iroquois federation of nations that he adapted that model into our system of state and federal government. Or that the Indian tribes were systematically betrayed and massacred by a greedy young nation that stole their land and called it the United States.

4   I never heard one word about how Asian immigrants were among the first to turn California's desert into fields of plenty. Or about Chinese immigrant Ah Bing, who bred the cherry now on sale in groceries across the nation. Or that plantation owners in Hawaii imported labor from China, Japan, Korea and the Philippines to work the sugar cane fields. I never learned that Asian immigrants were the only immigrants denied

U.S. citizenship, even though they served honorably in World War I. All the immigrants in my textbook were white.

5 I never learned about Frederick Douglass, the runaway slave who became a leading abolitionist and statesman, or about black scholar W.E.B. Du Bois. I never learned that black people rose up in arms against slavery. Nat Turner wasn't one of the heroes in my childhood history class.

6 I never learned that the American Southwest and California were already settled by Mexicans when they were annexed after the Mexican-American War. I never learned that Mexico once had a problem keeping land-hungry white men on the U.S. side of the border.

7 So when other children called me a slant-eyed chink and told me to go back where I came from, I was ready to believe that I wasn't really an American because I wasn't white.

8 America's bittersweet legacy of struggling and failing and getting another step closer to democratic ideals of liberty and equality and justice for all wasn't for the likes of me, an immigrant child from Korea. The history books said so.

9 Well, the history books were wrong.

10 Educators around the country are finally realizing what I realized as a teenager in the library, looking up the history I wasn't getting in school. America is a multicultural nation, composed of many people with varying histories and varying traditions who have little in common except their humanity, a belief in democracy and a desire for freedom.

11 America changed them, but they changed America too.

12 A committee of scholars and teachers gathered by the New York State Department of Education recognizes this in their recent report, "One Nation, Many Peoples: A Declaration of Cultural Interdependence."

13 They recommend that public schools provide a "multicultural education, anchored to the shared principles of a liberal democracy."

14 What that means, according to the report, is recognizing that America was shaped and continues to be shaped by people of diverse backgrounds. It calls for students to be taught that history is an ongoing process of discovery and interpretation of the past, and that there is more than one way of viewing the world.

15 Thus, the westward migration of white Americans is not just a heroic settling of an untamed wild, but also the conquest of indigenous peoples. Immigrants were not just white, but Asian as well. Blacks were not merely passive slaves freed by northern whites, but active fighters for their own liberation.

16 In particular, according to the report, the curriculum should help children "to assess critically the reasons for the inconsistencies between the ideals of the U.S. and social realities. It should provide information and intellectual tools that can permit them to contribute to bringing reality closer to the ideals."

17 In other words, show children the good with the bad, and give them the skills to help improve their country. What could be more patriotic?

18 Several dissenting members of the New York committee publicly worry that America will splinter into ethnic fragments if this multicultural curriculum is adopted. They argue that the committee's report puts the focus on ethnicity at the expense of national unity.

19 But downplaying ethnicity will not bolster national unity. The history of America is the story of how and why people from all over the world came to the United States, and

how in struggling to make a better life for themselves, they changed each other, they changed the country, and they all came to call themselves Americans.

20   *E pluribus unum.* Out of many, one.

21   This is why I, with my Korean background, and my childhood tormentors, with their lost-in-the-mist-of-time European backgrounds, are all Americans.

22   It is the unique beauty of this country. It is high time we let all our children gaze upon it.

Questions for Close Reading

1. What is the selection's thesis? Locate the sentence(s) in which Yuh states her main idea. If she doesn't state the thesis explicitly, express it in your own words.

2. Yuh makes the rather shocking claim that "the history books were wrong" (paragraph 9). Why does she make this statement? What evidence does she offer to support it?

3. According to Yuh, what changes are needed in U.S. history courses?

4. Why does Yuh feel it is critical that U.S. students receive more than the traditional whites-only version of our nation's history? Who will be served by making history books more multicultural?

5. Refer to your dictionary as needed to define the following words used in the selection: *albeit* (paragraph 1), *tinge* (1), *galore* (2), *multicultural* (10, 13, 18), *interdependence* (12), *indigenous* (15), *dissenting* (18), *ethnicity* (18), and *bolster* (19).

Questions About the Writer's Craft

1. **The pattern.** Where in her argument does Yuh present the opposing viewpoint? Why do you suppose she waits so long to deal with the dissenting opinion? What effect does this delay have on her argument's effectiveness?

2. **Other patterns.** Why might Yuh have decided to use so many *examples* in paragraphs 2 through 6? How do these examples contribute to the persuasiveness of her position? Why might she have placed these examples before her thesis statement?

3. Yuh mixes the subjective and the objective in her argument. Where does she use specifics from her own life? How do these personal details help persuade readers to accept her viewpoint?

4. Yuh often uses parallelism and repetition of phrases, particularly in paragraphs 1 through 6 and paragraph 15. What effect do you think she intended these two stylistic devices to have on her readers?

Writing Assignments Using Argumentation-Persuasion as a Pattern of Development

1. Using the resources of the library and/or Internet, read several articles about the ongoing debate over multiculturalism's role in contemporary education. In addition to locating coverage of the 1991 New York State Department of Education Study (cited by Yuh in paragraph 12) and historian Arthur Schlesinger's *Time* essay "The Cult of Ethnicity: Good and Bad" (July 8, 1991), you should review many more recent sources on this issue. Review your research, and decide whether or not you support the idea of a multicultural curriculum. Then write an essay in which you argue your position, refuting as many of the opposing views as possible. Draw upon your own experiences as well as your research when developing your point of view.

2. Yuh cites a problem she encountered in her education. What problems or insufficiencies have you found in your own education? Perhaps you perceive an overemphasis on athletics, a reliance on rote memorization, a tendency to discourage female students from pursuing an interest in math and science. Select a single problem at one level of education, and brainstorm with others to gather material about the problem. Then write an essay directed at those who think all is well in our educational system. Be sure your argument illustrates the inaccuracy of these individuals' overly positive view. Before writing your paper, you may want to read Clifford Stoll's

"Cyberschool", and James Barszcz's "Can You Be Educated From a Distance?" because they offer critiques of U.S. education.

Writing Assignments Combining Patterns of Development

3. Because the mainstream culture they lived in didn't recognize the presence of minorities, the author's classmates considered Yuh an outsider, almost a nonbeing. To what extent, in your opinion, does television contribute to the dehumanization of minorities? For several days, watch a variety of television shows, noting how a particular ethnic or minority group (such as African-Americans, Hispanic-Americans, or the elderly) is portrayed. Then write an essay *arguing* that the depiction of this group on television is either accurate *or* distorted. Support your main idea with plentiful *examples* of specific television shows, including newscasts, situation comedies, talk shows, and so forth.

4. In her essay, Yuh refers to a report issued by the New York State Department of Education. The report argues that curriculum should encourage students to examine "the reasons for the inconsistencies between the ideals of the U.S. and social realities." Like most people, you probably detected such disparities when you were growing up. Perhaps as a youngster, you heard an admired neighbor brag about "scamming" the government or a business of owed money. As a high school student, you might have learned that an esteemed coach took kickbacks from college recruiters. Focus on one such clash between the ethical ideal and the everyday reality, and write about the incident's *effect* on you. Provide dramatic *details* to show how you reacted, what you did to explain the discrepancy to yourself, and whether you asked adults to help you understand the situation. At the end, reach some conclusions about the way children can be helped to deal with such collisions between ideals and reality.

Writing Assignment Using a Journal Entry as a Starting Point

5. Write an essay in which you argue for *or* against schools' revealing harsh historical realities to children. Review your pre-reading journal entry, and select *one* historical event to focus on. Provide plentiful reasons to support your position, whenever possible pointing out weaknesses in opposing viewpoints.

READING

James Barszcz

After earning his doctoral degree in English at Rutgers University, James Barszcz (1955–) taught college for several years. He is now employed at a major telecommunications company and pursues writing and independent scholarship in his spare time. In addition to issues related to technology and the classroom, his research interests include nineteenth-century American literature, especially Hawthorne, Melville, and Emerson. He lives with his wife and two children in Maplewood, New Jersey.

Pre-Reading Journal Entry

While many students readily acknowledge the practical reasons for attending college, fewer consider the intangible opportunity for personal development that higher education can provide. Take a few moments to consider what personal qualities you seek to cultivate in the course of your college education. Freewrite about this subject in your pre-reading journal, listing the various characteristics you hope to develop by the time you get your diploma. Discussing your thoughts with peers might help broaden your perspective on this question.

Can You Be Educated From a Distance?

1   By almost any measure, there is a boom in Internet-based instruction. In just a few years, thirty-four percent of American colleges and universities have begun offering some form of what's called "distance learning" (DL), and among the larger schools, it's closer to ninety percent. If you doubt the popularity of the trend, you probably haven't heard of the University of Phoenix. It grants degrees entirely on the basis of online instruction. It enrolls 90,000 students, a statistic used to support its claim to be the largest private university in the country.

2   While the kinds of instruction offered in these programs will differ, DL usually signifies a course in which the instructors post syllabi, reading assignments, and schedules on websites, and students send in their written assignments by e-mail. Other forms of communication often come into play, such as threaded messaging, which allows for posting questions and comments that are publicly viewable, as a bulletin board would, as well as chat rooms for real-time interchanges. Generally speaking, face-to-face communication with an instructor is minimized or eliminated altogether.

3   The attraction for students might at first seem obvious. Primarily, there's the convenience promised by courses on the Net: you can do the work, as they say, in your pajamas. But figures indicate that the reduced effort results in a reduced commitment to the course. While the attrition rate for all freshmen at American universities is around twenty percent, the rate for online students is thirty-five percent. Students themselves seem to understand the weaknesses inherent in the setup. In a survey conducted for eCornell, the DL division of Cornell University, less than a third of the respondents expected the quality of the online course to be as good as the classroom course.

4   Clearly, from the schools' perspective, there's a lot of money to be saved. Although some of the more ambitious programs require new investments in servers and networks to support collaborative software, most DL courses can run on existing or minimally upgraded systems. The more students who enroll in a course but don't come to campus, the more the school saves on keeping the lights on in the classrooms, paying custodians, and maintaining parking lots. And, while there's evidence that instructors must work harder to run a DL course for a variety of reasons, they won't be paid any more, and might well be paid less.

5   But as a rule, those who champion distance learning don't base their arguments on convenience or cost savings. More often, they claim DL signals an advance in the effectiveness of education. Consider the vigorous case made by Fairleigh Dickinson University (FDU), in Madison, New Jersey, where students—regardless of their expectations or desires—are now required to take one DL course per year. By setting this requirement, FDU claims that it recognizes the Internet as "a premier learning tool" of the current technological age. Skill in using online resources "prepares our students, more than others, for life-long learning—for their jobs, their careers, and their personal growth." Moreover, Internet-based courses will connect FDU students to a "global virtual faculty," a group of "world-class scholars, experts, artists, politicians, and business leaders around the world."

6   Sounds pretty good. But do the claims make much sense? First, it should be noted that students today and in the future might well use the Internet with at least as much facility as the faculty. It's not at all clear that they need to be taught such skills. More to the point, how much time and effort do you suppose "world-class scholars" (much less

politicians and business leaders) will expend for the benefit of students they never meet or even see? Probably a lot less than they're devoting to the books, journal articles, and position papers that are already available to anyone with access to a library.

7   Another justification comes from those who see distance learning as the next step in society's progress toward meritocracy. A recent article in *Forbes* magazine cites Professor Roger Schank of Northwestern University, who predicts that soon "students will be able to shop around, taking a course from any institution that offers a good one. . . . Quality education will be available to all. Students will learn what they want to learn rather than what some faculty committee decided was the best practical compromise." In sum, says Professor Schank, who is also chairman of a distance-learning enterprise called CognitiveArts, "Education will be measured by what you know rather than by whose name appears on your diploma."

8   Statements like these assume education consists in acquiring information ("what you know"). Accept that and it's hard to disagree with the conclusions. After all, what does it matter how, or through what medium, you get the information? But few truly educated people hold such a mechanistic view. Indeed, traditionally, education was aimed at cultivating intellectual and moral values, and the "information" you picked up was decidedly secondary. It was commonplace for those giving commencement speeches to note that, based on etymology, education is a drawing out, not a putting in. That is, a true education *educes,* or draws out, from within a person qualities of intellect and character that would otherwise have remained hidden or dormant.

9   Exactly how this kind of educing happens is hard to pin down. Only in part does it come from watching professors in the classroom present material and respond to student questions, the elements of education that can be translated to the Net with reasonable fidelity. Other educational experiences include things like watching how professors joke with each other (or not!) in the hallways, seeing what kinds of pictures are framed in a professor's office, or going out for coffee after class with people in your dorm. Such experiences, and countless others, are sometimes labeled (and dismissed) as "social life on campus." But they also contribute invaluably to education. Through them, you learn a style, in the noblest sense of that term, a way of regarding the information you acquire and the society you find yourself in. This is what the philosopher Alfred North Whitehead meant when he called style the ultimate acquisition of a cultivated mind. And it's the mysterious ways of cultivating that style that the poet Robert Frost had in mind when he said that all that a college education requires is that you "hang around until you catch on." Hang around campus, that is, not lurk on the Net.

Questions for Close Reading

1. What is the selection's thesis? Locate the sentence(s) in which Barszcz states his main idea. If he doesn't state the thesis explicitly, express it in your own words.
2. According to Barszcz, what primarily attracts students and schools to distance learning?
3. What does Barszcz say are the most common arguments made by proponents of distance learning?
4. How does Barszcz define *education?* Do you agree with his definition, or do you see education functioning in a different way? Explain.
5. Refer to your dictionary as needed to define the following words used in the selection: *attrition* (3), *virtual* (5), *facility* (6), *meritocracy* (7), *mechanistic* (8), *etymology* (8), *dormant* (8), and *fidelity* (9).

Questions About the Writer's Craft

1. **The pattern.** What sort of audience—supportive, wavering, or hostile—does Barszcz seem to have geared his argument toward? How can you tell?

2. **Other patterns.** Barszcz develops paragraph 2 through *division-classification*. What larger topic does he divide into categories? What are these categories? What organizational order does he use in this paragraph?

3. Barszcz quotes literature from Fairleigh Dickinson University (FDU) in some detail. Considering that FDU's position represents an opposing point of view, why do you think he quotes FDU at such length? What is the effect of this quoting?

4. **Other patterns.** In paragraphs 2 and 8, Barszcz provides two *definitions* that fundamentally differ in purpose and tone. Describe the differences.

Writing Assignments Using Argumentation-Persuasion as a Pattern of Development

1. Barszcz posits that a central component of education should be the cultivation of "moral values." Do you agree? Take the case of public elementary schools. Write an essay in which you argue that these schools should *or* should not instruct students in morality as part of the curriculum. Be sure as you develop your argument to acknowledge and refute opposing points of view. You might benefit from reading Yuh Ji-Yeon's "Let's Tell the Story of All America's Cultures" (page 255), in which the author advocates a certain type of moral education.

2. Barszcz suggests that the true motivation of some who champion distance learning is financial. Think of some other phenomenon—say, the invasion of one country by another, the marketing of a new medication, advertisements for life insurance—and write an essay *arguing* that a financial motive underlies lofty rhetoric ("We will liberate the people of . . . ," "We care about your health," "Invest in your children's future"). Support your case with at least three major *examples* that *illustrate* your assertion. You should also consider citing facts, statistics, and/or expert opinions derived from visiting the library and/or going online to lend additional authority to your position.

Writing Assignments Combining Patterns of Development

3. In Barszcz's view, educated people are intellectually and morally cultivated. Write an essay *describing* someone you know (or know of) who, in your view, epitomizes an educated person. What are the person's intellectual qualities? What are his or her character traits? What are his or her moral values and tastes? As you answer these questions about the person, provide vivid *examples* to *illustrate* the characteristics you're describing.

4. As Barszcz indicates, on-campus experiences contribute to college students' education. In an essay of your own, *narrate* a school-related experience from any time in your life that left you significantly better educated. The experience you describe, though school-related, need not be strictly academic. For example, you might discuss developing a friendship with someone from a different culture, coming to appreciate an initially disliked instructor, participating in an inspiring class, and so on. *Describe* those details that convey what made the experience so enlightening. How did the experience make you more understanding, aware, critical, sensitive, or appreciative? How did it alter your worldview?

Writing Assignment Using a Journal Entry as a Starting Point

5. A "true education," according to Barszcz, "*educes,* or draws out, from within a person qualities of intellect and character that would otherwise have remained hidden or dormant" (8). What personal qualities do you hope a college education will educe from you? Reviewing what you wrote in your pre-reading journal entry, write an essay in which you identify at least two or three qualities you hope to nurture during your college years and explain why you hope to do

so. For instance, you might discuss your aspiration to become more intellectually objective, more assertive, more articulate, and so on. And, in order to demonstrate the progress you hope to make, for each quality, you should *contrast* yourself at the outset of your college education with where you hope to be by the end. For some general reflections on the role of education in students' lives, read any of the following: Clifford Stoll's "Cyberschool", Mary Sherry's "In Praise of the 'F' Word", and Yuh Ji-Yeon's "Let's Tell the Story of All America's Cultures".

READING

Mark Twain

Mark Twain is a central figure in American literature. Published in 1884, *The Adventures of Huckleberry Finn,* Twain's finest work, recounts a journey down the Mississippi by two memorable figures: a White boy and a Black slave. Twain was born Samuel Langhorne Clemens in 1835 and was raised in Hannibal, Missouri. During his early years, he worked as a riverboat pilot, newspaper reporter, printer, and gold prospector. Although his popular image is as the author of such comic works as *The Adventures of Tom Sawyer* (1876), *Life on the Mississippi* (1883), and *The Prince and the Pauper* (1882), Twain had a darker side that may have resulted from the bitter experiences of his life: financial failure and the deaths of his wife and daughter. His last writings are savage, satiric, and pessimistic. The following selection is taken from *Letters From the Earth,* one of Twain's later works.

Pre-Reading Journal Entry

What would you identify as the major differences between human beings and other animals? What are the similarities? In your journal, list as many items for each as you can, from the obvious to the subtle. Be as specific as you can.

The Damned Human Race

1   I have been studying the traits and dispositions of the "lower animals" (so-called), and contrasting them with the traits and dispositions of man. I find the result humiliating to me. For it obliges me to renounce my allegiance to the Darwinian theory of the Ascent of Man from the Lower Animals; since it now seems plain to me that the theory ought to be vacated in favor of a new and truer one, this new and truer one to be named the *Descent* of Man from the Higher Animals.

2   In proceeding toward this unpleasant conclusion I have not guessed or speculated or conjectured, but have used what is commonly called the scientific method. That is to say, I have subjected every postulate that presented itself to the crucial test of actual experiment, and have adopted it or rejected it according to the result. Thus I verified and established each step of my course in its turn before advancing to the next. These experiments were made in the London Zoological Gardens, and covered many months of painstaking and fatiguing work.

3   Before particularizing any of the experiments, I wish to state one or two things which seem to more properly belong in this place than further along. This in the interest of clearness. The massed experiments established to my satisfaction certain generalizations, to wit:

1. That the human race is of one distinct species. It exhibits slight variations—in color, stature, mental caliber, and so on—due to climate, environment, and so forth; but it is a species by itself, and not to be confounded with any other.

2. That the quadrupeds are a distinct family, also. This family exhibits variations—in color, size, food preferences and so on; but it is a family by itself.

3. That the other families—the birds, the fishes, the insects, the reptiles, etc.—are more or less distinct, also. They are in the procession. They are links in the chain which stretches down from the higher animals to man at the bottom.

4   Some of my experiments were quite curious. In the course of my reading I had come across a case where, many years ago, some hunters on our Great Plains organized a buffalo hunt for the entertainment of an English earl—that, and to provide some fresh meat for his larder. They had charming sport. They killed seventy-two of those great animals; and ate part of one of them and left the seventy-one to rot. In order to determine the difference between an anaconda and an earl—if any—I caused seven young calves to be turned into the anaconda's cage. The grateful reptile immediately crushed one of them and swallowed it, then lay back satisfied. It showed no further interest in the calves, and no disposition to harm them. I tried this experiment with other anacondas; always with the same result. The fact stood proven that the difference between an earl and an anaconda is that the earl is cruel and the anaconda isn't; and that the earl wantonly destroys what he has no use for, but the anaconda doesn't. This seemed to suggest that the anaconda was not descended from the earl. It also seemed to suggest that the earl was descend-ed from the anaconda, and had lost a good deal in the transition.

5   I was aware that many men who have accumulated more millions of money than they can ever use have shown a rabid hunger for more, and have not scrupled to cheat the ignorant and the helpless out of their poor servings in order to partially appease that appetite. I furnished a hundred different kinds of wild and tame animals the opportunity to accumulate vast stores of food, but none of them would do it. The squirrels and bees and certain birds made accumulations, but stopped when they had gathered a winter's supply, and could not be persuaded to add to it either honestly or by chicanery. In order to bolster up a tottering reputation the ant pretended to store up supplies, but I was not deceived. I know the ant. These experiments convinced me that there is this difference between man and the higher animals: he is avaricious and miserly, they are not.

6   In the course of my experiments I convinced myself that among the animals man is the only one that harbors insults and injuries, broods over them, waits till a chance offers, then takes revenge. The passion of revenge is unknown to the higher animals.

7   Roosters keep harems, but it is by consent of their concubines; therefore no wrong is done. Men keep harems, but it is by brute force, privileged by atrocious laws which the other sex were allowed no hand in making. In this matter man occupies a far lower place than the rooster.

8   Cats are loose in their morals, but not consciously so. Man, in his descent from the cat, has brought the cat's looseness with him but has left the unconsciousness behind—the saving grace which excuses the cat. The cat is innocent, man is not.

9   Indecency, vulgarity, obscenity—these are strictly confined to man; he invented them. Among the higher animals there is no trace of them. They hide nothing; they are

not ashamed. Man, with his soiled mind, covers himself. He will not even enter a drawing room with his breast and back naked, so alive are he and his mates to indecent suggestion. Man is "The Animal that Laughs." But so does the monkey, as Mr. Darwin pointed out; and so does the Australian bird that is called the laughing jackass. No—Man is the Animal that Blushes. He is the only one that does it—or has occasion to.

10   At the head of this article[1] we see how "three monks were burnt to death" a few days ago, and a prior "put to death with atrocious cruelty." Do we inquire into the details? No; or we should find out that the prior was subjected to unprintable mutilations. Man—when he is a North American Indian—gouges out his prisoner's eyes; when he is King John, with a nephew to render untroublesome, he uses a red-hot iron; when he is a religious zealot dealing with heretics in the Middle Ages, he skins his captive alive and scatters salt on his back; in the first Richard's time he shuts up a multitude of Jew families in a tower and sets fire to it; in Columbus's time he captures a family of Spanish Jews and—but *that* is not printable; in our day in England a man is fined ten shillings for beating his mother nearly to death with a chair, and another man is fined forty shillings for having four pheasant eggs in his possession without being able to satisfactorily explain how he got them. Of all the animals, man is the only one that is cruel. He is the only one that inflicts pain for the pleasure of doing it. It is a trait that is not known to the higher animals. The cat plays with the frightened mouse; but she has this excuse, that she does not know that the mouse is suffering. The cat is moderate—unhumanly moderate: she only scares the mouse, she does not hurt it; she doesn't dig out its eyes, or tear off its skin, or drive splinters under its nails—man-fashion; when she is done playing with it she makes a sudden meal of it and puts it out of its trouble. Man is the Cruel Animal. He is alone in that distinction.

11   The higher animals engage in individual fights, but never in organized masses. Man is the only animal that deals in that atrocity of atrocities, War. He is the only one that gathers his brethren about him and goes forth in cold blood and with calm pulse to exterminate his kind. He is the only animal that for sordid wages will march out, as the Hessians did in our Revolution, and as the boyish Prince Napoleon did in the Zulu war, and help to slaughter strangers of his own species who have done him no harm and with whom he has no quarrel.

12   Man is the only animal that robs his helpless fellow of his country—takes possession of it and drives him out of it or destroys him. Man has done this in all the ages. There is not an acre of ground on the globe that is in possession of its rightful owner, or that has not been taken away from owner after owner, cycle after cycle, by force and bloodshed.

13   Man is the only Slave. And he is the only animal who enslaves. He has always been a slave in one form or another, and has always held other slaves in bondage under him in one way or another. In our day he is always some man's slave for wages, and does that man's work; and this slave has other slaves under him for minor wages, and they do *his* work. The higher animals are the only ones who exclusively do their own work and provide their own living.

14   Man is the only Patriot. He sets himself apart in his own country, under his own flag, and sneers at the other nations, and keeps multitudinous uniformed assassins on

---

[1]Twain originally began his article with newspaper clippings containing telegrams that reported atrocities in Crete (editors' note).

hand at heavy expense to grab slices of other people's countries, and keep *them* from grabbing slices of *his*. And in the intervals between campaigns he washes the blood off his hands and works for "the universal brotherhood of man"—with his mouth.

15   Man is the Religious Animal. He is the only Religious Animal. He is the only animal that has the True Religion—several of them. He is the only animal that loves his neighbor as himself, and cuts his throat if his theology isn't straight. He has made a graveyard of the globe in trying his honest best to smooth his brother's path to happiness and heaven. He was at it in the time of the Caesars, he was at it in Mahomet's time, he was at it in the time of the Inquisition, he was at it in France a couple of centuries, he was at it in England in Mary's day, he has been at it ever since he first saw the light, he is at it today in Crete—as per the telegrams quoted above[2]—he will be at it somewhere else tomorrow. The higher animals have no religion. And we are told that they are going to be left out, in the Hereafter. I wonder why? It seems questionable taste.

16   Man is the Reasoning Animal. Such is the claim. I think it is open to dispute. Indeed, my experiments have proven to me that he is the Unreasoning Animal. Note his history, as sketched above. It seems plain to me that whatever he is he is *not* a reasoning animal. His record is the fantastic record of a maniac. I consider that the strongest count against his intelligence is the fact that with that record back of him he blandly sets himself up as the head animal of the lot: whereas by his own standards he is the bottom one.

17   In truth, man is incurably foolish. Simple things which the other animals easily learn, he is incapable of learning. Among my experiments was this. In an hour I taught a cat and a dog to be friends. I put them in a cage. In another hour I taught them to be friends with a rabbit. In the course of two days I was able to add a fox, a goose, a squirrel and some doves. Finally a monkey. They lived together in peace; even affectionately.

18   Next, in another cage I confined an Irish Catholic from Tipperary, and as soon as he seemed tame I added a Scotch Presbyterian from Aberdeen. Next a Turk from Constantinople; a Greek Christian from Crete; an Armenian; a Methodist from the wilds of Arkansas; a Buddhist from China; a Brahman from Benares. Finally, a Salvation Army Colonel from Wapping. Then I stayed away two whole days. When I came back to note results, the cage of Higher Animals was all right, but in the other, there was but a chaos of gory odds and ends of turbans and fezzes and plaids and bones and flesh—not a specimen left alive. These Reasoning Animals had disagreed on a theological detail and carried the matter to a Higher Court.

19   One is obliged to concede that in true loftiness of character, Man cannot claim to approach even the meanest of the Higher Animals. It is plain that he is constitutionally incapable of approaching that altitude; that he is constitutionally afflicted with a Defect which must make such approach forever impossible, for it is manifest that this defect is permanent in him, indestructible, ineradicable.

20   I find this Defect to be *the Moral Sense*. He is the only animal that has it. It is the secret of his degradation. It is the quality *which enables him to do wrong*. It has no other office. It is incapable of performing any other function. It could never have been

---

[2]See note, page 222 (editors' note).

intended to perform any other. Without it, man could do no wrong. He would rise at once to the level of the Higher Animals.

21　　Since the Moral Sense has but the one office, the one capacity—to enable man to do wrong—it is plainly without value to him. It is as valueless to him as is disease. In fact, it manifestly *is* a disease. *Rabies* is bad, but it is not so bad as this disease. Rabies enables a man to do a thing which he could not do when in a healthy state: kill his neighbor with a poisonous bite. No one is the better man for having rabies: The Moral Sense enables a man to do wrong. It enables him to do wrong in a thousand ways. Rabies is an innocent disease, compared to the Moral Sense. No one, then, can be the better man for having the Moral Sense. What, now, do we find the Primal Curse to have been? Plainly what it was in the beginning: the infliction upon man of the Moral Sense; the ability to distinguish good from evil; and with it, necessarily, the ability to *do* evil; for there can be no evil act without the presence of consciousness of it in the doer of it.

22　　And so I find that we have descended and degenerated, from some far ancestor—some microscopic atom wandering at its pleasure between the mighty horizons of a drop of water perchance—insect by insect, animal by animal, reptile by reptile, down the long highway of smirchless innocence, till we have reached the bottom stage of development—namable as the Human Being. Below us—nothing.

Questions for Close Reading

1. What is the selection's thesis? Locate the sentence(s) in which Twain states his main idea. If he doesn't state the thesis explicitly, express it in your own words.
2. Because of their intelligence, humans are usually called the highest animal. What, according to Twain, are the specific traits that make humans the lowest animal?
3. How does the story of the earl who hunted down seventy-two buffalo show that an anaconda is superior to an earl?
4. What does Twain mean when he points out that humankind is the only animal that "has occasion to" blush? What are some of the occasions for blushing that he highlights in the essay?
5. Refer to your dictionary as needed to define the following words used in the selection: *confounded* (paragraph 3), *anaconda* (4), *wantonly* (4), *chicanery* (5), *heretics* (10), *constitutionally* (19), *ineradicable* (19), and *smirchless* (22).

Questions About the Writer's Craft

1. **The pattern.** Most writers don't tell the reader outright the reasoning process they used to arrive at their essay's proposition. But Twain claims that he reached his conclusion about human beings inductively—through the use of the "scientific method." Why does Twain make this claim?
2. Where in the essay does Twain try to shock the audience? Why do you think he adopts this technique?
3. **Other patterns.** In some paragraphs, Twain provides numerous *examples* of political and religious atrocities. Why do you suppose he supplies so many examples?
4. Black humor is defined as "the use of the morbid and the absurd for comic purposes." What elements of the morbid and the absurd do you find in Twain's essay? Would you say "The Damned Human Race" is an example of black humor? Explain.

Writing Assignments Using Argumentation-Persuasion as a Pattern of Development

1. In an essay, argue that human beings are worthy of being considered the "highest animal." The paper should acknowledge and then refute Twain's charges that people are miserly, vengeful, foolish, and so on. To support your proposition, use specific examples of how human beings can be kind, caring, generous, and peace-loving.

2. Write an essay agreeing with Twain that it is our everyday meannesses, unkindnesses, and cruelties that make us the "lowest animal." Use compelling examples to support your argument, including description and dialogue whenever appropriate. You might focus on one of the following topics:

   Violence toward children
   Abuse of animals
   Hurtful sarcasm
   Insults of a racial, sexist, or religious nature
   Indifference to the unfortunate

   Somewhere in the essay, you should acknowledge the view that humans are capable of considerable kindness and compassion. For more perspectives like Twain's, read Stephen King's "Why We Crave Horror Movies".

Writing Assignments Combining Patterns of Development

3. What failings of human decency do you see around you every day in your town, on your campus, or at your job? Write an essay *arguing* that inhumanity resides not just in atrocities but also in ordinary acts of indifference. Providing compelling *examples* or *anecdotes* will be crucial as you make your argument. In your essay, you may use Twain's kind of bitter sarcasm, or you may adopt a more objective, less vitriolic tone. You might also read John M. Darley and Bibb Latané's "Why People Don't Help in a Crisis", another essay specifically exploring the causes of inhumanity.

4. How could humans become less cruel? Write an essay outlining a new *process* for raising children or "re-civilizing" adults—a process that, if instituted, would have a clearly beneficial *effect* on human morality.

Writing Assignment Using a Journal Entry as a Starting Point

5. Write an essay in which, unlike Twain, you illustrate the *similarities* between human beings and other species of animals. Using your pre-reading journal entry, select the most compelling similarities. Try to explore likenesses that go beyond such obvious ones as eating, sleeping, reproduction, etc.; focus instead on behaviors and traits that are elusive but telling. Your essays, which may be humorous or serious, should reveal your attitude toward the similarities you discuss. Do they reflect favorably or negatively on the human species?

READING

Nat Hentoff

Nat Hentoff was born in Boston in 1925 and attended Northwestern University, followed by Harvard. His writings for the *Village Voice* and the *New Yorker*, his columns for the *Washington Post*, and his more than twenty-five books of fiction and nonfiction have earned him the reputation as a respected voice of the political Left. Privacy, drug testing, racism, the draft, abortion, and educational reform have all come under Hentoff's keen observation. In 1987,

Hentoff published his autobiography, *Boston Boy*, and 1989 saw the publication of his book *The First Freedom: The Tumultuous History of Free Speech in America*. Other publications include *Free Speech for Me—But Not for Thee* (1993), *Listen to the Stories* (1996), *Speaking Freely: A Memoir* (1997), *Living the Bill of Rights: How to Be an Authentic American* (1998), *The Nat Hentoff Reader* (2001), and *The War on the Bill of Rights and the Gathering Resistance* (2003). Despite his political stance as a leftist, Hentoff has criticized the zeal of the Left in suppressing speech it finds offensive. Such concerns led him to write the following essay, first published in the *Progressive* in May 1989.

Pre-Reading Journal Entry

How do you feel about freedom of speech on campus? In your journal, list several controversial issues that might be debated in a college setting. For each issue, indicate whether you feel that divergent, even inflammatory views should have an opportunity to be heard on campus—for example, in class, in the college newspaper, in a lecture series. Jot down why you feel as you do.

Free Speech on Campus

1   A flier distributed at the University of Michigan some months ago proclaimed that blacks "don't belong in classrooms, they belong hanging from trees."

2   At other campuses around the country, manifestations of racism are becoming commonplace. At Yale, a swastika and the words WHITE POWER! were painted on the building housing the University's Afro-American Cultural Center. At Temple University, a White Students Union has been formed with some 130 members.

3   Swastikas are not directed only at black students. The Nazi symbol has been spray-painted on the Jewish Student Union at Memphis State University. And on a number of campuses, women have been singled out as targets of wounding and sometimes frightening speech. At the law school of the State University of New York at Buffalo, several women students have received anonymous letters characterized by one professor as venomously sexist.

4   These and many more such signs of the resurgence of bigotry and knownothingism throughout the society—as well as on campus—have to do solely with speech, including symbolic speech. There have also been physical assaults on black students and on black, white, and Asian women students, but the way to deal with physical attacks is clear: call the police and file a criminal complaint. What is to be done, however, about speech alone—however disgusting, inflammatory, and rawly divisive that speech may be?

5   At more and more colleges, administrators—with the enthusiastic support of black students, women students, and liberal students—have been answering that question by preventing or punishing speech. In public universities, this is a clear violation of the First Amendment. In private colleges and universities, suppression of speech mocks the secular religion of academic freedom and free inquiry.

6   The Student Press Law Center in Washington, D.C.—a vital source of legal support for student editors around the country—reports, for example, that at the University of Kansas, the student host and producer of a radio news program was forbidden by school officials from interviewing a leader of the Ku Klux Klan. So much for free inquiry on that campus.

7   In Madison, Wisconsin, the *Capital Times* ran a story in January about Chancellor Sheila Kaplan of the University of Wisconsin branch at Parkside, who ordered her cam-

pus to be scoured of "some anonymously placed white supremacist hate literature." Sounding like the legendary Mayor Frank ("I am the law") Hague of Jersey City, who booted "bad speech" out of town, Chancellor Kaplan said, "This institution is not a lamppost standing on the street corner. It doesn't belong to everyone."

8   Who decides what speech can be heard or read by everyone? Why, the Chancellor, of course. That's what George III[1] used to say, too.

9   University of Wisconsin political science professor Carol Tebben thinks otherwise. She believes university administrators "are getting confused when they are acting as censors and trying to protect students from bad ideas. I don't think students need to be protected from bad ideas. I think they can determine for themselves what ideas are bad."

10   After all, if students are to be "protected" from bad ideas, how are they going to learn to identify and cope with them? Sending such ideas underground simply makes them stronger and more dangerous.

11   Professor Tebben's conviction that free speech means just that has become a decidedly minority view on many campuses. At the University of Buffalo Law School, the faculty unanimously adopted a "Statement Regarding Intellectual Freedom, Tolerance, and Political Harassment." Its title implies support of intellectual freedom, but the statement warned students that once they enter "this legal community," their right to free speech must become tempered "by the responsibility to promote equality and justice."

12   Accordingly, swift condemnation will befall anyone who engages in "remarks directed at another's race, sex, religion, national origin, age, or sex preference." Also forbidden are "other remarks based on prejudice and group stereotype."

13   This ukase is so broad that enforcement has to be alarmingly subjective. Yet the University of Buffalo Law School provides no due-process procedures for a student booked for making any of these prohibited remarks. Conceivably, a student caught playing a Lenny Bruce, Richard Pryor, or Sam Kinison[2] album in his room could be tried for aggravated insensitivity by association.

14   When I looked into this wholesale cleansing of bad speech at Buffalo, I found it had encountered scant opposition. One protester was David Gerald Jay, a graduate of the law school and a cooperating attorney for the New York Civil Liberties Union. Said the appalled graduate: "Content-based prohibitions constitute prior restraint and should not be tolerated."

15   You would think that the law professors and administration at this public university might have known that. But hardly any professors dissented, and among the students only members of the conservative Federalist Society spoke up for free speech. The fifty-strong chapter of the National Lawyers Guild was on the other side. After all, it was more important to go on record as vigorously opposing racism and sexism than to expose oneself to charges of insensitivity to these malignancies.

16   The pressures to have the "right" attitude—as proved by having the "right" language in and out of class—can be stifling. A student who opposes affirmative action, for instance, can be branded a racist.

---

[1]King of England at the time of the American Revolution, George III reportedly lost his sanity in his later years (editors' note).

[2]Lenny Bruce was a stand-up comic popular in the 1950s and early 1960s. Bruce's caustic social commentary and his use of language that many considered offensive established the precedent for the confrontational style of many later comedians, including Richard Pryor and Sam Kinison (editors' note).

17   At the University of California at Los Angeles, the student newspaper ran an editorial cartoon satirizing affirmative action. (A student stops a rooster on campus and asks how the rooster got into UCLA. "Affirmative action," is the answer.) After outraged complaints from various minority groups, the editor was suspended for violating a publication policy against running "articles that perpetuate derogatory or cultural stereotypes." The art director was also suspended.

18   When the opinion editor of the student newspaper at California State University at Northridge wrote an article asserting that the sanctions against the editor and art director at UCLA amounted to censorship, he was suspended too.

19   At New York University Law School, a student was so disturbed by the pall of orthodoxy at that prestigious institution that he wrote to the school newspaper even though, as he said, he expected his letter to make him a pariah among his fellow students.

20   Barry Endick described the atmosphere at NYU created by "a host of watchdog committees and a generally hostile classroom reception regarding any student comment right of center." This "can be arguably viewed as symptomatic of a prevailing spirit of academic and social intolerance of . . . any idea which is not 'politically correct.'"

21   He went on to say something that might well be posted on campus bulletin boards around the country, though it would probably be torn down at many of them: "We ought to examine why students, so anxious to wield the Fourteenth Amendment, give short shrift to the First. Yes, Virginia, there are racist assholes. And you know what, the Constitution protects them, too."

22   Not when they engage in violence or vandalism. But when they speak or write, racist assholes fall right into this Oliver Wendell Holmes[3] definition—highly unpopular among bigots, liberals, radicals, feminists, sexists, and college administrators: "If there is any principle of the Constitution that more imperatively calls for attachment than any other, it is the principle of free thought—not free only for those who agree with us, but freedom for the thought we hate."

23   The language sounds like a pietistic Sunday sermon, but if it ever falls wholly into disuse, neither this publication nor any other journal of opinion—right or left—will survive.

24   Sometimes, college presidents and administrators sound as if they fully understand what Holmes was saying. Last year, for example, when the *Daily Pennsylvanian*[4]—speaking for many at the University of Pennsylvania—urged that a speaking invitation to Louis Farrakhan[5] be withdrawn, University President Sheldon Hackney disagreed.

25   "Open expression," said Hackney, "is the fundamental principle of a university." Yet consider what the same Sheldon Hackney did to the free-speech rights of a teacher at his own university. If any story distills the essence of the current decline of free speech on college campuses, it is the Ballad of Murray Dolfman.

26   For twenty-two years, Dolfman, a practicing lawyer in Philadelphia, had been a part-time lecturer in the Legal Studies Department of the University of Pennsylvania's Wharton School. For twenty-two years, no complaint had ever been made against him; in-

[3]Holmes was Associate Justice of the Supreme Court (1902–32) (editors' note).

[4]The student newspaper at the University of Pennsylvania (editors' note).

[5]The leader of the Black Nation of Islam, Farrakhan holds controversial views that have been called anti-Semitic and racially inflammatory (editors' note).

deed his student course evaluations had been outstanding. Each year students competed to get into his class.

27   On a November afternoon in 1984, Dolfman was lecturing about personal-service contracts. His style somewhat resembles that of Professor Charles Kingsfield in *The Paper Chase*.[6] Dolfman insists that students he calls on be prepared—or suffer the consequences. He treats all students this way—regardless of race, creed, or sex.

28   This day, Dolfman was pointing out that no one can be forced to work against his or her will—even if a contract has been signed. A court may prevent the resister from working for someone else so long as the contract is in effect but, Dolfman said, there can "be nothing that smacks of involuntary servitude."

29   Where does this concept come from? Dolfman looked around the room. Finally, a cautious hand was raised: "The Constitution?"

30   "Where in the Constitution?" No hands. "The Thirteenth Amendment," said the teacher. So, what does *it* say? The students were looking everywhere but at Dolfman.

31   "We will lose our liberties," Dolfman often told his classes, "if we don't know what they are."

32   On this occasion, he told them that he and other Jews, as ex-slaves, spoke at Passover of the time when they were slaves under the Pharaohs so that they would remember every year what it was like not to be free.

33   "We have ex-slaves here," Dolfman continued, "who should know about the Thirteenth Amendment." He asked black students in the class if they could tell him what was in that amendment.

34   "I wanted them to really think about it," Dolfman told me recently, "and know its history. You're better equipped to fight racism if you know all about those post-Civil War amendments and civil rights laws."

35   The Thirteenth Amendment provides that "neither slavery nor involuntary servitude . . . shall exist within the United States."

36   The black students in his class did not know what was in that amendment, and Dolfman had them read it aloud. Later, they complained to university officials that they had been hurt and humiliated by having been referred to as ex-slaves. Moreover, they said, they had no reason to be grateful for a constitutional amendment which gave them rights which should never have been denied them—and gave them precious little else. They had not made these points in class, although Dolfman—unlike Professor Kingsfield—encourages rebuttal.

37   Informed of the complaint, Dolfman told the black students he had intended no offense, and he apologized if they had been offended.

38   That would not do—either for the black students or for the administration. Furthermore, there were mounting black-Jewish tensions on campus, and someone had to be sacrificed. Who better than a part-time Jewish teacher with no contract and no union? He was sentenced by—George Orwell[7] would have loved this—the Committee on Academic Freedom and Responsibility.

---

[6]Charles Kingsfield was the demanding law professor in both the film and the television show *The Paper Chase*. The series, popular in the 1970s, chronicled the struggles of first-year law students at a prestigious university (editors' note).

[7]British essayist and novelist George Orwell often wrote about the fragile line separating democratic and despotic institutions (editors' note; for more information on Orwell, see page 140).

39   On his way to the stocks, Dolfman told President Sheldon Hackney that if a part-time instructor "can be punished on this kind of charge, a tenured professor can even-tually be booted out, then a dean, and then a president."

40   Hackney was unmoved. Dolfman was banished from the campus for what came to be a year. But first he was forced to make a public apology to the entire university and then he was compelled to attend a "sensitivity and racial awareness" session. Sort of like a Vietnamese reeducation camp.

41   A few conservative professors objected to the stigmatization of Murray Dolfman. I know of no student dissent. Indeed, those students most concerned with making the campus more "sensitive" to diversity exulted in Dolfman's humiliation. So did most lib-erals on the faculty.

42   If my children were still of college age and wanted to attend the University of Penn-sylvania, I would tell them this story. But where else could I encourage them to go?

Questions for Close Reading

1. What is the selection's thesis? Locate the sentence(s) in which Hentoff states his main idea. If he doesn't state the thesis explicitly, express it in your own words.
2. What evidence does Hentoff present to support his statement that there's a "resurgence of big-otry and knownothingism throughout the society"?
3. According to Hentoff, how have officials on campuses at the University of Kansas, the University of Wisconsin, and the University of California at Los Angeles interfered with free in-quiry and free speech? What reasons did university officials give for their actions?
4. Why, in Hentoff's opinion, should college campuses permit all types of speech? According to Hentoff, what problems arise when free speech is curtailed?
5. Refer to your dictionary as needed to define the following words used in the selection: *ven-omously* (paragraph 3), *knownothingism* (4), *ukase* (13), *dissented* (15), *malignancies* (15), *sanc-tions* (18), *pall* (19), *pariah* (19), *pietistic* (23), *distills* (25), *stocks* (39), and *stigmatization* (41).

Questions About the Writer's Craft

1. **The pattern.** Writing on a complex and controversial issue, Hentoff wisely confronts the op-posing viewpoint—in this case, the position that the free speech of extremists should be sup-pressed. What strategies does Hentoff use to deal with this view?
2. **Other patterns.** Where in the selection does Hentoff use *examples* and a *narrative* account to support his argument? How do the examples and the narrative help him support his case?
3. What tone does Hentoff employ when describing those who believe that sometimes it is neces-sary to limit free speech? How do Hentoff's sentence structure and word choice help create this tone?
4. Examine the quotations in paragraphs 20 through 22. Why do you think Hentoff chooses to quote these two particular individuals—law student Barry Endick and Supreme Court Justice Oliver Wendell Holmes? What does he achieve by juxtaposing Endick's words with those of Holmes?

Writing Assignments Using Argumentation-Persuasion as a Pattern of Development

1. Consider the stereotyping, the economic deprivations, and the personal slurs that many mem-bers of minority groups continue to suffer. Then decide which you believe is more important: totally free speech or the protection of the rights, feelings, and status of groups that have been discriminated against. Write an essay in which you argue that on college campuses protecting "equality and justice" either is or isn't more important than protecting freedom of speech.

Provide specific examples to defend your position, and don't forget to deal with opposing viewpoints.

2. Hentoff mentions that on one campus student journalists were punished for publishing a satirical cartoon that proved offensive to several minority groups. But satire and comedy, especially when they have some bite, often offend one group or another. Carefully consider the comedy and satire currently in vogue. What are they? Do they provide harmless entertainment? Do they perpetuate negative stereotypes? Do they open up helpful discussion and debate? Prepare an essay in which you argue your position, supporting it with a number of persuasive examples. And don't forget to acknowledge (and, if possible, to refute) opposing viewpoints at some point in your paper.

Writing Assignments Combining Patterns of Development

3. What procedures has your college or university established so that people on campus—faculty, staff, and/or students—can file grievances if they feel they have been discriminated against in some way? In an essay, describe this *process* and indicate whether you feel it's adequate. If it isn't, explain what steps need to be taken to improve the procedures. No matter what position you take, you should provide *examples* to illustrate your point of view.

4. Stereotyping isn't restricted to minorities. Most of us have felt unfairly stereotyped at some time or another, perhaps because of gender, physical or intellectual abilities, even a hobby or interest. Write an essay *recounting* a time you were treated unfairly or cruelly because of some personal characteristic. Be sure to show how the event *affected* you. The following essays will provide insight into the potentially corrosive effect of labels and stereotypes: Alice Walker's "Beauty: When the Other Dancer Is the Self".

Writing Assignment Using a Journal Entry as a Starting Point

5. Write an editorial for your college newspaper arguing that a college campus is *or* is not the place to air conflicting, even inflammatory views about *one* of the controversial issues listed in your pre-reading journal entry. Perhaps you feel that the issue warrants a public forum in one campus setting but not another. If so, explain why. To lend authority to your position, interview students who don't share your point of view. Be sure to acknowledge their position in your editorial.

READING

Camille Paglia

Before 1990, Camille Paglia, professor of humanities at Philadelphia's University of the Arts, was known primarily for her electrifying performance in the classroom. Then came the publication of Paglia's *Sexual Personae: Art and Decadence From Nefertiti to Emily Dickinson,* a sweeping book that moves with dizzying speed from the days of cave art to the nineteenth century. *Sexual Personae* makes the case that man creates art as a defensive response to woman's terrifying cosmic power—specifically, her sexual and procreative force. Suddenly Paglia became an international celebrity and had many opportunities to express her controversial views. She has been both revered and reviled for making statements like these: "Male aggression and lust are the energizing factors in culture" and "If I ever got into a dating situation where I was overpowered and raped, I would say, 'Oh well, I misread the signals.'" Born in 1947, Paglia earned her doctorate from Yale University, where her Ph.D. thesis was an early version of *Sexual Personae. Sex, Art, and American Culture: Essays* (1992), *Vamps and Tramps: New Essays* (1994), and *Alfred Hitchcock's "The Birds"* (1998) are Paglia's latest works. Formerly a columnist for *Salon* online magazine, she is a contributing editor to *Interview* magazine and appears frequently on television programs to provide commentary on pop culture and gender issues. The following selection, written in Paglia's characteristically provocative style, first appeared in *New York Newsday* in 1991.

Pre-Reading Journal Entry

How would you define "date rape"? Use your journal to formulate a preliminary definition. Working as quickly as you can, jot down your preliminary thoughts about what it is and what it isn't.

Rape and Modern Sex War

1   Rape is an outrage that cannot be tolerated in civilized society. Yet feminism, which has waged a crusade for rape to be taken more seriously, has put young women in danger by hiding the truth about sex from them.

2   In dramatizing the pervasiveness of rape, feminists have told young women that before they have sex with a man, they must give consent as explicit as a legal contract's. In this way, young women have been convinced that they have been the victims of rape. On elite campuses in the Northeast and on the West Coast, they have held consciousness-raising sessions, petitioned administrations, demanded inquests. At Brown University, outraged, panicky "victims" have scrawled the names of alleged attackers on the walls of women's rest rooms. What marital rape was to the '70s, "date rape" is to the '90s.

3   The incidence and seriousness of rape do not require this kind of exaggeration. Real acquaintance rape is nothing new. It has been a horrible problem for women for all of recorded history. Once, father and brothers protected women from rape. Once, the penalty for rape was death. I come from a fierce Italian tradition where, not so long ago in the motherland, a rapist would end up knifed, castrated, and hung out to dry.

4   But the old clans and small rural communities have broken down. In our cities, on our campuses far from home, young women are vulnerable and defenseless. Feminism has not prepared them for this. Feminism keeps saying the sexes are the same. It keeps telling women they can do anything, go anywhere, say anything, wear anything. No, they can't. Women will always be in sexual danger.

5   One of my male students recently slept overnight with a friend in a passageway of the Great Pyramid in Egypt. He described the moon and sand, the ancient silence and eerie echoes. I am a woman. I will never experience that. I am not stupid enough to believe I could ever be safe there. There is a world of solitary adventure I will never have. Women have always known these somber truths. But feminism, with its pie-in-the-sky fantasies about the perfect world, keeps young women from seeing life as it is.

6   We must remedy social injustice whenever we can. But there are some things we cannot change. There are sexual differences that are based in biology. Academic feminism is lost in a fog of social constructionism. It believes we are totally the product of our environment. This idea was invented by Rousseau.[1] He was wrong. Emboldened by dumb French language theory, academic feminists repeat the same hollow slogans over and over to each other. Their view of sex is naive and prudish. Leaving sex to the feminists is like letting your dog vacation at the taxidermist's.

---

[1]A French political writer and philosopher (1712–78) (editors' note).

7   The sexes are at war. Men must struggle for identity against the overwhelming power of their mothers. Women have menstruation to tell them they are women. Men must do or risk something to be men. Men become masculine only when other men say they are. Having sex with a woman is one way a boy becomes a man.

8   College men are at their hormonal peak. They have just left their mothers and are questing for their male identity. In groups, they are dangerous. A woman going to a fraternity party is walking into Testosterone Flats, full of prickly cacti and blazing guns. If she goes, she should be armed with resolute alertness. She should arrive with girl-friends and leave with them. A girl who lets herself get dead drunk at a fraternity party is a fool. A girl who goes upstairs alone with a brother at a fraternity party is an idiot. Feminists call this "blaming the victim." I call it common sense.

9   For a decade, feminists have drilled their disciples to say, "Rape is a crime of vio-lence but not of sex." This sugar-coated Shirley Temple nonsense has exposed young women to disaster. Misled by feminism, they do not expect rape from the nice boys from good homes who sit next to them in class.

10   Aggression and eroticism, in fact, are deeply intertwined. Hunt, pursuit and cap-ture are biologically programmed into male sexuality. Generation after generation, men must be educated, refined, and ethically persuaded away from their tendency toward anarchy and brutishness. Society is not the enemy, as feminism ignorantly claims. Soci-ety is woman's protection against rape. Feminism, with its solemn Carry Nation[2] re-pressiveness, does not see what is for men the eroticism or fun element in rape, espe-cially the wild, infectious delirium of gang rape. Women who do not understand rape cannot defend themselves against it.

11   The date-rape controversy shows feminism hitting the wall of its own broken promises. The women of my '60s generation were the first respectable girls in history to swear like sailors, get drunk, stay out all night—in short, to act like men. We sought total sexual freedom and equality. But as time passed, we woke up to cold reality. The old double standard protected women. When anything goes, it's women who lose.

12   Today's young women don't know what they want. They see that feminism has not brought sexual happiness. The theatrics of public rage over date rape are their way of restoring the old sexual rules that were shattered by my generation. Yet nothing about the sexes has really changed. The comic film *Where the Boys Are* (1960), the ultimate ex-pression of '50s man-chasing, still speaks directly to our time. It shows smart, lively women skillfully anticipating and fending off the dozens of strategies with which horny men try to get them into bed. The agonizing date-rape subplot and climax are brilliantly done. The victim, Yvette Mimieux, makes mistake after mistake, obvious to the other girls. She allows herself to be lured away from her girlfriends and into isolation with boys whose character and intentions she misreads. *Where the Boys Are* tells the truth. It shows courtship as a dangerous game in which the signals are not verbal but subliminal.

13   Neither militant feminism, which is obsessed with politically correct language, nor academic feminism, which believes that knowledge and experience are "constituted by" language, can understand preverbal or nonverbal communication. Feminism, focusing on sexual politics, cannot see that sex exists in and through the body. Sexual desire and arousal cannot be fully translated into verbal terms. This is why men and women mis-understand each other.

---

[2]A nineteenth-century reformer who advocated the abolition of alcohol (editors' note).

14   Trying to remake the future, feminism cut itself off from sexual history. It discarded and suppressed the sexual myths of literature, art and religion. Those myths show us the turbulence, the mysteries and passions of sex. In mythology we see men's sexual anxiety, their fear of woman's dominance. Much sexual violence is rooted in men's sense of psychological weakness toward women. It takes many men to deal with one woman. Woman's voracity is a persistent motif. Clara Bow,[3] it was rumored, took on the USC[4] football team on weekends. Marilyn Monroe, singing "Diamonds Are a Girl's Best Friend," rules a conga line of men in tuxes. Half-clad Cher, in the video for "If I Could Turn Back Time," deranges a battleship of screaming sailors and straddles a pink-lit cannon. Feminism, coveting social power, is blind to woman's cosmic sexual power.

15   To understand rape, you must study the past. There never was and never will be sexual harmony. Every woman must be prudent and cautious about where she goes and with whom. When she makes a mistake, she must accept the consequences and, through self-criticism, resolve never to make that mistake again. Running to mommy and daddy on the campus grievance committee is unworthy of strong women. Posting lists of guilty men in the toilet is cowardly, infantile stuff.

16   The Italian philosophy of life espouses high-energy confrontation. A male student makes a vulgar remark about your breasts? Don't slink off to whimper with the campus shrinking violets. Deal with it. On the spot. Say, "Shut up, you jerk! And crawl back to the barnyard where you belong!" In general, women who project this take-charge attitude toward life get harassed less often. I see too many dopey, immature, self-pitying women walking around like melting sticks of butter. It's the Yvette Mimieux syndrome: make me happy. And listen to me weep when I'm not.

17   The date-rape debate is already smothering in propaganda churned out by the expensive Northeastern colleges and universities, with their overconcentration of boring, uptight academic feminists and spoiled, affluent students. Beware of the deep manipulativeness of rich students who were neglected by their parents. They love to turn the campus into hysterical psychodramas of sexual transgression, followed by assertions of parental authority and concern. And don't look for sexual enlightenment from academe, which spews out mountains of books but never looks at life directly.

18   As a fan of football and rock music, I see in the simple, swaggering masculinity of the jock and in the noisy posturing of the heavy-metal guitarist certain fundamental, unchanging truths about sex. Masculinity is aggressive, unstable, combustible. It is also the most creative cultural force in history. Women must reorient themselves toward the elemental powers of sex, which can strengthen or destroy.

19   The only solution to date rape is female self-awareness and self-control. A woman's number-one line of defense against rape is herself. When a real rape occurs, she should report it to the police. Complaining to college committees because the courts "take too long" is ridiculous. College administrations are not a branch of the judiciary. They are not equipped or trained for legal inquiry. Colleges must alert incoming students to the problems and dangers of adulthood. Then colleges must stand back and get out of the sex game.

---

[3]A movie star from the Roaring Twenties era (editors' note).

[4]University of Southern California (editors' note).

Questions for Close Reading

1. What is the selection's thesis? Locate the sentence(s) in which Paglia states her main idea. If she doesn't state the thesis explicitly, express it in your own words.
2. In Paglia's opinion, why are women more "vulnerable and defenseless" now than in the past?
3. According to Paglia, what "truth about sex" has feminism hidden from young women?
4. What does Paglia believe is "the only solution to date rape"?
5. Refer to your dictionary as needed to define the following words used in the selection: *inquests* (paragraph 2), *testosterone* (8), *constituted* (13), *grievance* (15), and *judiciary* (19).

Questions About the Writer's Craft

1. **The pattern.** Examine the way Paglia develops her argument in paragraphs 6 and 8. Which of her assertions in these paragraphs can be assumed to be true without further proof? Why do you think Paglia includes these essentially incontestable statements? Conversely, which of her assertions in paragraphs 6 and 8 require further proof before their truth can be demonstrated? Does Paglia provide such support? Explain.
2. **Other patterns.** How does Paglia use the *comparison-contrast* pattern to develop her argument?
3. Paglia's style is frequently characterized by short sentences strung together with few transitions. Locate some examples of this style. Why might Paglia have chosen this style? What is its effect?
4. Where does Paglia use emotional, highly connotative language? Where does she employ strongly worded absolute statements? Do you think that this use of pathos makes Paglia's argument more or less convincing? Explain.

Writing Assignments Using Argumentation-Persuasion as a Pattern of Development

1. Read an article that discusses date rape as a crime in which the woman has no responsibility. Then write an essay arguing that the *other writer* has trouble making a strong case for her position. Consider the merits and flaws (including any logical fallacies) in the argument, plus such issues as the writer's credibility, strategies for dealing with the opposing view, and use of emotional appeals. Throughout, support your opinion with specific examples drawn from the selection. Keep in mind that you're critiquing the effectiveness of the writer's argument. It's not appropriate, then, simply to explain why you agree or disagree with the writer's position or merely to summarize what the writer says.
2. Paglia criticizes those who claim that the environment, or social climate, is primarily responsible for shaping gender differences. She believes that such differences "are based in biology." Write an essay arguing your own position about the role that environment and biology play in determining sex-role attitudes and behavior. Remembering to acknowledge opposing views, defend your own viewpoint with plentiful examples based on your experiences and observations. You may also need to conduct some library research to gather support for your position.

Writing Assignments Combining Patterns of Development

3. Paglia writes in paragraph 7 that "men become masculine only when other men say they are. Having sex with a woman is one way a boy becomes a man." Write an essay constructing your own *definition* of masculinity. Comment on the extent to which you feel being sexually active is an important criterion, but also include other hallmarks and *examples* of masculinity.
4. Date rape seems to be on the rise. Brainstorm with others to identify what may be leading to its growing occurrence. Focusing on several related *factors*, write an essay showing how these factors contribute to the problem. Possible factors include the following: the way males and females are depicted in the media (advertisements, movies, television, rock videos); young people's use of alcohol; the emergence of coed college dorms. At the end of the essay, offer some recommendations about *steps* that can be taken to create a safer climate for dating. You should consider supporting your speculations with information about date rape gathered in the library and/or on the Internet.

Writing Assignment Using a Journal Entry as a Starting Point

5. Drawing upon the material in your pre-reading journal entry, write an essay in which you present a carefully considered definition of the term "date rape." Explain clearly what constitutes date rape and what doesn't. To deepen your understanding of this thorny issue, consider brainstorming with others as well as conducting research in the library and/or on the Internet. One issue to consider: Do males and females define the term differently? If so, how do they define it, and why might their definitions differ?

ADDITIONAL WRITING TOPICS

ARGUMENTATION-PERSUASION

General Assignments

Using argumentation-persuasion, develop one of the topics below in an essay. After choosing a topic, think about your purpose and audience. Remember that the paper's thesis should state the issue under discussion as well as your position on the issue. As you work on developing evidence, you might want to do some outside research. Keep in mind that effective argumentation-persuasion usually means that some time should be spent acknowledging and perhaps refuting opposing points of view. Be careful not to sabotage your argument by basing your case on a logical fallacy.

1. Euthanasia
2. Hiring or college-admissions quotas
3. Giving birth-control devices to teenagers
4. Prayer in the schools
5. Living off campus
6. The drinking age
7. Spouses sharing housework equally
8. Smoking in public places
9. Big-time sports in college
10. Pornography on the Internet
11. Single parents with young children
12. Acid rain
13. Drugs on campus
14. Political campaigns
15. Requiring college students to pass a comprehensive exam in their majors before graduating
16. Reinstating the military draft
17. Putting elderly parents in nursing homes
18. An optional pass-fail system for courses
19. The homeless
20. Nonconformity in a neighborhood: allowing a lawn to go wild, keeping many pets, painting a house an odd color, or some other atypical behavior

Assignments With a Specific Purpose, Audience, and Point of View

On Campus

1. Your college's Financial Aid Department has decided not to renew your scholarship for next year, citing a drop in your grades last semester and an unenthusiastic recommendation from one of your instructors. Write a letter to the director of financial aid arguing for the renewal of your scholarship.
2. You strongly believe that a particular policy or regulation on campus is unreasonable or unjust. Write a letter to the dean of students (or other appropriate administrator) arguing that the policy needs to be, if not completely revoked, amended in some way. Support your contention with specific examples showing how the regulation has gone wrong. End by providing constructive suggestions for how the policy problem can be solved.

At Home or in the Community

3. You and one or more family members don't agree on some aspect of your romantic life (you want to live with your boyfriend/girlfriend and they don't approve; you want to get married and they want you to wait; they simply don't like your partner). Write a letter explaining why your preference is reasonable. Try hard to win your family member(s) over to your side.

4. Assume you're a member of a racial, ethnic, religious, or social minority. You might, for example, be a Native American, an elderly person, a female executive. On a recent television show or in a TV commercial, you saw something that depicts your group in an offensive way. Write a letter (to the network or the advertiser) expressing your feelings and explaining why you feel the material should be taken off the air.

On the Job

5. As a staff writer for an online pop-culture magazine, you've been asked to nominate the "Most Memorable TV Moment of the Last 50 Years" to be featured as the magazine's lead article. Write a letter to your supervising editor in support of your nominee.

6. As a high school teacher, you support some additional restriction on students. The restriction might be "no radios in school," "no T-shirts," "no food in class," "no smoking on school grounds." Write an article for the school newspaper, justifying this new rule to the student body.

237